The Gospel of St. John
And Its Relation to the Other Gospels

The Gospel of St. John
And Its Relation to the Other Gospels

Fourteen Lectures delivered in Kassel
June 24–July 7, 1909

By Rudolf Steiner

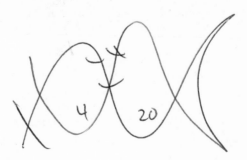

The Anthroposophic Press
Spring Valley,   New York

The fourteen lectures presented here were given in
Kassel from June 24 to July 7, 1909. In the Collected
Edition of Rudolf Steiner's works, the volume containing the German texts is entitled, *Das Johannes-
Evangelium im Verhaltnis zu den drei anderen Evangelien, besonders zu dem Lukas-Evangelium* (Vol.
number 112 in the Collected Edition). They were translated from the German by Samuel and Loni Lockwood
and revised by Maria St. Goar. This edition was edited
by Stewart C. Easton, Ph.D.

First Edition 1948
Second Edition (Revised Translation) 1982
Copyright © 1982

Steiner, Rudolf, 1861-1925.
    The Gospel of St. John and its relation to the
other Gospels.

    Rev. translation of: Johannes Evangelium im
Verhältnis zu den drei anderen Evangelien.
    1. Anthroposophy—Addresses, essays, lectures.
2. Bible. N.T. John—Criticism, interpretation, etc.—
Addresses, essays, lectures. I. Title. II. Title:
Gospel of Saint John and its relation to the other
Gospels.
BP595.S854433 1982   226'.506   82-18500
ISBN 0-88010-015-X
ISBN 0-88010-014-1 (pbk.)

Cover Design by Betty Joanna Humphreys

Printed in the United States of America

CONTENTS AND SYNOPSIS

Lecture One 1
Christ Jesus and His forerunner—the Christ Event as the
greatest event in all earthly evolution—the task of Anthroposophy in revealing the meaning and content of Christ
Event, formerly known only by Rosicrucians or Johannine
Christians. Writer of John Gospel recognizes Christ as
Logos, Luke stresses descent from Adam, the son of God,
thus of divine origin—Matthew traces back to Abraham.
Relation between coming of Christ Jesus and awakening of
higher ego in man, as understood also by Rosicrucians and
in Mystery of Holy Grail—through Event of Palestine
higher ego can be born for all men who prepare themselves
for it—birth of immortal ego in mortal ego. Christ already
perceived as Vishva Karman in ancient Indian civilization,
as Ahura Mazdao by Zarathustra and by Moses in burning
bush. Jesus of Nazareth as exalted initiate, specially
prepared, and recognized as such by Three Kings from the
East and by Simeon in the Temple, later to receive the
Christ at Baptism in Jordan. Diminution of John the Baptist
after descent of the Christ.

Lecture Two 20
Spiritual science does not interpret documents but reads the
Akasha Chronicle—nature of this Chronicle—history often

only *fable convenue* because of absence of necessary documents—attempts to complete Goethe's Nausicaa fragment. Man gradually descended from gods but his task is to return to them—preceded in this task by initiate leaders. Example of Buddha already enlightened at birth—long preparation of Jesus of Nazareth through many incarnations—necessity for reaching intellectual soul age (28-35) before becoming able to receive the Christ—beginning of John Gospel and beginning of Genesis—description in Luke of the maturing of three soul qualities in Jesus of Nazareth before entry of Christ.

Fourfold nature of man in waking and sleeping and its reflection in man's physical organism—physical body as oldest component of man, more perfect than etheric and astral bodies. Physical body perfected through earlier stages of evolution—stages of planetary evolution, Old Saturn, Old Sun and Old Moon—separation of sun and moon during Old Moon evolution and its significance for "men" of that epoch—Bull, Lion and Eagle "men" on Old Moon, their spiritual counterparts on the sun. Old Moon followed by "devachan" or "pralaya" until emergence of Earth, when ego is added to man. Recapitulation of earlier epochs on Earth—separation of sun and moon—this succession described in Prologue of John Gospel, first Logos (Saturn), then Life (Sun), then Light (Moon). Luke's informants as "servants of the Word" or Logos—rediscovery of these truths through spiritual science.

Continued influence of sun beings on men, especially when they are asleep—sacrifice of their substance by Thrones on Old Saturn to create human physical body in cooperation

with Archai (Spirits of Personality)—Kyriotetes and Archangels create etheric body during Old Sun—role of back-
ward Spirits of Personality in creating animal kingdom—
Spirits of Motion and Angels on Old Moon—recapitulation
of these stages at beginning of Earth evolution—creation of
mineral kingdom through activity of Spirits of Personality
while moon still united with earth—desolation of the earth,
difficulty of souls to incarnate—Kant-Laplace theory a fanci-
ful hypothesis, a modern materialistic mythology less true
than earlier mythologies—separation of sun and development
of planets, result of work of spiritual beings—souls waiting
on these planets until departure of moon—gradual repeopling
of earth—all beings returning too quickly to earth less perfect than those that waited, minerals, plants and animals all
before man—higher beings incorporated in some men of
early epochs of civilization but highest Being, the Christ
waited. The man who had waited longest incarnated in Jesus
of Nazareth, having developed through many incarnations—
into this individuality descended the Christ at Baptism in
Jordan—Christ, formerly known as Vishva Karman and
Ahura Mazdao, when incarnated could say truly "I am the
Light of the World."

Man's present physical perfection a consequence of coincidence between physical and etheric bodies—evolution
through Polarian, Hyperborean, Lemurian and Atlantean
ages—neither earth nor man solid before Atlantis—after
moon left in Lemurian times souls gradually descended to
earth—clairvoyant until intervention of Lucifer—Luciferic
influence and how it manifested in different ways—through
Lucifer developed human potentiality for freedom. After
man became physical, entry of Ahrimanic or Mephistophelean
influence—through Ahriman came belief that external world

only material—role of Atlantean initiates and Hebrew people in combatting Luciferic development of personal ego—Christ as higher ego with task of transforming Luciferic influence into good—retardation of Luciferic spirits represents sacrifice by them for man's ultimate good.

Characterization of kind of consciousness prevalent in Atlantean times when etheric body did not yet coincide with physical—gradual solidification of physical body—influence of Lucifer and efforts of Atlantean leaders to guard against it—the Atlantean Oracles—relations of their initiates with their pupils—sinking of Atlantis and its consequences—continuation of Oracles in Mysteries of post-Atlantis—study of what is now Anthroposophy in Mysteries—methods of initiation in all post-Atlantean Mysteries until Christian times—living revelation of spiritual worlds in early post-Atlantean times combined with dim clairvoyance—love of earthly world as necessary step forward in evolution—progress of earthly orientation through first four post-Atlantean epochs culminating in Greeks—approach of Christ toward Earth seen by Zarathustra and Moses—similarity between baptism by John and pre-Christian type of initiation—spiritual experience of those baptized by John—recognition of the approaching "I am" by some—Christ Impulse as spiritual love brought to earth by Christ to counteract egotism of Lucifer—undertone of Christ Impulse in Tolstoi—contrast of Tolstoi's Christianity with that of Solovyev—Anthroposophy needed for long ages to come to give understanding of Christ.

Similarity between baptism by John and old form of initiation—symbolic for some while others attained to perception of spiritual worlds—contrast with Christ's "baptism by fire and the Holy Spirit." How spirit acts in material world—psycho-spiritual processes of shame and fear affecting the physical body—William James and his materialistic explanations—importance of understanding how spirit underlies everything physical—distinction between hereditary tendencies and forces derived from previous incarnations—spirit capable of overcoming heredity but ought not to overestimate its actual power in an individual life. How anthroposophical world-outlook and true knowledge of human evolution nourish human spirit. Christ-Being central to all understanding of evolution—Christ Impulse working through man as inner force is new form of initiation. New Christ initiates also attain to vision of spiritual worlds—Lazarus, the "disciple whom Jesus loved," as first Christ initiate, becoming author of St. John's Gospel, thus accounting for its profundity.

Special case of "initiation" of Lazarus by Christ, Lazarus becoming John, writer of Gospel. All Gospels agree on facts of Baptism in Jordan, Mark and John beginning with it. Withdrawal of ego of Jesus of Nazareth, Christ, the Logos, entering the sheaths—nature of Jesus of Nazareth—his genealogy according to Matthew and Luke—influence of Zarathustra ego within sheaths taken over by Christ, especially the astral body—Zarathustra and Ahura Mazdao—the Logos spoken of in Persian initiation. Bull, Lion, Eagle, and Man spirits active in evangelists, all comprehending Christ differently, different descriptions in Gospels according to particular initiations of writers (Luke–Bull; Mark–Lion; Matthew–Man; John–Eagle). Experience of St. Paul perceiving Christ in earth aura and thus knowing that Christ had indeed resurrected—"If Christ be not

Risen, then is your faith vain." Solovyev's acceptance of Paul's viewpoint, but inability to reach beyond philosophical concepts to spiritual science.

The seven miracles or signs of John Gospel—healing in ancient times characteristic of older forms of consciousness—magical power of blood ties in ancient times—"I and Father Abraham are one."—evolution from consanguineous to exogamous marriage—Marriage in Cana of Galilee, joint power of Christ and his Mother needed for first sign, turning water into wine—intensification of Christ force in progression of signs to culmination in healing of man blind from birth (6th sign)—Christ force working on eternal individuality through karma.

Baptism of Jesus in Jordan as supreme event in earth evolution—entry of Christ force right down to skeleton—the dove visible to clairvoyant sight as spiritual element detaching itself from Jesus of Nazareth at Baptism. Other influences of Baptism—on the Earth, on the Mother of Jesus. Contrast with old form of initiation, identification of initiate with female principle, the Folk Soul—Nathaniel as initiate of fifth degree, one with Folk Soul of his people. Recovery of virginity by Mother of Jesus at Baptism leading to transformation of water into wine as first sign, for which Mother was needed. Intensification of Christ power and greater control of sheaths in succeeding signs, to the healing of the blind man. "I am the Light of the World." Lazarus as John, writer of the Gospel, initiated by Christ Himself.

body by Christ filling it with life and counteracting death tendencies. Evolution of science from clairvoyance to modern scientific thought—failure of Celsus to understand anything about Christ—difficulty for Christ impulse to penetrate into brain—"God-forsaken" world of modern mechanistic thinking—Galileo—Darwinian concepts squeezed-out lemons—task of Anthroposophy in vivifying desiccated brains—first impetus given by Christ for revitalization of man—expulsion of Lucifer and Ahriman from physical body of Jesus—"the prince of this world is cast out."

Early evolution of earth—splitting off of sun, and then moon in Lemurian epoch—sun and moon forces thereafter working from without—distortion of man's picture of world by Luciferic and Ahrimanic influences—death as maya or illusion—erroneous views about death—Death as Father-Principle distorted by Lucifer and Ahriman—Christ's death as demonstration that death in reality is giver of life—significance of blood flowing on Golgotha—earth beginning to radiate astral light visible only to clairvoyance, eventually to diffuse physical light as luminous body in distant future—Christ light streaming into human etheric bodies; part of etheric body survives death to form spiritual sphere around earth, eventually to become sun—distorted view of death in pre-Christian times—union of Christ with death is birth of a new life and new sun—death as germ of life—Christ's teachings about death and the Father in John Gospel—contrast with teachings of "auxiliary" books, each with its own purpose in different ages—Mark for early Christians, then Luke, now in our age Matthew—Jesus of Nazareth in Matthew as man. Anthroposophy tries to lead man upward to understand Gospel of Gospels: John. Paul's vision of the living Christ on road to Damascus.

Not until Earth evolution did world of nature exist apart
from divine spiritual being—retarded spirits expelled by
divinity ensconced themselves in all nature and men. In
Atlantis solidification for first time, man also developing
self-consciousness. Luciferic beings cast down by Michael
into man—purposes of Luciferic and Ahrimanic beings—
man independent but cut off from spiritual worlds—death
bringing man back into spiritual worlds—Christ making
possible for man to take his eternal egoity into world of
death—all future evolution possible only because of Christ—
since Golgotha Christ has been in earth and in everything it
brings forth—earth as body of Christ—"This is my body,
this is my blood."—Saul/Paul's recognition of Christ as
present in earth's aura made possible by his premature birth
—clairvoyance of Mary of Magdala at the tomb when Christ
spoke to her. Stages of Christian initiation leading to vision
of Christ—impossibility for men to understand seventh
stage, the Ascension, which showed also advance of Christ
Himself—Christ and karma—healing of blind man and for-
giving of adulteress—feeding of Five Thousand—"I am the
Bread of Life." Role of Mark and Luke Gospels in evolution of Christianity—purpose of cycle like this is not to give
knowledge only but to transform understanding into feeling
and will—above all bearing fruit in lives of hearers.

Introduction

The fourteen lectures given by Rudolf Steiner at Kassel in June and July, 1909 bearing the title *The Gospel of St. John and Its Relation to the Other Gospels* have to a certain extent been neglected in the English-speaking world. Only one edition has ever been published in the English language, and that was as late as 1948. When that first American edition was exhausted it was never reprinted until now, when the cycle is appearing again in a revised translation. Yet it could reasonably be considered as the most comprehensive of all Steiner's cycles on the Gospels, covering as it does a very wide range of topics, and placing the Christ event in the perspective of the whole of earthly evolution in such a way that the cycle can be used even as an introductory work for beginners. It covers many of the subjects discussed in the much more popular 1908 cycle on the Gospel of St. John given at Hamburg, but never in exactly the same manner. Thus there is relatively little duplication between the two cycles, while the later lectures in this beautiful cycle, especially those on what is meant by the overcoming of death by Christ are unique among Steiner's lectures, and ought not to be missed by any student of Anthroposophy.

The title, although the cycle has always borne it, including the German original, is not a very accurate description of the contents, and this may have discouraged some students from reading it. The references to the Gospels other than that of St. John are in fact quite scarce, and appear only in a few of the lectures. The cycle is, indeed, concerned with the Gospel of St. John just as much as is the Hamburg cycle, but from a different point of view, and stressing entirely different topics. Very much more is to be found here on the working of the Christ impulse in earth evolution than in the earlier cycle, and as far as the cosmic significance of the Mystery of Golgotha it is to be compared only with the much later cycle on St. Mark (Basel, 1912). So it forms an integral part of the remarkable lectures on the Gospels and the essence of Christianity that began in 1907 and came to an end with the War. A list of these lectures is printed at the end of this book.

The cycle also constitutes a watershed in Steiner's works on Christology, since it was the last to be given before his revelations concerning the two Jesus children. From one or two passages in this cycle it will be clear that Steiner was already well aware of the fact that there had been two different Jesus children: the child of the royal line descended from Solomon, described in Matthew, who was visited by the Three Kings, and the child of the priestly line descended from Nathan, described by Luke, who was born in a stable and visited by the shepherds. However, he was not yet ready to speak even to members about this fact which is so often found startling by traditionally minded Christians, although he was to divulge it later in 1909, in his cycle on the Gospel of St. Luke, and revealed it to the public in a lecture originally given at Copenhagen, and edited by him for general publication later in the same year (*The Spiritual Guidance of Man and Humanity*). In the present cycle Rudolf Steiner does not have much to say about the childhood of Jesus, and when he does speak about it, it is evident he is talking about the Solomon Jesus child, in whom the ancient Persian initiate Zarathustra had reincarnated. Even so, if the reader is already aware that there had been two Jesus children, some of what Steiner has to say here will be understood at a deeper level. For this reason, if for no other, no serious student of Anthroposophy should ever stop with one or even two Gospel cycles, but should read and study them all, since all have something different and essential to tell him. After all, it should never be forgotten that Steiner's teachings about Christ constitute the core of Anthroposophy, nothing in it making any real sense if it is not understood within the context of the working of the Christ impulse in humanity in the age of the consciousness soul and on into the future.

With the coming of the War in 1914, Rudolf Steiner entered into a different phase of his work, and he is reported to have said that conditions in the spiritual world during these years were not conducive to drawing down new knowledge of the period of the Mystery of Golgotha, which had been given so abundantly in the years up to the War. Steiner seems to have taken it more or less for granted that his hearers were familiar with what he had given; and all that he spoke about the Christ in the postwar years was based on this assumption. He therefore devoted his postwar lectures to special aspects of Christianity and the Christ impulse in preference to giving any more formal cycles on biblical subjects. Yet in all his work until the very end the Christ was never absent from the forefront of his consciousness, whether he was lecturing on the philosophy of Thomas Aquinas or on Rosicrucianism, discussing Cosmology, Philosophy and Religion in the French Course, carving the great statue of the Representative of Mankind for the Goetheanum, founding the General Anthroposophical Society, or writing those intimate letters in the last year of his life telling us of the work of Michael, whom he called "the countenance of Christ."

So the work of the years from 1907 to 1914 remains an indispensible study for the serious student of Anthroposophy, and will surely remain so for the indefinite future.

—Stewart C. Easton

xvii

Preface to First Edition

As a comment on the publication of the spoken lectures that were first published privately at the urgent request of members of the Anthroposophical Society and are now being made available to the public in book form, we cite the following excerpt from Rudolf Steiner's *The Course of My Life*.*

"There are two categories of works that are the fruit of my anthroposophical activities: first, my published books, available to the world at large, and second, a great number of lecture courses first intended to be printed privately and for sale to members of the Anthroposophical Society only. These were taken down with varying accuracy in shorthand, but lack of time always prevented me from correcting them. I should have preferred to have the spoken word remain such; but the members clamored for the private printing of the lectures, and so this came about. If I had had time to correct them the restriction 'for members only' would have been unnecessary from the start. Now, for over a year, it has been abandoned.

"Here in *The Course of My Life* it is necessary to make clear the relative position of these two categories—the published books and the private printings—in what I have developed as anthroposophy.

"Whoever would follow my inner struggles and labors to bring anthroposophy to present-day consciousness must do so by means of my published writings intended for the world

***The Course of My Life* (trans. O.D. Wannamaker. New York: Anthroposophic Press, 1951), Chapter XXXVI.

at large. There I have dealt with all we have today in the way of striving for knowledge; and there is also set forth what took ever clearer shape in me through spiritual vision, what became the edifice of anthroposophy, albeit in many respects imperfectly.

"But side by side with this call to build up anthroposophy and, in doing so, to serve only what resulted from the duty to impart communications from the spirit world to the general educated public of today, there arose the obligation to meet the spiritual needs of the soul, the spiritual longings, of our members.

"There was above all an urgent demand to have the Gospels and the substance of the Bible in general presented in the light that had become the anthroposophical light. People wanted lecture courses on these revelations that have been vouchsafed mankind.

"These privately given courses led to something else. Only members were present, and these were familiar with the elementary disclosures of anthroposophy. One could talk to them as to advanced students, and these private lectures were given in a way that would not have done for writings intended for the public. In this inner circle I could talk of things in a way different from what it would necessarily have been, had the presentation been intended for the public.

"There exists, then, something in this duality—the public and the private writings—that really springs from two sources: the wholly public writings are the result of what struggled and worked in me alone, whereas in the private printings the Society struggles and works with me. I listen to the vibrations in the soul life of the members, and the character of the lectures is determined by my living vividly in what I hear there.

"If for no other reason than that I worked from the reality

of the members' soul needs, the privately printed lectures must be judged by a different standard than those given full publicity from the start. The contents of the former were intended as oral communications, not as books; and the subjects discussed were gleaned in the course of time by listening for the soul needs of the members.

"The substance of the published books conforms with the demands of anthroposophy as such. The manner in which the privately printed works unfold is something in which the soul configuration of the whole Society collaborated, in the sense set forth."

I

My dear Friends:

A special festival has long been celebrated on this particular day of the year by a great number of those seeking
higher wisdom; and many friends of our anthroposophical
movement here in this city have wished this series of lectures
to begin on this day, St. John's Day.

The day of the year bearing this name was a festival as
far back as the time of ancient Persia. There, on a day corresponding to a June day of today, the so-called Festival of the
Baptism by Water and Fire was celebrated. In ancient Rome
the Festival of Vesta was held on a similar day in June, and
that again was a festival of the baptism by fire. Going back
to the time of pre-Christian culture in Europe and including
the period before Christianity had become widely dissemi-
nated, we find a similar June festival coinciding with the
time when the days are longest and the nights shortest,
when the days start to become shorter again, when the sun
once more begins to lose some of the power that provides for
all earthly growth and flourishing. This June festival seemed
to our European forefathers like a withdrawal, a gradual disappearance of the God Baldur who was thought of as associated with the sun. Then in Christian times this June festival gradually became the Festival of St. John in memory of
the Forerunner of Christ Jesus. In this way it can form the
starting point, as it were, for our discussions during the
coming days of that most significant event in human evolution which we call the deed of Christ Jesus. This deed, its
whole significance for the development of mankind, the way

1

it is revealed primarily in the most important Christian document, the Gospel of St. John, and then a comparison of this with the other Gospels—a study of all this will form the subject of this lecture cycle.

St. John's Day reminds us that the most exalted Individuality that ever took part in the evolution of mankind was preceded by a forerunner. This touches at once an important part which—again like a forerunner—we must place at the beginning of our lectures as a subject of discussion. In the course of human evolution, profoundly important events occur again and again, which shine with a stronger light than other events. From epoch to epoch we see history recording such vital events; and ever and anon we are told that there are men who, in certain respects, know of such events in advance and can foretell them. This implies that such events are not arbitrary, but rather, that one who discerns the whole sense and spirit of human history knows how such events must unfold, and how he himself must work and prepare in order that they may come to pass.

We shall have occasion in the next few days to refer repeatedly to the Forerunner of Christ Jesus. Today we will consider him only as one of those who, by means of special spiritual gifts, are able to see deep into the relations within the evolution of mankind, and who thus know that there are pre-eminent moments in this evolution. For this reason he was able to clear the path for Christ Jesus. But if we turn to Christ Jesus Himself, thus coming to the main subject of our discussions, as it were, we must understand that not without reason does a large part of mankind divide the record of time into two epochs separated by the appearance of Christ Jesus on earth. This discloses a feeling for the incisive importance of the Christ Mystery. But all truth, all reality, must ever be proclaimed to humanity in new forms, in new ways, for the needs of men change from one epoch to

2

another. In certain respects our epoch calls for a new revelation even of this greatest event in the earthly evolution of man, the Christ Event; and it is anthroposophy's aim to be this revelation.

As far as its content is concerned, the anthroposophical revelation of the Christ Mystery is nothing new, not even for us today; but its form is new. All that is to be disclosed here in the next few days has been known for centuries within certain restricted circles of our cultural and spiritual life. Only one feature distinguishes today's revelation from all those that have gone before: it can address itself to a larger circle. Those smaller circles, in which for centuries the same message was proclaimed within our European spiritual life, had recognized the same symbol that confronts you here (in this lecture hall) today: the Rose Cross. For this reason it is fitting that today, when this message goes forth to a larger public, the Rose Cross should again be its symbol.

First let me characterize once more in a symbolical way the basis of these Rosicrucian revelations concerning Christ Jesus. The Rosicrucians are a brotherhood that has fostered a genuinely spiritual Christianity within the spiritual life of Europe ever since the 14th Century. This Rosicrucian community, which, aside from all outer historical forms, has endeavored to bring to light the deepest truth of Christianity, always called its members also "Johannine Christians." If we come to understand this term, the whole spirit and trend of the following lectures will be—if not intellectually explained, at least imaginatively grasped.

As you know, the Gospel of St. John—that mighty document of the human race—begins with the words:

In the beginning was the Word, and the Word was with God, and a God was the Word.

The same was in the beginning with God.

The Word, then—or the *Logos*—was in the beginning

3

with God. And we are further told that the light shone in the darkness, and that the darkness at first comprehended it not; that this light was in the world among men, but that these men counted but few among their number who were able to comprehend the Light. Then the Word made flesh appeared as a Man, a Man Whose forerunner was the Baptist John. And then we see how those who had some understanding of this appearance of Christ on earth endeavored to make clear what Christ really was. We see the author of the John Gospel pointing directly to the fact that what dwelt in Jesus of Nazareth as profoundest essence was nothing different from that in which originate all other beings that surround us: the living Spirit, the living Word, the *Logos* itself.

And the other Evangelists as well, each in his own way, have been at pains to characterize what it really was that appeared in Jesus of Nazareth. We see, for example, the writer of the Luke Gospel endeavoring to show that something quite special manifested itself when, at the Baptism of Christ Jesus by John the Baptist, the Spirit united with the body of Jesus of Nazareth. Then the same writer tells us that this Jesus of Nazareth was the descendant of ancestors reaching far, far back; that his genealogy went back to David, to Abraham, to Adam—even to God Himself. Note well that the Luke Gospel points emphatically to this line of descent:

Jesus was the son of Joseph, Joseph was the son of Eli, he was a son of Matthat . . . then: he was a son of David, and further it then says:* he was a son of Adam, and Adam was of God! (Luke 3)

---

*Ordinarily in this edition the King James version will be used for Biblical translations. However, since the Luther Bible quoted by Dr. Steiner is significantly different, the passage in the text is a re-translation from the latter.

4

This means that the author of the Luke Gospel considers it of special importance that a direct line runs from Jesus of Nazareth, with whom the spirit united at the Baptism by John, to Him Whom he calls the Father of Adam, to God. Such things must be taken entirely literally.

Again, in the Matthew Gospel, the attempt is made to trace the descent of this Jesus of Nazareth back to Abraham, to whom God revealed Himself.

In this way and in many others, through many statements we can find in the Gospels, the individuality that is the bearer of the Christ, as well as the whole manifestation of Christ, is set before us not only as one of the greatest, but as the very greatest of all manifestations in the evolution of humanity. Clearly this means, does it not? what can be expressed quite simply as follows: If Christ Jesus is regarded by those who divined something of His greatness as the most significant manifestation in the evolution of man upon earth, then this Christ Jesus must in some way be connected with what is most vital and sacred in man himself. In other words, there must be something in man himself that can be brought into relation with the Christ event. Can we not ask, if Christ Jesus, as the Gospels maintain, is really the most important event in human evolution, does it not follow that always, in every human soul, there is something that is related to Christ Jesus?

And that is precisely what the Johannine Christians of the Rosicrucian brotherhood deemed of greatest import and significance: that there *is* in every human soul something directly related to the events in Palestine as brought about through Christ Jesus. If the coming of Christ Jesus can be called the greatest event for mankind, then what corresponds in the human soul to the Christ event must be the greatest and most significant as well. And what can that be? The dis-

5

ciples of the Rosicrucians answered: There exists for every human soul something that is called *awakening*, or *rebirth*, or *initiation*.

Let us see what is meant by these terms. Looking at the various things around us—things we see with our eyes, touch with our hands—we observe them coming into being and perishing. We see the flower, the whole annual plant life, come up and then wither; and though there are such things in the world as rocks and mountains that seem to defy the centuries we need only consider the proverb, "a steady drip hollows out the rock" to realize that the human soul senses the laws of transience as governing even the majestic boulders and mountains. And we know that even what is built of the elements comes into being and perishes: not only what we call our corporeality, but what we know as our perishable ego is engendered and then passes. But those who know how a spiritual world can be reached know also that this is not attained by means of eyes or ears or other senses, but by the path of awakening, of rebirth, of initiation.

And what is it that is reborn? When a man observes his inner self he finally comes to realize that what he sees there is that to which he says "I." Its very name differentiates it from anything in the outer world. To everything in the outer world a name can be applied externally. Everyone can call a table a table or a clock a clock; but never in the world could the name "I" fall on our ear if it were intended to denote ourself, for "I" must be spoken within us: to everyone else we are "you." This in itself shows us that our ego-being is distinct from all else that is in or around us.

But in addition, we now come to something that spiritual scientists of all times have emphasized from their own experience for the benefit of mankind: that within this ego another, a higher ego, is born, as the child is born of the mother. A man as he appears in life is first encountered as a

6

child, awkward in his surroundings but gradually learning to understand things: he gains in sense, his intellect and his will grow, and his strength and energy increase. But there have always been people who grow in other ways as well, who attain to a stage of development beyond the average, who find, so to say, a second I that can say "you" to the first one in the same way that the I itself says "you" to the outer world and to its own body—that looks upon this first I from above, as it were.

As an ideal, then, for the soul of man, and as a reality for those who follow the instructions of spiritual science, we have the thought: the ego I have hitherto known takes part in the whole outer world, and together with this it is perishable; but there slumbers within me a second ego of which men are unaware but can become aware. It is linked with the imperishable, just as the first ego is bound up with the perishable, the temporal; and by means of rebirth this higher ego can behold a spiritual world just as the lower ego can perceive the physical world through eyes and ears.

This awakening, rebirth, initiation, as it is called, is the greatest event for the human soul—a view shared by those who called themselves adherents of the Rose Cross. These knew that this event of the rebirth of the higher ego, which can look from above on the lower ego as man looks on outer forms, must have some connection with the event of Christ Jesus. This means that just as a rebirth can occur for the individual in his development, so a rebirth for all humanity came about through Christ Jesus. That which is an inner event for the individual—a mystical-spiritual event, as it is called, something he can experience as the birth of his higher ego—corresponds to what occurred in the outer world, in history, for all mankind in the event of Palestine through Christ Jesus.

How did this appear to a man like, for instance, the

7

author of the Luke Gospel? He reasoned as follows: The genealogy of Jesus of Nazareth goes back to Adam and to God himself. What today is mankind, what now inhabits a physical human body, once descended from divine heights: it was born of the spirit, it was once with God. Adam was he who had been sent down out of spiritual heights into matter, and in this sense he is the son of God. So there was at one time a divine-spiritual realm—thus the author of the Luke Gospel told himself—that condensed, as it were, into the mortal earthly realm: Adam came into being. Adam was an earthly reflection of the son of God, and from him are descended the human beings that dwell in a physical body. And in a special way there lived in Jesus of Nazareth not only what exists in every man and all that pertains to it, but something the essence of which can be found only when one is aware that the true being of man derives from the divine. In Jesus of Nazareth something of this divine descent is still apparent. For this reason the writer of the Luke Gospel feels constrained to say, Behold him who was baptized by John! He bears special marks of the divine out of which Adam was originally born. This can come to life again in him. Just as the God descended into matter and disappeared as such from the human race, so He reappears. In Jesus of Nazareth mankind could be reborn in its innermost divine principle. What the author of the Luke Gospel meant was this: If we trace the genealogy of Jesus of Nazareth to its source, we find the divine origin and the characteristics of the son of God appearing in him in a new way, and in a higher degree than would hitherto have been possible for mankind.

And the writer of the John Gospel emphasizes only more strongly the existence of something divine in man, as well as the fact that this appeared in its most grandiose form as the God and the *Logos* itself. The God Who had been buried, as it were, in matter is reborn as God in Jesus of Nazareth. That is what was meant by those who introduced their Gospels in this way.

And those who endeavored to perpetuate the wisdom of these Gospels—what did they say? How did the Johannine Christians put it? They said: In the individual human being a great and mighty event can take place that can be called the rebirth of the higher ego. As the child is born of the mother, so the divine ego is born of man. Initiation, awakening, is possible; and when once this has come to pass—so said those who were competent to speak—a new standard of values will arise.

Let us try to understand by a comparison what it is that henceforth becomes important. Suppose we have before us a man seventy years old—an "awakened" man who has attained to his higher ego—and suppose he had been in his fortieth year when he experienced rebirth, the awakening of his higher ego. Had someone approached him at that time with the intention of describing his life he could have reflected: I have before me a man who has just given birth to his higher ego. It is the same man I knew five years ago in certain circumstances, and ten years ago in others. And if he had wanted to portray the identity of this man, if he had wanted to show that this man had a quite special start, even at birth, he would trace back the forty years with his physical existence in mind and describe the latter as far as pertinent, in the manner of one who sees matters from the spiritual-scientific viewpoint. But in his fortieth year a higher ego was born in this man, and henceforth this higher ego irradiates all the circumstances of his life. He is a new man. That which existed previously is of no further importance. What is now important is to understand, above all things, how the higher ego grows from year to year and develops further. Now, when this man had arrived at the age of seventy, we would enquire into the path taken by the higher ego from the fortieth to the seventieth year; and if we believe in what was born in the soul of this man thirty years before, it would be of importance to us that it is the true spiritual ego he presents to us in his seventieth year. That is the way the Evangelists went about it; and it was thus, and in connection with the Gospels, that the Johannine Christians of Rosicrucianism dealt with the Being we know as Christ Jesus.

The Gospel writers had set themselves the task of showing, first of all, that Christ Jesus had His origin in the primordial World Spirit, in the God Himself. The God that had dwelt unseen in all mankind is specifically manifested in Christ Jesus; and that is the same God of Whom the John Gospel tells us that He was in the beginning. It was the Evangelist's concern to show that it was precisely this God that dwelt in Jesus of Nazareth. But those whose task it was to continue the eternal wisdom right into our own time now were interested in showing that man's higher ego, the divine spirit of mankind—born in Jesus of Nazareth through the event in Palestine—has remained the same and has been preserved by all who possessed true understanding for it. Just as in our comparison we described how the man bore his higher ego in his fortieth year, so the Evangelists pictured the God that dwells in man up to the event of Palestine—how the God developed, how he was reborn, and so forth. But those who had to demonstrate that they are the successors of the Evangelists, had to point out that this is the time for the rebirth of the higher ego, where one is dealing only with the spiritual part that outshines all else.

Those who called themselves the Johannine Christians and whose symbol was the Rose Cross held that precisely what was reborn for mankind as the secret of its higher ego has been preserved—preserved by the close community which grew out of Rosicrucianism. This continuity is symbolically indicated by that sacred vessel from which Christ Jesus ate and drank with His disciples, and in which Joseph of Arimathea caught the blood that flowed from the wound— the Holy Grail which, as the story is told, was brought to Europe by angels. A temple was built to contain this vessel, and the Rosicrucians became the guardians of what it contained, namely, the essence of the reborn God.

The mystery of the reborn God held sway in humanity. It is the Mystery of the Grail, a mystery propounded like a new Gospel, proclaiming: We look up to a sage such as the writer of the John Gospel who was able to say:

In the beginning was the Word, and the Word was with God, and a God was the Word.

That which was with God in the beginning was born again in Him Whom we have seen suffer and die on Golgotha and Who is risen. This continuity throughout all time of the divine principle and its rebirth, that is what the author of the John Gospel aimed to set forth. Something known to all those who endeavored to proclaim this truth was that what was in the beginning has been preserved. In the beginning was the mystery of the higher ego; it was preserved in the Grail; with the Grail it has remained linked. And in the Grail lives the ego united with the eternal and immortal, just as the lower ego is bound to the ephemeral and mortal. He who knows the secret of the Holy Grail knows that from the wood of the Cross there springs ever new life, the immortal ego, symbolized by the roses on the black wood of the cross.

The secret of the Rose Cross can thus appear like a continuation of the John Gospel; and in reference to the latter and to its continuation it can truly be said:

In the beginning was the Word, and the Word was with

11

God, and a God was the Word. The same was in the beginning with God. All things were made by It;* and without It was not any thing made that was made. In It was life; and the life was the light of men. And the light shineth in the darkness; and the darkness comprehended it not. [John 1:1-5]

Only a few men—those who possessed something of what is not born of the flesh—comprehended the light that shone in the darkness. But then the light became flesh and dwelt among men in the form of Jesus of Nazareth. Here we can say, wholly within the meaning of the John Gospel: That which dwelt as the Christ in Jesus of Nazareth was the higher divine ego of all humanity, of the reborn God Who, in Adam, as His image, became earthly. This reborn human ego continued on; it was preserved as a holy secret under the symbol of the Rose Cross, and is now proclaimed as the secret of the Holy Grail, as the Rose Cross.

The principle which can be born in every human soul as the higher ego points to the rebirth of the divine ego, in the evolution of mankind as a whole, through the Event of Palestine. Just as the higher ego is born in the individual, so the higher ego of all mankind, the divine ego, is born in Palestine; and it is preserved and further developed in what lives concealed in the sign of the Rose Cross.

But if we study the evolution of man we find not only this one great event, the rebirth of the higher ego, but a

---

*John 1: 3–4. Luther's translation, used here by Dr. Steiner, differs from the King James Version. "It" (the Word) remains the subject throughout the passage, not "he" (God), as in the English. That this is the correct translation is made clear by Dr. Steiner in the first and fourth lectures of his other cycle on the St. John Gospel (Hamburg, 1908), and it is therefore incorporated in the passage above. It should also be noted that the words "were made by" do not correctly reflect the Greek. A better translation would be "came into being." A perfectly good word exists in Greek for "were made by," but the Evangelist did not use it.

12

number of lesser ones as well. Before man can give birth to his higher ego, before this mighty, comprehensive, pervasive experience can come to the soul—the birth of the immortal ego in the mortal ego—extensive preparatory stages must have been passed through. A man must prepare himself in many different ways. And after the great experience has come to him that enables him to say to himself, Now I feel within myself something that looks down from above on my ordinary ego, just as my ordinary ego looks upon the things of the senses; now I am a second being within my first; now I have attained to the realms in which I am united with the divine beings—when the human being has had this experience, then he faces further stages that must be passed through, stages differing in their nature from the preparatory ones, but which none the less must be traversed.

Thus there is for each individual the one great incisive event, the birth of the higher ego; and there is a similar birth as well for the whole of mankind: the rebirth of the divine ego. Also, there are stages leading to this incisive event and others that must follow it. To find the former, we look back in time beyond the Christ event. There we encounter other great manifestations in human evolution. We become aware of the gradual approach of the Event of Christ, as indicated by the writer of the Luke Gospel when he says, In the beginning there was a God, a spirit-being in spiritual heights. It descended into the material world and became man, became humanity. True, one could discern in man, as he developed, his origin in the God, but the God Himself could not be perceived by observing human evolution with outer physical eyes alone. He was behind the earthly-physical world, as it were; and there He was seen by those who knew where He is, by those who could behold His kingdoms.

Let us turn back for a moment to the first civilization

that followed upon a great catastrophe, to the ancient Indian civilization. There we find seven great and holy teachers known as the Holy Rishis. They point upwards to a higher being of whom they said, Our wisdom can divine this lofty being, but it cannot perceive it. The vision of the Holy Rishis is great, but the exalted being they called Vishva Karman is beyond their sphere. Vishva Karman, though permeating the spiritual world, is a being beyond what the clairvoyant human eye of that time could reach.

Then followed the civilization called after its great leader, Zarathustra, and Zarathustra spoke as follows to those whom it was his mission to guide: When the clairvoyant eye contemplates the things of this world—minerals, plants, animals, men—it perceives behind these things all sorts of spiritual beings. The being, however, to whom man is indebted for his very existence, who in the future is destined to dwell in man's deepest self, remains hidden as yet from the physical eye and the clairvoyant eye when one contemplates the things of this earth. But when Zarathustra raised his clairvoyant sight to the sun, then—so he said— more than the sun is seen; as an aura is perceived surrounding man, so, in contemplating the sun, the great sun aura is discerned—Ahura Mazdao. And it is the great sun aura that once brought forth man, in a manner to be characterized later. Man is the reflection of the sun spirit, of Ahura Mazdao; but as yet Ahura Mazdao did not dwell on earth. Then comes the time when man, who is becoming clairvoyant, begins to see Ahura Mazdao in what surrounds him on earth. The great moment has arrived when something could take place that had not been possible in Zarathustra's time. When Zarathustra discerned clairvoyantly what was manifested in earthly lightning and thunder, it was not Ahura Mazdao, the great sun spirit who is the prototype of mankind, that he saw; but when he turned to the sun he saw

14

Ahura Mazdao. When Zarathustra had found a successor in Moses, Moses' clairvoyant vision could see in the burning bush and in the fire on Sinai the spirit who proclaimed himself to him as *ehjeh asher ehjeh*, as the "I am, He Who was, He Who is, He Who shall be: *Jahve*, or *Jehova*."

What had taken place? Since that primordial time, since the appearance of Zarathustra and before that of Moses upon earth, the Spirit Who previously had dwelt only on the sun had moved downward to earth. He flamed up in the burning bush and shone in the fire on Sinai: He was in the elements of the earth. And then another period passed; and the Spirit Whose presence the great holy Rishis divined, but of Whom they had to say: Our clairvoyance does not suffice to see Him—the Spirit Whom Zarathustra had to seek in the sun, Who revealed Himself to Moses in thunder and lightning—this Spirit appeared in a human being: in Jesus of Nazareth. That was the evolution: first a descent from the cosmos into the physical elements, then into a human body. Only then was reborn the divine ego from which man descended, and to which the writer of the Luke Gospel traces the genealogy of Jesus of Nazareth. This was the great event of the rebirth of the God in man.

Thus we look back upon the preparatory stages. Mankind, too, passed through these. And those who had advanced with mankind as its earlier leaders also had to pass through these preparatory stages until one of them had advanced to where he could become the bearer of the Christ. Such is the evolution of mankind as seen through spiritual eyes.

And there is another point. What the holy Rishis revered as Vishva Karman, what Zarathustra addressed as the Ahura Mazdao of the sun, and what Moses reverenced as *ehjeh asher ehjeh*—this had to appear in a single human being, in Jesus of Nazareth, in physically circumscribed humanness. This is how far it had to come. But to enable so exalted a being

15

to dwell in such a man as Jesus of Nazareth, many circumstances had to contribute. For one thing, Jesus of Nazareth himself had to have arrived at an exalted level. Not every man could be the vehicle of such a being that comes into the world in the manner described. Now, we who have made contact with spiritual science know that there is reincarnation. Therefore, we must realize that Jesus of Nazareth—not the Christ—had experienced many incarnations and that he had passed through the most manifold stages in his previous incarnations before he could become Jesus of Nazareth.

This means nothing less than that Jesus of Nazareth had himself to become a high initiate before he could become the Christ bearer. Now, when a lofty initiate is born, how do such a birth and the subsequent life differ from the birth and life of an ordinary man? In a general way it can be assumed that when a man is born he bears the characteristics, at least approximately, of what derives from a previous incarnation. But that is not the case with an initiate. The initiate could not be a leader of mankind if he bore within him only what wholly corresponds to the external, for man must build up his external nature according to the conditions of his external environment. When an initiate is born there must enter his body a lofty soul that in past times has had mighty experiences in the world. That is why legend has it that the birth of all initiates occurs in a manner differing from that of other human beings.

As to why and how this is so, we have already touched upon the answer to the first of these questions. It is because a comprehensive ego that had already passed through significant experiences in the past now unites with a body, but this body is at first unable to receive what seeks to incarnate in it as spiritual nature. For this reason it is necessary, in the case of a lofty being incarnating as a high initiate in a perishable human being, that the reincarnating ego should from the start envelop the physical form more intensely than in the case of other men. While in the ordinary human being the physical form resembles and adapts itself soon after birth to the spiritual form, or human aura, the human aura of a reborn initiate is luminous. It is the spiritual part that proclaims that here more is present than can be seen in the ordinary sense. What does it proclaim? That not only has a child been born in the physical world, but that something has occurred in the spiritual world. The stories that attach to the birth of all reincarnating initiates express the idea, Not only is a child born: something is born in the spirit as well, something that cannot be encompassed by what is born down below.

But who can discern this? Only one who himself has a clairvoyant eye for the spiritual world. Hence it is said that in the birth of Buddha an initiate recognized an event differing from an ordinary birth. Hence it is related of Jesus of Nazareth that the Baptist had first to foretell his coming. One who has insight into the spiritual world knows that the initiate must come and be reborn; and he knows that this is an event in the spiritual world. The three kings from the East who came to offer sacrifice at the birth of Jesus of Nazareth knew it too. And the same truth is indicated when the initiated Priest of the Temple says: Now I can die gladly, since mine eyes have beheld the One Who will be the salvation of mankind.

Clearly, then, we must here differentiate accurately. We have an exalted initiate reborn as Jesus of Nazareth, of whose birth it must be said that a child was born; but with this child there appeared something that will not be encompassed by his physical body. This discloses at the same time something in this Jesus of Nazareth that has significance in the spiritual world, something that will gradually develop this body upward to the point where it will be fit to receive this

17

spirit. And when this was fulfilled, the event did occur in which the Baptist approaches Jesus of Nazareth, and a loftier spirit descends and unites with this Jesus of Nazareth: the Christ enters Jesus of Nazareth. And then the Baptist, the Forerunner of Christ Jesus, can well say: I came into the world. It was I who prepared the way for a loftier one. With the words of my mouth I proclaimed the coming of the Kingdom of God, the Realm of the Heavens, and I exhorted men to change their hearts. I came among men, and it was vouchsafed me to bring them tidings of a special impulse that is to come to mankind. As in the springtime the sun mounts higher to announce the budding of something new, so did I appear to bring tidings of what is burgeoning in mankind as the reborn ego of humanity.

Then, when the human principle had reached its height in Jesus of Nazareth, his human body having become an expression of his spirit, he was ripe to receive within himself the Christ at the Baptism by John. The body of Jesus of Nazareth had unfolded like the bright sun on St. John's Day in June. That had been foretold. Then the spirit was to be born out of the darkness, just as the sun steadily gains in strength and power up to St. John's Day, and then begins to decline. That was what the Baptist had to proclaim. He had to continue to bear witness until—pointing to the sun's ever-increasing splendor—he could say, He of Whom the old Prophets told, He Who in the spiritual realms has been called the Son of the Spiritual Realms, He has appeared!—Up to this point John the Baptist was active. But then—when the days become shorter and darkness begins to gain the upper hand—then the inner spiritual light is to shine as a result of right preparation, is to become ever brighter as the Christ shines in Jesus of Nazareth.

That is the way John the Baptist saw the approach of Jesus of Nazareth; and he felt the growth of Jesus of Nazareth as his own diminution and as the increase in the power of the sun. From now on I shall wane, he said, even as the sun wanes after St. John's Day. But He will wax—He the spiritual sun—and shine out of the darkness.—Thus was the Christ heralded; and thus began the rebirth of the ego of mankind, upon which depends the rebirth of every individual higher human ego.

This characterizes the most important event in the development of the individual human being: the rebirth of what can proceed from the ordinary ego as the immortal principle. It is linked with the greatest event, the Christ event, to which the next lectures will be devoted.

II

When a subject such as our present one is discussed from the standpoint of spiritual science, this is not done by basing the facts upon some document or other exposition come into being in the course of human development, and by then illuminating the facts in question on the authority of such a document. That is not the way of spiritual science. On the contrary, entirely independent of all documents, spiritual science investigates what has occurred in human evolution; and only then—after the spiritual scientist has completed his research by means independent of any documents, and knows how to describe what he has found—only then is the document in question examined with a view to discovering whether it agrees with what has first been discovered by spiritual research independently of any tradition whatever. So all the statements made in these lectures concerning the course of this or that event are by no means to be taken as merely deriving from the Bible, from one of the four Gospels, but rather as the results arrived at by spiritual research independent of the Gospels. But no opportunity will be missed to show that everything the spiritual scientist can fathom and observe is to be found in the Gospels, particularly in the Gospel of St. John.

We have a curious utterance by the great mystic Jacob Boehme which puzzles all who are not in touch with spiritual science. Jacob Boehme once drew attention to his way of discussing past epochs in human evolution—say, the figure of Adam—as though they had been within the scope of his own experiences, and he said: "Many might ask, Were you then present when Adam walked the earth?" And Jacob Boehme answers unequivocally: "Yes, I was present." Now, that is a noteworthy statement; for actually, spiritual science is in a position really to observe with the eyes of the spirit whatever has occurred, be it ever so far back. And in these introductory remarks I should like to touch briefly upon the reason for this.

Everything that happens in the physical sensorial world has, of course, its counterpart in the spiritual world. When a hand moves there is present not only what your eye sees as a moving hand, but behind this moving hand, this visible image of the hand, there are, for example, my thought and my will: the hand is to move. In short, a spiritual element underlies it all. But while the visible image, the sense impression of the hand motion, passes, its spiritual counterpart remains inscribed in the spiritual world and always leaves a trace; so if our spiritual eyes are opened we can trace all things that have happened in the world by the imprints left by their spiritual counterparts. Nothing can occur in the world without leaving such traces.

Suppose the spiritual scientist gazes back to Charlemagne, or to the time of Rome, or to Greek Antiquity: everything that took place there has been preserved in the spiritual world as imprints of its spiritual prototypes, and can be seen there. This viewing of the traces, which all events leave behind in the spiritual world, is called the "reading in the *Akasha Chronicle*." There exists this living script which the spiritual eye can see; and when the spiritual scientist describes the events of Palestine or the observation of Zarathustra he is not describing what is found in the Bible or in the Gathas, but what he himself is able to read in the *Akasha Chronicle*. Only then does he investigate whether the disclosures of the *Akasha Chronicle* are to be found in the documents as well— in our case, the Gospels.

The attitude, therefore, of spiritual research toward documents is wholly unhampered; and for this very reason spiritual research will be the true judge of what documents have to tell. But when we find the same information in the documents as we were able to glean from the *Akasha Chronicle* we infer first, that the documents are true, and second, that someone must have written them who was also able to read in the *Akasha Chronicle*. Many religious and other documents of the human race are retrieved by spiritual science in this way. What has just been said shall now be clarified by the study of a special chapter in human evolution, the Gospel of St. John, and its relation to the other Gospels. But you must not imagine that the *Akasha Chronicle*, the spiritual history which lies open like a book before the seer's eyes, resembles any script of the ordinary world. It is a living kind of script, and we will try to understand this through what is to follow.

Suppose the seer gazes back in time—say, to the time of Caesar. Caesar did certain deeds, and in so far as they occurred on the physical plane his contemporaries witnessed them. But they all left their traces in the *Akasha Chronicle*; and when the seer looks back he sees them as spiritual shadow-pictures or prototypes. Call to mind again the movement of the hand: as a seer you do not perceive the picture this presents to the eye, but you will always see the intention to move the hand, the invisible forces that move it. In the same way is to be seen everything that went on in Caesar's thoughts, be it certain steps he intended to take or some battle he planned. Everything seen by his contemporaries originated in the impulses of his will and was executed by the invisible forces underlying the sense images. But the latter really appear in the *Akasha Chronicle* as the Caesar who moved and acted, as the spiritual image of Caesar.

Here someone inexperienced in such matters might object: Your tales of past ages are nothing but daydreams—you know from your history what Caesar did, and now your mighty imagination makes you believe you are seeing all sorts of invisible *akashic* pictures. But one who has experience in these things knows that the less familiar one is with such events through outer history, the easier it is to read in the *Akasha Chronicle*; for outer history and a knowledge of it are actually confusing for the seer. When we have reached a certain age we are hampered by various aspects of our education connected with the age in which we live. In the same way the seer, equipped with the education provided by his epoch, arrives at the point when he can give birth to his clairvoyant ego. He has studied history; he has learned how things are handed down in geology, biology, archeology, and the history of culture. All this actually interferes with his vision and may prejudice him in his reading of the *Akasha Chronicle*; for in outer history one can by no means expect to find the same objectivity and certainty that are to be achieved in deciphering the *Akasha Chronicle*.

Consider for a moment what it is that causes this or that event to become what is called history: it may be that certain documents have been preserved relating to some events, while others—and perhaps the most important ones—have been lost. An example will show how unreliable all history can be. Among a number of poems Goethe had planned but did not finish—and for the deeper student these constitute a beautiful supplement to the great and glorious finished works he left us—there is the fragment of a poem on *Nausicaa*. There exist only a few sketches in which Goethe had noted how he intended to deal with this poem. He often worked that way, jotting down a few sentences of which frequently but little is preserved. That was the case with the *Nausicaa*. A few slips of paper exist with some notes written on them. Now, there were two men who endeavored to complete this work, both of them research men: Scherer, the literary historian, and Herman Grimm. But Herman Grimm was not only a researcher but an imaginative thinker—the man who wrote *The Life of Michelangelo* and the *Goethe*. Herman Grimm went about the task by trying to find his way into Goethe's spirit, and he asked himself: Goethe being what he was, how would he have conceived of a figure like the Nausicaa of the *Odyssey*? Whereupon, with a certain disregard of that historical document, he created a *Nausicaa* in the spirit of Goethe. Scherer, on the other hand, who always sought what was to be found among the documents in black and white, argued that a *Nausicaa* begun by Goethe must be completed purely on the basis of the material available; and he, too, tried to construct a *Nausicaa*, but exclusively out of what these scraps of paper had to offer. Of this procedure Herman Grimm remarked: What if Goethe's servant used some of these scraps of paper—perhaps just the ones containing something every important—for lighting the fire? Have we any guarantee that the surviving scraps of paper are of any value at all compared with those that may have been used for lighting the fire?

All history based on documents may be analagous to this illustration, and indeed it often is. When building on documents we must never lose sight of the possibility that just the most important ones may have perished. Indeed, what passes for history is nothing more nor less than a *fable convenue*. But when the seer is hampered by this convention and at the same time sees everything quite differently in the *Akasha Chronicle*, it is difficult for him to have faith in the *akashic* picture; and the public will voice its resentment when he tells a different story out of the *Akasha Chronicle*. Hence one who is experienced in these things likes best to speak of ancient times of which there exist no documents, of the remote stages in the evolution of our earth. There are no documents relating to those epochs; and that is where the *Akasha Chronicle* reports most faithfully, because the seer is not confused by outer history. You will be able to gather from these remarks that it could never occur to anyone familiar with these matters that the pictures provided by the *Akasha Chronicle* might be an echo of what is already known to him from outer history.

If we now search the *Akasha Chronicle* for the great event to which we alluded yesterday, we find the following salient points. The whole human race, in as far as it lives on the earth, is descended from a divine realm, from a divine-spiritual existence. It can be stated that before any possibility existed for a physical eye to see human bodies, for a hand to touch human bodies, man was present as a spiritual being; and in the earliest ages he existed as a part of the divine-spiritual beings. As a being, man is born out of divine-spiritual beings. The Gods are the ancestors of men, so to speak, and men the descendants of the Gods. The Gods had need of men as their issue, because without them they would have been unable to descend, as it were, into the sensorial physical world. In that remote time the Gods continued their existence in other worlds, acting from without upon man who gradually evolved upon the earth.

And now men had to overcome, step by step, the obstacles placed in their path by their earth life. What is the nature of these obstacles? The essential point in regard to the human being is the fact that the Gods remained spiritual, while men, as their descendants, became physical. All the obstacles presented specifically by physical existence had to be surmounted by man, who possessed spirit only as the inner phase of the physical, and who as an outer being had become physical. It was within the confines of material existence that he had to develop; and it was in this way that he progressed upward step by step, steadily maturing until he should be-

25

come increasingly able to turn to the Gods in whom he had his genesis. A descent from the Gods, and then a turning back to them, in order to reach and re-unite with them, that is man's path through life on earth. But if this evolution was to come about, certain human individualities always had to develop more rapidly than the rest, to hurry on ahead in order to become their leaders and teachers. Such men, then, have their being in humanity's midst and find their way back to the Gods, as it were, in advance of others. We can picture it in this way: In a given epoch men have attained to a certain degree of maturity in their development. They may have the premonition of a return to the Gods, but they have a long way to go before achieving it. Every man has within him a spark of the divine, but in the leaders it is always brighter: they are closer to that divine principle to which man must ultimately attain again. And this that dwells in the leaders of mankind is perceived, by those whose eyes have been opened to the spirit, as their essence and chief attribute.

Let us suppose some great leader of mankind confronted another man, not his equal but above the average. The latter feels vividly that the other is a great leader, permeated to a high degree by the spirituality to which other men must eventually attain. How would such a man describe this leader? He might say: Before me stands a man, a man in a physical body like everyone else; but his physical body is negligible, it need not be taken into account. When, however, I observe him with the eye of the spirit, I see united with him a mighty spiritual being, a divine-spiritual being which predominates to such an extent that my whole attention is focussed on it—not on what appears as body which he has in common with others.

To spiritual sight, then, there appears in a leader of mankind something which in its nature towers above the rest of

26

humanity, and which must be described in quite a different way: the description must be of what the spiritual eye sees. Nowadays public men whose word is law would undoubtedly be amused at the idea of such surpassing leaders of mankind: we already have the spectacle of various erudite scientists regarding the shining lights of humanity as psychiatric cases. Such a leader would only be recognized as such by those whose spiritual vision had been sharpened; but these would indeed know that he was neither a fool nor a visionary, nor simply a very gifted person, as the more benevolent might designate him, but rather, that he was among the greatest figures of human life in the spiritual sense.

That is the way it would be today; but in the past it was a different matter, even in the not too remote past. Human consciousness, as we know, has undergone various metamorphoses, and formerly all men were endowed with a dim, shadowy clairvoyance. Even at the time when Christ lived on earth clairvoyance was still developed to a certain degree, and in earlier centuries even more so, though it was but a shadow of the clairvoyance common in the Atlantean and the first post-Atlantean epochs. It disappeared only gradually. But a few isolated individuals still had it, and even today there are natural clairvoyants, whose dim higher vision enables them to distinguish the spiritual nature of men.

Let us turn to the time in which Buddha appeared to the ancient Indian people. Conditions were very different at that time. Today the appearance of a Buddha, especially in Europe, would arouse no particular respect. But in Buddha's age it was a different matter, for there were a great number of people who could discern the true nature of the event, namely, that this Buddha birth signified something other than does an ordinary birth. In oriental writings, especially in those treating the subject with the deepest understanding, the birth of Buddha is described in the grand manner, as one might put it. It is related that Queen Maya was "the image of the Great Mother," and that it was foretold she would bring a mighty being into the world. This being was then born prematurely. This is frequently the means of sending an outstanding being into the world, because thereby the human being, in which the higher spiritual being is to incarnate, is less closely united with matter than when the child is carried the full time of gestation. It is then further related in the notable records of the Orient that at the moment of birth Buddha was enlightened, that he opened his eyes at once and directed his gaze to the four points of the compass, to the north, south, east, and west. We are told that he then took seven steps, and that the marks of these steps are engraved in the ground he trod. It is further recorded that he spoke at once, and the words he spoke were these: "This is the life in which I shall rise from Bodhisattva to Buddha, the last incarnation I shall have to pass through on this earth!"

Strange as such a communication may appear to the materialistic-minded man of today, and impossible as it is to interpret offhand from a materialistic viewpoint, it is nevertheless the truth for one who is able to see things with the eye of the spirit; and at that time there still existed men who, by means of natural clairvoyance, could discern spiritually what it was that was born with Buddha. Those are strange excerpts I have quoted from the oriental writings: nowadays they are called legends and myths. But he who understands these things knows that something of spiritual truth is hidden therein; and events such as the Buddha birth have significance not only for the intimate circle of the personality in question but for the world as well, for they radiate spiritual forces, as it were. And those who lived at a time when the world was more receptive to spiritual forces perceived that at the birth of Buddha spiritual forces were actually rayed forth.

It would be a trivial question to ask: Why does that sort of thing not still occur today? As a matter of fact, it does happen; only it requires a seer to perceive it. It is not enough that there should be one to radiate these forces; there must also be someone there to receive them. When people were more spiritual than they are today they were also more receptive to such radiations. So again a profound truth underlies the story that healing and reconciling forces were at work when Buddha was born. It is not merely a legend but a report based on deep truths which tells us that when Buddha came into the world, those who had previously hated each other were now united in love, those who had quarreled now met with expressions of mutual esteem, and so forth.

To one who surveys the development of mankind with the eye of the seer this does not appear as it does to the historian—a level path, at most overtopped a bit here and there by figures accepted as historical. Men will not admit that spiritual peaks and mountains exist—that is more than they can bear. But the seer knows that there are lofty heights and mountains towering above the path of the rest of mankind: these are the leaders of humanity. Now, what is such leadership based on? It is based on man's gradually passing through the levels that lead to life in the spiritual world. One of the levels we pointed out yesterday as the most important one: the birth of the higher ego, the spiritual ego; and we said that this was preceded and followed by other stages. It is evident that what we designate the Christ event is the mightiest peak in the range of human evolution, and that a long preparation was indispensable before the Christ Being could incarnate in Jesus of Nazareth.

In order to understand this preparation we must visualize the same phenomenon on a smaller scale. Let us suppose a man starts on the path to spiritual cognition in any one of his incarnations—that is, he carries out some of the exercises (to be described later) which render the soul more and more spiritual, more receptive to what is spiritual, and guide it toward the moment when it bears the higher, imperishable ego that can see into the spiritual world. Man undergoes many experiences before that moment arrives. One must not imagine that anything pertaining to the spirit can be hurried, it must be passed through with patience and perseverance. Let us suppose, then, that someone starts a training of this kind. His aim is the birth of the higher ego, but he only succeeds in reaching a certain preliminary stage. Then he dies; and in due time he is born again. Here one of two things can happen: either he can feel the urge to seek a teacher who will show him how he can rapidly repeat what he had previously passed through and attain to the higher stages, or else, for one reason or another, he does not take this way. In the latter case, as well, the unfolding of his life will often be different from that of the lives of other men. The life of one, who has already undergone some part of the path of enlightenment, will quite of itself provide something resembling effects of the level of perception he had attained in his previous incarnation. He will have experiences of a different nature, and the impression of these on him will be different from that received by other men. Then he will attain anew, by means of these experiences, to what he had previously achieved through his efforts. In his former incarnation he had to strive actively from step to step; but now that life brings him as a recurrence, so to speak, what he had once acquired through effort, this approaches him from without, as it were; and it may be that he will experience the results of his previous incarnations in quite a different form.

Thus it may happen that even in his childhood some experience can make upon his soul an impression of such a nature as to re-engender the forces he had acquired in his previous life. Suppose such a man had attained to a certain degree of wisdom in a given incarnation. He is then born again as a child, like everyone else. But at the age of seven or eight he has some painful experience, and the consequence is that all the wisdom he had once acquired comes to the fore again: he is back at the stage he had reached before, and thence can advance to the next one. Now we will suppose further that he endeavors to proceed another few steps, and dies again. In his next incarnation the same thing can happen again: once more some outer experience can put him to the test, as it were, again revealing first, what he had achieved in his next to the last incarnation, and then, in his last one. And now he can climb another step.

You will see from this that only by taking account of such events can we understand the life of one who had already passed through certain stages of development. There is one stage, for instance, that is soon reached by serious striving along the path of enlightenment: the stage of the so-called homeless person, of him who has outgrown the prejudices of his immediate surroundings and has cast off the fetters imposed by his environment. This need not make him irreverent; he can be all the more reverent. But he must be free of the shackles of his immediate surroundings. Let us assume that this man dies at a stage in which he has already worked his way through to a modicum of freedom and independence. When he is born again it can happen that comparatively early in his life some experience will re-awaken this feeling of freedom and independence in him. As a rule, this is the result of losing his father or someone else to whom he is closely bound; or it might be a consequence of his father's reprehensible behavior toward him—he might have cast him out, or something of the sort. All this is faithfully reported in the legends of the various peoples, for in matters of this kind the folk myths and legends are really wiser than is modern science. Among the legends you will often find the type in which the child is cast out, is found by shepherds, nourished and brought up by them, and later restored to his station (Chiron, Romulus and Remus). The fact that their own home plays them false serves to re-awaken in them the fruits of former incarnations. The legend of the casting out of Oedipus belongs in this category, too. You will now understand that the more advanced a man is—whether at the stage when his higher ego is born or even farther—the richer in experience his life must be if he is to be capable of a new experience, one he has not yet had.

He who was destined to embody in himself the mighty Being we call the Christ could naturally not assume this mission at any random age; he had first to mature very gradually. No ordinary man could undertake this mission; it had to be one who in the course of many lives had attained to lofty degrees of initiation. What was here demanded is faithfully told us in the *Akasha Chronicle*. This relates how a certain individuality had striven upward throughout many lives step by step to high degrees of initiation. Then this individuality was born again, and in this earthly embodiment passed first through preparatory experiences. But in this embodiment there lived an individuality who had already passed through high stages of initiation, an initiate destined in a later period of his life to receive into himself the Individuality of the Christ. And the first experiences of this initiate are repetitions of his former degrees of initiation, whereby all the previous achievements of his soul are re-evoked.

Now, we know that the human being consists of physical body, etheric body, astral body, and ego. But we also know that in the course of human life only the physical body is born at physical birth, and that up to the seventh year the etheric body is still enclosed in a sort of etheric maternal sheath which is then discarded, at the time of the change of teeth, in the same way as is the physical maternal sheath when the physical body is born into the outer physical world.

32

Similarly, at puberty, an astral sheath is thrown off and the astral body is born. And approximately in the twenty-first year the ego is born, but again only gradually.

Having considered the birth of the physical body, of the etheric body in the seventh year, and of the astral body in the fourteenth or fifteenth year, we must similarly take into account a birth of the sentient soul, the intellectual soul, and the consciousness soul; and the ages at which these births occur are approximately the twenty-first, the twenty-eighth, and the thirty-fifth year respectively. From this it is evident that the Christ Being could not incarnate in a man of this earth, could not find room in such a man, before the intellectual soul was completely born: the Christ Being could not embody in the initiate into whom He was born before this initiate had reached his twenty-eighth year. Spiritual investigation confirms this. It was between the twenty-eighth and thirty-fifth years that the Christ Being entered the individuality who walked the earth as a great initiate, and who gradually, in the light and radiance of this great Being, unfolded all that otherwise man develops without this radiance, this light; namely, the etheric body, the astral body, the sentient soul, and the intellectual soul. Thus we can say that up to this age we see before us in him who was called to be the Christ bearer a lofty initiate who gradually passed through the experiences that finally evoked all he had undergone in previous incarnations—the sum of his conquests in the spiritual world. Only then could he say, Now I am here; now will I sacrifice all that I have. I no longer desire an independent ego, but will make of myself the bearer of the Christ: henceforth He shall dwell in me, shall fill me completely.

All four Gospels stress this moment when the Christ incorporated in a personality of this earth. However much they may differ in other respects, they all point to this event of the Christ slipping into the great initiate, as it were: the

Baptism by John. In that moment, so clearly defined by the author of the John Gospel when he says that the Spirit descended in the form of a dove and united with Jesus of Nazareth, in that moment occurred the birth of Christ; as a new and higher Ego the Christ is born in the soul of Jesus of Nazareth. Until then, another ego, that of a great initiate, had developed to the lofty plane on which it was ripe for this event.

And Who was it that was to be born in the being of Jesus of Nazareth? This was indicated yesterday: the God Who was there from the beginning, Who had remained aloof in the spiritual world, so to speak, leaving mankind to its evolution. He it was Who was now to descend and incarnate in Jesus of Nazareth. Can we find this indicated by the writer of the John Gospel? We need only take the words of the Gospel very seriously; and with this in mind let us read the beginning of the Old Testament.

In the (primordial) *beginning God created the heaven and the earth.*

And the earth was without form, and void; and darkness was upon the face of the deep. And the Spirit of God moved upon the face of the waters.

Let us visualize the situation: *The Spirit of God moved upon the face of the waters.* Below, the earth with its kingdoms as the issue of the divine Spirit; and among these one individual evolves to the point of being able to take into himself this Spirit that moved upon the face of the waters. What does the author of the John Gospel say? He tells us that John the Baptist realized that the Being spoken of in the Old Testament was here. He says:

I saw the Spirit descending from heaven like a dove, and it abode upon him. [John 1:32]

He knew that upon whomsoever the Spirit should descend was He that was to come: the Christ. There you have the beginning of world evolution: the Spirit moving upon the face of the waters; and there you have John who baptizes with water, and the Spirit that in the beginning moved upon the face of the waters and now descends into the individuality of Jesus of Nazareth. It would be impossible to connect the event of Palestine in a more grandiose way than does the writer of the John Gospel with that other event, told at the beginning of the same document to which the Gospel relates itself.

But in other ways as well we find the John Gospel linked with this oldest of documents. The writer effects this by pointing out that with Jesus of Nazareth is merged the same principle that from the beginning worked creatively at all earth evolution. We know that the opening words of the Gospel of St. John read:

In the beginning was the Word (or *Logos*), *and the Word* (or *Logos*) *was with God, and a God was the Word* (or *Logos*).

What is this *Logos*, and in what sense was it with God? Let us turn to the beginning of the Old Testament, to the passage presenting this Spirit of whom it is written:

And the Spirit of God moved upon the face of the waters. And the divine Spirit said, Let there be light: and there was light.

Let us keep that in mind and express it somewhat differently; let us listen to the divine Spirit intoning the creative Word through the world. What is this Word? In the beginning was the *Logos*, and the divine Spirit called out, and what the Spirit called out came to pass. That means that in the Word there was life; for had there been no life in it, nothing could have come to pass. And what was it that came to pass? We are told:

And God said, Let there be light: and there was light.
Turn back here to the John Gospel:

In the beginning was the Word, and the Word was with God, and a God was the Word.

35

Now the Word had streamed into matter, where it became the outer form of the Godhead, as it were.

In it was life; and the life was the light of men.

In this way the author links his Gospel to that oldest of documents, the *Book of Genesis*. He refers to the same divine Spirit, only in different words. Then he makes it clear to us that this is the divine Spirit Who appears in Jesus of Nazareth. All four Evangelists agree that with the Baptism by John the Christ was born in Jesus of Nazareth, and that for the consummation of this event Jesus of Nazareth had needed comprehensive preparation. We must understand that everything previously told us concerning the life of Jesus of Nazareth is nothing but the sum of experiences portraying his ascent into the higher worlds during previous incarnations: the gradual preparation of everything embraced in his astral body, etheric body, and physical body for the eventual reception of the Christ.

The Evangelist who wrote the Gospel of St. Luke even says, somewhat emphatically, that Jesus of Nazareth had prepared himself in every respect for this great event, the birth of Christ in him. The individual experiences that led him upward to the Christ event will be discussed tomorrow. Today I shall merely point out that the author of the Luke Gospel told us in a single sentence that he who received the Christ into himself had indeed prepared himself in the previous years: that his astral body had achieved the virtue, nobility and wisdom indispensable for the birth of the Christ in him; and furthermore, that he had brought his etheric body to such a degree of maturity, and had developed such pliancy and beauty in his physical body, that the Christ could dwell in him.—One need only understand the Gospel aright. Take the second Chapter of Luke, verse 52. True, the wording of this verse in most of the Bible translations will not tell you what I just said. There it says:

36

And Jesus increased in wisdom and age*, and in favor with God and man.

It would still make sense if such a man as the writer of the Luke Gospel had related of Jesus of Nazareth that he increased in wisdom; but when he reports as a solemn fact that he increased in age—well, that is not clear on its face, for it is a circumstance calling for no special emphasis. That it is nevertheless mentioned suggests that something more must be involved. Let us examine the verse in question in the original text:

Kai Jesous proekopten en te sophia, kai helekia kai chariti para theo kai anthropois.

As a matter of fact, here is what this means: "He increased in wisdom" signifies that he developed his *astral body*; and anyone who knows what the Greek mind associated with the word *helekia* can tell you that the term refers to the development of the *etheric body*, whereby wisdom gradually becomes skill. As you know, the astral body develops the qualities called upon for individual occasions: we understand something once and for all. The etheric body, on the other hand, shapes what it develops into habits, inclinations, and capabilities. This occurs by means of constant repetition. Wisdom becomes a habit: it is practised because it has become second nature. So what this "increase in age" means is an increase in *maturity*: just as the astral body has grown in wisdom, so the etheric body has increased in pure habits in the realm of goodness, nobility, and beauty. And the third quality that increased in Jesus of Nazareth, *charis*, really means that which manifests itself and becomes visible as beauty. No other translations are right. In translating this verse we

---

**TRANSLATOR'S NOTE: In Luther's translation "age" is the word that corresponds to the "stature" of our King James version. It is retained here in order to avoid altering the term adhered to by Dr. Steiner.

37

must indicate that Jesus gained in *gracious beauty*; in other words, that his *physical body*, too, grew in beauty and nobility.

And Jesus increased in wisdom (in his astral body), *in maturity of disposition* (in his etheric body), *and in gracious beauty* (in his physical body), *in a way manifest to God and man.*

There you have the delineation given by St. Luke. Clearly, he knew that he who was to receive the Christ into himself had first to develop the threefold sheath—physical body, etheric body, and astral body—to its highest capacity.

In this way we shall learn how one can rediscover in the Gospels what spiritual science tells us independent of them. For this reason spiritual science constitutes a cultural current capable of recapturing the religious documents; and this recapture will not remain a mere milestone in human knowledge and cognition, but will stand as a conquest of soul and mind in the realm of feeling and mood. And that is precisely the sort of understanding we need if we are to grasp the intervention of the Christ in the evolution of humanity.

III

Those of you who have been attending my lecture cycles or single lectures on spiritual-scientific subjects have had various facts of the higher worlds presented from many different aspects, and various beings as well were introduced to us in one realm or another and were shown from different sides. In order to anticipate any possible misconceptions that might arise I should like to point out today that when these beings and facts are considered, now from one angle, now from another, a superficial view might see contradictions. But if you look more closely you will see that these complicated facts of the spiritual world can be clarified only by throwing light on them from many sides. It is necessary to say this because certain facts with which most of you are already familiar from one aspect must in part be illuminated today from another, a new angle. We need only turn to that most profound document of the New Testament, familiar as the Gospel according to St. John, and read the pregnant words, which we quoted yesterday, in order to sense the literally endless enigmas of cosmic and human evolution hidden in the opening words of this Gospel. In the course of our observations the opportunity may present itself to show why the great narrators of spiritual events often expressed precisely the mighty, comprehensive truths in such a concise, paradigmatical form as we find in the opening verses of the John Gospel. Today we will return to certain well-known facts of spiritual science, treating them from an aspect differing from yesterday's, and see in what form we meet them

39

again in the Gospel of St. John. Let us take our point of departure from the most elementary facts of spiritual science, comparatively speaking.

As we know, man in his ordinary state consists of four principles: physical body, etheric or life body, astral body, and ego, and we know that his daily life alternates in such a way that during his waking hours these four members of his being are organically interconnected and penetrate each other, whereas during sleep, while the physical and etheric bodies remain in bed, the astral body and the ego bearer—we may call it simply the ego—are removed. Now, there is one point we must thoroughly understand today. The human being of the present stage of evolution contains this fourfoldness of interpenetrating bodies as a necessary condition. As he lies in bed at night with only his physical and etheric bodies present he has, in a sense, the value of a plant, for the plant, as it appears in the outer world, consists only of physical body and etheric or life body; it bears no astral body or ego, and is thus differentiated from the animal and from man. The animal is the first to have an astral body, and man, an ego. Hence it can be said that during sleep, when his physical and etheric bodies alone remain in bed, man is in a sense a plantlike being. But again, he is not like a plant, and this must be rightly understood. In the present age a free and independent being having neither astral body nor ego, but consisting solely of etheric body and physical body, must have the appearance of a plant—must, in fact, be a plant. On the other hand man, as he lies asleep in bed, has grown beyond the value of a plant, because during the course of evolution he has added to his physical and etheric body an astral body—bearer of joy and sorrow, pleasure and pain, impulses, desires, and passions—and also the bearer of the ego. But the acquisition of a higher principle always involves a corresponding alteration in all that pertains to the

40

lower principles. If an astral body were added to the plant we see today as a being of outer nature, if this astral body were not only to hover over the plant but to permeate it, then what we see penetrating the plant in its substance would have to become animal flesh. That is because upon entering, the astral body would transform the plant in such a way as to convert the substance into animal flesh. And the addition of an ego in the physical world would entail an analogous transformation.

We may therefore say that in a being like man, whose nature embraces not only a physical body but invisible, higher, supersensible principles as well, the supersensible members find expression in the lowest ones. Just as the inner qualities of your soul are superficially expressed in your features, in your physiognomy, so your physical body is an expression of the work performed by your astral body and ego; and the physical body does not represent merely itself; it stands as the physical expression of the human principles that are physically invisible. Thus the glandular system and all that pertains to it is an expression of the etheric body, everything connected with the nervous system is an expression of the astral body, and all that is comprised in the circulation is an expression of the ego bearer. So in the physical body itself we again have to take into account a fourfold organization; and only one who worships a crass materialistic world conception could classify the various substances in the human body as equivalent. The blood pulsating in our veins became the substance it is as a result of the fact that an ego dwells in us; the form and substance of the nervous system are due to the presence of an astral body; and the glandular system is the outcome of the etheric body.

If you will take all this into consideration you will readily see that between falling asleep at night and waking up in the morning the human being is really a being inwardly filled

41

with contradictions. One is inclined to call him a plant, yet he is not a plant because the physical substance of a plant lacks the expression of the astral body—the nervous system —as well as the expression of the ego—the circulatory system. A physical being such as man, equipped with a glandular, a nervous, and a circulatory system, can exist only by means of an etheric body, an astral body, and an ego; but in the night you forsake your physical and etheric bodies—that is, in as far as your astral body and ego constitute you a human being. You basely abandon them, as it were, making them into a self-contradictory being. Were nothing of a spiritual nature to intervene at this time, while you simply withdraw your astral body and ego from your physical and etheric bodies, you would find your nervous and circulatory systems destroyed when you woke up in the morning; for these cannot exist without your having an astral body and an ego within you. Therefore the following takes place, perceptible to clairvoyant consciousness:

In proportion to the withdrawal of the ego and astral body the clairvoyant sees a divine ego and a divine astral body enter into man. Actually there is during sleep, too, an astral body and an ego—or at least a substitute for these—in the physical and etheric bodies. When man's astral principle passes out, a higher one moves in—as does similarly a substitute for the ego. From this it is evident that within the realm of our lives, within their sphere, beings are at work that have no immediate expression in the physical world. What comes to expression in the physical world are minerals, plants, animals, and human beings. The last are at present the highest of the beings within our physical sphere, for they alone have physical body, etheric body, astral body, and ego. The fact that in sleep the astral body and ego withdraw from the physical and etheric bodies shows us that even today the former retain a certain independence; that they detach themselves, so to speak, and can live for a certain length of time every day thus sundered from the physical and etheric vehicles.

At night, then, we have the following condition: Just as the human physical body and the human etheric body are by day the bearers of the human ego and the human astral body—in other words, of the innermost principles—so by night they become the bearers, or the temple, of higher astral and ego beings. Now we look with different eyes at the sleeper, for the astral principle within him is a divine-spiritual principle, and there is also an ego, but a divine-spiritual ego. In a sense it can be said that while we are asleep in respect of our astral body and ego, we are watched over and the structure of our organization is maintained by these beings that thus become a part of our life, beings that enter our physical and etheric bodies when we ourselves abandon these. A great deal can be learned from a fact of this sort; and especially if taken in conjunction with certain clairvoyant observations it can elucidate much concerning the evolution of man. What we shall now do is to correlate this difference between waking and sleeping with the great spiritual facts of evolution.

The astral body and the ego appear, to be sure, as the highest and most intimate principles of man's nature, but by no means do they prove to be the most perfect. Even to superficial observation the physical body is more perfect than the astral body. Two years ago already, I pointed out here* that the more closely we examine man's physical body, the more admirable it appears in its entire structure. Not only does the marvel of the human heart or the human brain

---

*Lecture cycle, held in Kassel from June 16–29, 1907; published in Bibl. #100 in German as *Human Evolution and Christ-Perception. Theosophy and Rosicrucianism. The St. John Gospel.*

when examined anatomically satisfy the mind's acute, intellectual thirst for knowledge, but whoever approaches these with his soul feels an aesthetic and moral uplift when he realizes how sublime and wise are the provisions made in this physical body. The astral body is as yet less advanced. It is the bearer of joy and sorrow, of impulses, desires, indulgence, and so forth; and we must admit that in order to satisfy his desires man turns to all sorts of things hardly calculated to further the wise and ingenious workings of the heart or the brain. His craving for enjoyment leads him to seek satisfaction in things like coffee, that are poison for the heart, thereby proving the astral body's craving for pleasures that harm the wisely contrived human heart; yet for decades the heart withstands such poisons consumed by man as a result of his astral body's craving for enjoyment.

This proves that the physical body is more nearly perfect than the astral body. At some time in the future the astral body will be incomparably the more perfect of the two, but at present the development of the physical body is the most advanced. That is because it is actually the oldest principle of man's nature. The physical body itself furnishes the evidence that it was worked upon long before our earth came into being.

The modern doctrine of the origin of the world grew out of purely materialistic conceptions, and what it teaches is nothing but a materialistic fantasy; nor does it matter whether it is called the Kant-Laplace theory or, in the case of a later one, something else. For comprehending the outer structure of our world system these materialistic flights are undoubtedly useful, but they are of no avail in helping us understand anything higher than what the outer eye sees. Spiritual research shows that just as the human being passes from incarnation to incarnation, so a cosmic body like our earth has experienced other configurations, other planetary conditions, in the remote past. Before our earth came into being it was in a different planetary condition, called by spiritual science the "old *Moon.*"* This does not refer to our present moon but to an ancestor of our earth as a planetary being; and just as the human being has developed from an earlier form of embodiment into what he is today, so our earth has developed from old *Moon* to *Earth:* the old *Moon* is a sort of previous incarnation of the *Earth.* Going still farther back: a previous incorporation of the old *Moon* was the *Sun*—again not the present sun but an ancestor of our present earth; and finally, the precursor of this old *Sun* was the old *Saturn.* Those are the states our *Earth* passed through: a *Saturn* state, a *Sun* state, and a *Moon* state, and now it has reached its earth state.

The first germ of our physical body appeared on the old *Saturn.* In other words, while nothing of all that surrounds us today existed on that primeval cosmic body we designate the old *Saturn* (not the present planet)—nothing of our ani-

*TRANSLATOR'S NOTE: In his translation of *Occult Science, an Outline,* by Rudolf Steiner, Mr. Henry B. Monges provided an ingenious device for eliminating the confusion that arises so easily in connection with the study of planetary evolution. The following footnote, quoted from *Occult Science,* explains the device, which will be used also in this translation.

"In order to make clear the difference between the designations for the Planetary Evolutions and our present planetary bodies, which bear the same names, the following device has been determined on: *Saturn, Sun, Moon, Earth, Jupiter, Venus, Vulcan* printed in italics with initial capitals designate the great cosmic planetary cycles of evolution. In the *Sun* evolution, after the separation of the main cosmic body into two parts, the designation is Sun and Saturn, spelt with capitals, but not with italics. In the *Moon* evolution, when a separation takes place, the remaining body is spelt Moon, with an initial capital, the separating planetary sun is spelt with small letters. In the *Earth* evolution, the separated planetary bodies are spelt as is customary: The planets Saturn, Jupiter, Mars, Venus, Mercury with initial capitals: sun, moon, earth with small letters."

mal or plant life, or even of our mineral kingdom—yet there were the first rudiments of the present-day human physical body. This physical human body was constituted very differently from what it is today: it was present in its earliest germinal state, then developed during the *Saturn* evolution; and when the latter was completed the old *Saturn* passed through a sort of cosmic night in the same manner in which man passes through a *devachan*★ in order to reach his next incarnation. Then *Saturn* became the *Sun*; and as the plant arises out of the seed, so the human physical body reappeared on the old *Sun*. Gradually this physical body became permeated by an etheric or life body, so that on the old *Sun* the germinal physical body was joined by the etheric or life body. Man was then not a plant, but he had the status of a plant. He consisted of physical body and etheric body, and his consciousness resembled that of sleep, the consciousness of the carpet of plants that is spread out around us in the physical world today.

The *Sun* existence came to an end, and again there intervened a cosmic night, or world *devachan*, as we call it. When the *Sun* had passed through this cosmic *devachan* it was transformed into the old *Moon* state. Again we find the human physical and etheric bodies that had entered on *Saturn* and the *Sun* respectively, but during the *Moon* evolution the astral body was added. Now the human being possessed a physical, an etheric, and an astral body. Thus you see that the physical body, having come into being on *Saturn*, was

---

★In this and the following pages Rudolf Steiner uses the word "devachan" instead of the word "pralaya," which he ordinarily uses for the condition of rest between two planetary conditions, whereas devachan is ordinarily used to designate a "region" of the spiritual world. It would appear from this lecture that the two Sanskrit terms can also be used interchangeably, as he explains later.

46

already passing through its third state on the *Moon*; and the etheric body that had been added on the *Sun* now rose to its second stage of perfection. The astral body, just engendered, was in its first stage in the *Moon* period.

Something now happened on the *Moon* that would not have been possible during the *Saturn* and *Sun* development. While during the latter man had been a comparatively homogeneous being, the following event occurred when the old *Moon* had reached a certain condition of evolution: The whole heavenly body split into two members, a sun and its satellite, the Moon; so that while in the case of *Saturn* and the *Sun* we have the evolution of a single planet, only the first part of the *Lunar* evolution can be thus characterized. That is because in the beginning everything that constitutes our present earth, sun, and moon was united in one single primordial cosmic body. Then, two bodies came into being. What came into being as sun at that time was not our sun, nor was it the old *Sun*, mentioned above. It was a special condition that detached itself from the old *Moon* as a sun condition; and along with it there came into being a planet, outside of the sun and circling it, which again we call the "old *Moon*."

Now, what is the significance of this division that took place in our earth's predecessor during the evolution of the old *Moon*? It lies in the fact that along with the sun the higher beings and the finer substances withdrew from the whole stellar mass as sun, while the coarser substances and the lower beings remained with the Moon. So during the evolution of the old *Moon* we have two heavenly bodies instead of one: a sun body, harboring the higher beings, and a Moon body, the dwelling place of the lower beings. Had the whole remained united, with no separation occurring, certain beings who developed on the sundered Moon could not have kept pace with the sun beings: they were not sufficiently

47

mature, and therefore had to detach the coarser substances and build for themselves a sphere of action apart. Nor could the higher beings have remained united with these coarser substances, for it would have obstructed their more rapid progress. They, too, required a special field for their development, and that was the Sun.

Now let us turn to the beings dwelling on the old sun and those on the old *Moon*, after the separation. We have learned that the potential human physical body had its inception during the *Saturn* state, that on the *Sun* the etheric body was added, and on the *Moon*, the astral body. Now, these human beings—or human ancestors, if we may so call them—on the *Moon* had, in fact, remained with the Moon when it split off; and these were the ones who could not keep pace with the rapid development of the sun beings—those who had gone with the sun and now dwelt within the finer substances and matter on the sun. This also accounts for their becoming coarser during the *Moon* evolution. During this period, then, we have man in a state consisting of physical body, etheric body, and astral body; in other words, he had attained to the evolutionary stage of a present-day animal, for an animal has the physical, etheric, and astral bodies. But you must not imagine man on the old *Moon* as having been really an animal: his form was very different in appearance from anything in the present animal world, and it would strike you as utterly fantastic if I were to describe it.

Summing up, then: On the old *Moon* we find what may be called the ancestors of present-day man, equipped with physical, etheric, and astral bodies, in whom these principles tended to become rigid after the division—to become coarser than they would have become had they remained with the sun. But all that had split off with the sun had also passed through this threefold development, the *Saturn*, *Sun*, and *Moon* evolutions. This, however, proceeded in the direction

48

taken by the sun, whereas the ancestors of men followed the Moon. These beings that went with the sun show a threefold organism closely paralleling that of man. On the sun, too, were beings who had acquired three principles, so to speak; but these had become finer instead of coarser after the separation. Think of the process as follows: After the split the human ancestors became denser beings than they were before, they tended to solidify; while corresponding beings on the sun became more rarefied. Through having acquired an astral body during the *Moon* evolution, man in a sense descended to the level of an animal; but the beings that did not take part in this development—those that carried the finer substances with them to the sun—became finer.

So while man was hardening on the Moon, beings of lofty spirituality arose on the sun. In spiritual science these beings may be regarded as the counter-images of what evolved on the Moon. On the Moon men developed up to the rank of the animal, so to speak, although they were not animals. Now, in dealing with the animal kingdom people have always quite justifiably distinguished between different grades of animals, and the animal men on the Moon appeared in three grades differing essentially from one another. In spiritual science these are termed the grades of the "Bull," the "Lion," and the "Eagle." Those are typical configurations, as it were, of the animal world. The old Moon was inhabited by the three groups: Bull men, Lion men, and Eagle men. Although these connotations apply in no way to our present bulls, lions, and eagles, the deteriorated character of those primordial Moon men which we call Lion-men is nevertheless expressed, to a certain extent, in the feline species; in the character of the hoofed animals there comes to expression the degenerated nature of the so-called Bull men, and so forth. That describes the densified nature of man after a three-stage development.

But on the sun dwelt the spiritual counter-images of these, also consisting of three groups. While the development of the astral principle on the Moon was shaping these three different animal men, the corresponding spiritual men arose on the sun as Angelical beings, spirit beings. These, too, are known as Lion, Eagle, and Bull, but as the spiritual counter-images of the others. So when you contemplate the sun you see spiritual beings whom you envision as the beautiful proto-types conceived in wisdom, while on the Moon you find something like hardened replicas of what dwells on the sun.

But something in the nature of a mystery underlies all this. These replicas down on the Moon are not without connection with their spiritual counter-images on the sun. On the Moon we have a group of primordial men, the Bull men, and on the sun a group of spirit beings known as "Bull spirits"; and there is a spiritual connection between proto-type and replica, for the group soul is the prototype and acts as such upon the replicas. The forces proceed from the group soul and direct the replica down below; the Lion spirit directs the beings who, as Lion men, are its replica; the Eagle spirit guides the Eagle men, and so on. If these spirits up above had remained united with the Moon,* bound to their replicas and inhabiting them, their activity would have been paralyzed; they could not have exercised the forces needed for the salvation and development of the replicas. They understood that they had to foster on a higher level what was destined to evolve on the Moon. The Bull spirit felt, I must care for the Bull men; but on the Moon I cannot find the conditions for my own progress, hence I must dwell on the sun and from there send down my forces to the Bull men. And the same applies to the Lion spirit, and the Eagle spirit.

*The German has "Erde–earth" here, for the Moon minus the sun was the ancestor of our earth and so one could say this was the "moon-earth."

50

This is the reason for this development. Certain beings needed a more advanced sphere of action than those who were their physical replicas, so to speak. The latter required a lower, lesser field. In order to function effectually the spiritual beings had to sunder the sun from the Moon and then send down their forces from without. Thus we see on the one hand a development downward, so to say, and on the other, an upward development.

The evolution of the old *Moon* (as a cosmic period) proceeds. By acting upon their replicas from without, the spiritual beings spiritualize the Moon, with the result that the latter can in time reunite with the sun. The prototypes take their replicas back into themselves, absorb them, as it were. Another *world devachan* comes about, a cosmic night. (This is also known as a *pralaya*, whereas stages like *Saturn*, *Sun*, and *Moon* are called *manvantaras*.) Following this cosmic night there issues out of the obscurity of the cosmic womb our *Earth* stage, whose mission it is to advance man to the level at which he can add the ego, or ego bearer, to his physical, etheric, and astral bodies. First, however, all previous evolution must be repeated, for whenever a higher stage is to be reached a cosmic law demands the repetition of all that had already taken place. The *Earth* had thus to pass once more through the old *Saturn* stage: again the first potential beginnings of the physical body evolved as out of the cosmic germ; and then followed a repetition of the *Sun* and *Moon* stages.

At this time sun, earth, and moon still formed a single body; but now a repetition of previous events takes place: the sun again splits off, and again those loftier beings that need this higher sphere for their development depart with the sun, carrying with them the finer substances they need for creating their cosmic sphere of action. Thus the sun left the Earth, which at that time still bore the moon within its body, and took with it those beings who were sufficiently far advanced to find their further development on the sun. You will readily imagine that among these beings were to be found primarily those that had previously functioned as prototypes. All these beings, who during the old *Moon* period had attained to adequate maturity, progressed rapidly, with the result that they could no longer live in the denser substances and beings containing within themselves the earth plus moon: they had to detach themselves and establish a new existence on the sun—our present sun.

Who were these beings? They were the descendants of those who, back in the old *Moon* state, had developed on the sun as the Bull, Lion, and Eagle spirits; and the loftiest of these, the most advanced, were those who had merged within themselves the natures of Eagle, Lion, and Bull in a harmonious unity. They are the beings that can be regarded as the *human prototypes—spirit men* in the true sense of the term. Imagine that among the spiritual beings, who during the old *Moon* period were to be found on the sun as Bull, Eagle, and Lion spirits, some had attained to a higher plane of development, and these are the *Spirit Men* proper whose dwelling place is now principally the sun. They are spiritual counterparts, so to speak, of what is in the process of evolution down below on the severed earth-plus-moon; but those that are developing down there are the descendants of the beings that had lived on the old *Moon*. Now, you can imagine that since a certain condensation, a solidification of these beings had already set in on the old *Moon*, a tendency to condense, to solidify, to dry out would be all the more pronounced in their descendants. Indeed, a sad and dreary period commenced for this sundered portion which then comprised earth-plus-moon. Above, on the sun, an ever fresher and livelier development, ever fuller life; below, on the Earth, misery and barrenness, steadily increasing rigidity.

Something now occurred without which evolution would have been brought to a standstill: the moon as we know it today separated from the earth-plus-moon body, and what remained is our present earth. In this way the coarsest substances withdrew before rendering the earth completely hard, and the latter was saved from total desolation.

To summarize all this: At the beginning of our *Earth* evolution the *Earth* formed one body with our present sun and moon. Had the Earth (earth plus moon) remained with the sun, man would never have been able to reach his present stage of development: he could not have kept pace with a development such as the beings on the sun needed. What developed up there was not man as he is on earth, but his spiritual prototype of which, as he appears in his physical body, he is really but an image. And on the other hand, had the moon remained within the earth, man would have gradually dried out and mummified, and have found no possibility of further development on Earth. The Earth would have become a barren, arid cosmic body; and in place of human bodies as we know them today, something like lifeless statues would have developed, growing up out of the ground like desiccated men. This was prevented by the secession of the moon, which withdrew into cosmic space and took with it the coarsest substances. That made it possible for an ego to be added to the physical, etheric, and astral bodies already present in the descendants of the old *Moon* beings; and because the forces of sun and moon acted from without and there held each other in balance, man could experience fructification by the ego.

The earth was now the scene of further human evolution. All that had come over from the old *Moon* represented in a certain respect a devolution, a development into a lower stage; but now, the human being received a new impetus, an impulse upward.—And in the meantime the progress of those corresponding spiritual beings who had remained with the sun steadily continued.

What had become possible by means of the moon's separation from the earth? It can easily be pictured by making use of a comparison. Let us suppose we have a block of hard iron before us and that our muscles are of average strength. We pound and hammer the iron, trying to beat it flat, but we cannot manage to give it any form until we have softened the substance by heat. Something of this sort happened to the earth after the densest substances had withdrawn with the moon. Now the earth beings could be formed, and now the sun beings again took a hand—those beings who as early as the old *Moon* state had intervened there from the sun as the group souls. Before the moon split off, substances were too dense; but now these beings, whose sphere of action was the sun, asserted themselves as forces that gradually shaped and developed man to his present form.

Let us examine this more closely. Imagine you could have stood on this ancient planetary body that consisted of earth-plus-moon. You would have beheld the sun out in space; and if you had been clairvoyant you would also have seen the spiritual beings described above. On the Earth you would have perceived a sort of solidification, a desolation, and it would have struck you that all about on the Earth was nothing but aridity and death; for the forces of the sun could gain no influence over all this that was on its way to becoming a great cosmic graveyard. And then you would have seen the body of the moon detach itself from the Earth. You would have seen the substances of the earth becoming malleable and plastic, with the result that the forces descending from the sun were once more able to act. And you would have seen the Bull, Lion, and Eagle spirits regaining their influence over the human beings that were their replicas. You would have understood that the moon, isolated, had

54

lost some of its harmful influence through its withdrawal, for thenceforth it could act only from a distance; and that in this way it had rendered the earth capable of receiving what the spiritual beings had to give. Tomorrow we shall see what sort of a picture presents itself to the clairvoyant when he traces the more remote phases of evolution in the *Akasha Chronicle*.

We know that during the old *Saturn* stage the first beginning of the human physical body was formed. What today we see as the physical human form first took shape on *Saturn* as though emerging from cosmic chaos. Then came the *Sun* stage during which the etheric body was added to the first form of the physical; and on the old *Moon* these were joined by the astral element in the case of those beings who continued their development on the sundered Moon, as well as of the spirits who had remained with the sun. On the sun dwelt the spiritual prototypes, on the Moon, their counterparts on the animal level; and finally, upon the *Earth* there had gradually evolved a condition under which man was once more able to receive into himself the astral element developed on the sun during the *Moon* evolution, an element that now acted in him as a force.

Let us now trace these four states as described in the Gospel of St. John. The exalted power which during the *Saturn* stage provided the spiritual germ of the physical human form is called by the author of the John Gospel the *Logos*. The element that was added on the *Sun* and merged with what had arisen on *Saturn* he designates Life, known to us accordingly as the etheric or life body. And what was added on the *Moon* he terms the *Light*, for it is the spiritual light, the astral light. On the severed Moon this astral light effected a hardening, but on the sun itself, a spiritualization. What was thus engendered as spirit could and did continue to develop; and when during the *Earth* evolution the

55

sun again split off, the principle that had evolved during the third stage shone into men, but man was as yet unable to see what thus shone in from the sun. It took part in the shaping of man, acted as a force; but man could not see it.

What we have in this way come to recognize as the essence of the *Saturn* evolution we can now express in the words of the Gospel of St. John:

In the beginning was the Logos.

Now we pass to the *Sun*. To denote what came into being on *Saturn* and was further developed on the *Sun*, we say, the etheric body was added:

And the Logos was Life.

On the *Moon* the astral element entered into both the physical and the spiritual aspects of men:

Within the animated Logos Light arose.

When the separation occurred the light developed in two directions: on the sun into a clairvoyant light, among men into darkness. For when man was to receive the light he, who was the darkness, comprehended it not.

So if we illuminate the John Gospel by means of the *Akasha Chronicle*, what we read concerning cosmic evolution is as follows: In the beginning, during the *Saturn* evolution, everything had come into being out of the *Logos*; during the *Sun* evolution, *Life* was in the *Logos*; and out of this living *Logos* there arose *Light* during the *Moon* evolution. Finally, out of the living, light-filled *Logos* there appeared on the sun, during the *Earth* evolution, the Light in heightened form—but men were in a condition of darkness. And the beings who had become the advanced spirits of Bull, Lion, Eagle, and Man, shone down as light from the sun to the earth and into the forms of men that were taking shape. But these were the darkness, and they could not comprehend the light that shone down upon them. Naturally we must not think of this as the physical light, but rather, as the Light that was the sum of the radiations from the spiritual beings, the spirits of Bull, Lion, Eagle, and Man, who constituted the continuation of the spiritual evolution of the *Moon*. It was the spiritual Light that streamed down. Men could not receive it, could not comprehend it. Their whole development was advanced by it, but without their consciousness taking part. *The light shone in the darkness; and the darkness comprehended it not.*

Thus does the writer of the John Gospel present in an exemplary manner these great truths. Those, who knew them, have always been called the "servants or ministers of the Logos as it had been from the beginning." He who speaks thus was such a minister or servant of the *Logos* as it had been from the beginning. In the introduction to the Luke Gospel, we find basically the same reference. Just read understandingly what the writer of the Luke Gospel says: his purpose is to report events as they occurred from the beginning, *even as they delivered them unto us, who from the beginning were eyewitnesses, and ministers of the Word.*

And we believe that these documents were written by servants of the Word, or the *Logos*. We learn to believe this when by means of our own spiritual research we see what took place, when we see how our *Earth* evolution came about by way of *Saturn*, *Sun*, and *Moon*. And when we then find that we can rediscover, independently of all documents, what is presented in the comprehensive words of the John Gospel and in the words of the Luke Gospel, we learn anew to appreciate these documents and to find in them their own evidence that they were written by those who could read in the spiritual world. They provide a means of communication with men of remote times whom we can face, in a sense, and say, We recognize and know you—because what they knew we have found again in Spiritual Science.

57

IV

As the starting point of yesterday's discussion we took the alternation in our daily life that consists of waking and sleeping, and we pointed out that during sleep man's astral body and ego, as we term them, are out in space, while his physical and etheric bodies remain in bed. And at the same time we had to emphasize the fact that the principles remaining in bed could not continue to exist were it not for the entrance of a divine-spiritual astrality and a divine-spiritual ego. In other words, this alternation in the conditions of everyday human life means that at falling asleep man—with his human ego and human astral body—abandons his physical and etheric bodies, but that in their stead there enter divine-spiritual astral beings and divine spiritual ego beings. In the waking state, on the other hand, he himself fills out his physical and etheric bodies with his own astral body and ego.

That was one of our two points of departure yesterday. The other was the result of what we have gleaned from a comprehensive survey of our entire human evolution through the former embodiments of our *Earth*—through *Saturn*, *Sun*, and *Moon*. We also discussed certain details of this survey, and we found that as regards the progress of our planet earth a severance set in with the *Moon* evolution: certain beings who required baser, inferior substances, so to speak, for their further development divided off with the old *Moon*, while higher beings of a more spiritual nature detached themselves as an older form of the sun evolution. Next, we saw the two parts reunited later on, together passing through a world *devachan* or *pralaya*, and thus achieving their development. Then this *Earth* evolution proceeded in such a way that a repetition of the separation of the sun occurred, leaving for a time earth-plus-moon as a coarser, denser body, and the sun as a special, more rarefied body, dwelling place of higher, loftier beings. We learned further that if the earth had remained united with the moon substance it would inevitably have become barren and hard, and all living things would have died—or, more accurately, mummified. The moon, together with all that it embraces today, had to be cast out of the Earth evolution at a given time. The result was a rejuvenating process in the evolving human being. We saw that the lofty beings, who found the conditions for their advancement on the sun, could not influence human substances and beings until the moon had been sloughed off, but that then they could act upon them again with rejuvenating effect. This means that human evolution proper could not have commenced until after the separation of moon and earth. The sundering of the moon is of enormous importance for the whole of evolution, and today we will study it more closely. First, however, we shall show how our two starting points in yesterday's lecture merge, so to speak.

We observe a man as he stands before us in his daytime state: a being consisting of physical body, etheric body, astral body, and ego. But when clairvoyant consciousness observes him during sleep at night—his physical and etheric bodies in bed—higher beings are seen to enter this physical and etheric body. And who are these beings? Precisely those whose field of action we described as being on the sun. That is by no means impossible: only one who imagines all spirit as physical, and who fain would apply everything physical to his conception of spiritual beings—only such a person could doubt that solar beings, dwelling on the sun, can enter a man's physical and etheric bodies at night. For be-

59

ings so exalted as to inhabit the sun, no such spatial conditions exist as obtain for beings of the physical world. Such beings can very well inhabit the sun and yet send their forces down into human physical bodies at night.

We can put it this way, then: During the day the human being is awake—that is, he inhabits his physical and etheric bodies; at night he is asleep—that is, he is outside his physical and etheric bodies. During the night the Gods or other extra-terrestrial beings watch over man's physical and etheric bodies. That is expressed half figuratively, yet it is entirely pertinent. Thus we know whence come the beings who must enter our physical and etheric bodies at night, and this links up our two points. But we shall presently see that these beings are not only important for our life at night, but are gradually gaining in significance for our daytime life as well. First, however, we must consider a few other matters if we are clearly to understand the whole import of the moon's withdrawal from *Earth* evolution. Today we will occupy ourselves with the genesis of other beings that surround us.

Turning back once more to *Saturn*, we can say that it consisted exclusively of human beings. There was no animal, plant, or mineral kingdom. The whole sphere was composed of the earliest human germs in much the same form as a blackberry is made up of tiny individual berries; and everything that pertained to *Saturn* surrounded it and acted upon it from the environment. If we now ask, Whence came that which gave man this first impulse, on old *Saturn*, for his physical body, we can say in a certain sense that it derived from two sources. In the first instance, higher spiritual beings poured forth their own substance: a momentous sacrifice occurred on old *Saturn*, and the beings that achieved it are called *Thrones* in the sense of Christian esotericism. Human thinking or even human clairvoyance may scarcely presume to contemplate the august evolution the Thrones had to undergo before being able to sacrifice that which could form the germinal indication of the human physical body.*

Let us try to understand in some degree what such a sacrifice means. If today you contemplate the human being—the being with which you are best acquainted—it will occur to you that he demands certain things of the world, and gives it certain things. Goethe summarized this very beautifully in the words, "Human life runs its course in the metamorphosis between receiving and giving."† Man derives not only bodily nourishment but mental sustenance from the outer world; and in this way he grows and receives what he needs for his own development. But through this process he also develops the capacity for giving, in turn, what he has brought to maturity in the way of ideas and feeling, and ultimately, of love. By his taking something from the world and giving something else to his surroundings, his capacities keep constantly increasing: he becomes sensible and intelligent, able to develop concepts which he can sacrifice to the common life of humanity. He develops feelings and sensations that are transformed into love; and by offering these he stimulates his fellow creatures. We need only call to mind what a vitalizing effect love can have on our fellow beings—how one who is really able to pour forth love upon his fellow men can quicken and comfort and elevate them through his love alone.

Now man has attained to the virtue of sacrifice. But no matter how great a capacity for sacrifice we may acquire, it is slight when compared with that of the Thrones. Evolution, however, consists in constantly increasing this capacity

---

*Dr. Steiner gives a beautiful description of this deed of the Thrones in the cycle entitled *The Inner Realities of Evolution* (Berlin, 1911).

†*Das menschliche Leben verfliesst in der Metamorphose zwischen Nehmen und Geben.*

for sacrifice, until finally a being is able to sacrifice his own substance and essence, as it were, experiencing as highest blessedness the giving of all he had developed as matter and substance. There are august beings that rise to higher planes of existence by sacrificing their own substance. A materialistic soul will naturally object: When beings reach the point of sacrificing their own substance, how can they then rise to a higher plane? They would be sacrificing themselves, and nothing would be left of them! Thus speaks the materialistic soul, incapable of understanding that there is a spiritual existence, that such a being continues to exist through sacrificing what he had gradually received into himself. On *Saturn* the Thrones were on a plane where they were able to pour forth the substantiality they had acquired during their previous development; and thereby they themselves rose to a higher stage of evolution. And that which flowed from the Thrones—analogous, in a way, to what the spider secretes for weaving its web—was primarily the basis for the formation of the human physical body.

Then the Thrones were joined by another kind of beings, ranking lower than Thrones, whom we call the Spirits of Personality, or the Principalities—*Archai* in Christian esotericism. These Spirits of Personality worked over, as it were, what had flowed from the Thrones; and through the collaboration of these two kinds of beings the first inception of the human physical body came into being. This work continued over a long period of time. Then, as mentioned yesterday, a cosmic night, or world *devachan*, intervened, and there came about the second embodiment of the earth, the *Sun* phase. Human beings emerged again, and other spiritual beings appeared on the scene: the Spirits of Fire, or *Archangels*, as they are known in Christian esotericism, and the Spirits of Wisdom, or *Kyriotetes*. These were mainly concerned with the further development of what reappeared as the human physical body. Now it was the turn of the Kyriotetes—the Dominions, or Spirits of Wisdom—to sacrifice their substantiality; and what we call the etheric body flowed into the physical body. This etheric body was then worked upon by the Spirits of Fire, or Archangels, in collaboration with the Spirits of Personality; and thereby man became a being of the rank of a plant. We may say that on *Saturn* the human being had the status of a mineral, for our minerals have only a physical body, and so had the man of *Saturn*; hence he lived a mineral existence. On the *Sun* he had the status of a plant, for he had a physical and an etheric body.

Now we come to a concept which we must make our own as an especially important one if we are to understand evolution in its entirety. Here I always like to draw attention to the existence in the cosmos of something that corresponds to a certain daily commonplace—a source of anxiety and annoyance to parents—namely, that some children *fail*, do not arrive at the goal of their class, and must repeat the work. Certain beings do not reach the goal of a given cosmic grade; and in this sense certain Spirits of Personality, who should have reached their goal on *Saturn*, lagged behind. They had not done all that was necessary for raising man to the grade of a mineral, which would have brought him to perfection in that particular evolutionary stage. Such beings must then make up during the next grade what they had previously neglected.

Now, in what way could these retarded Spirits of Personality work during the *Sun* existence? They could not create a being such as man was due to become on the *Sun*, a being with physical body and etheric body: that called for the Spirits of Fire. Nor could they create on the *Sun* anything beyond what they had done on *Saturn*, namely, a potential physical body of mineral grade. So during the *Sun* period

63

their influence brought about the genesis of beings one grade lower. These beings now constituted a lower kingdom, inferior to the human kingdom; and they are the ancestors of our present animals. While our present human kingdom had already attained to the plant status on the *Sun*, our present animal kingdom was at that time on a level with mineral beings, having the physical body only. In this way the animal kingdom, in its first indications was added to the human kingdom.

So if we ask, what being among all those that surround us has passed through the longest development, who is the first born of creation, the answer is, man. And the other beings arose because the forces of development associated with human existence withheld what in a different stage might have become man, allowing it to become a lower being at a later stage. Had the retarded Spirits of Personality performed their task on *Saturn* instead of on the *Sun*, the animal kingdom would not have come into being.

In like manner—I need only sketch this—the *Moon* evolution showed the following: Man progressed upward by reason of having received an astral body from certain beings we call *Angels* and from other higher spirits, the Spirits of Motion, or *Dynamis* in Christian terminology. This gave man the rank of an animal during the *Moon* existence, while most of those beings who, during the *Sun* existence, had appeared as a second kingdom now arrived at the status of plants on the *Moon*. These were the precursors of our animals. And to these were added—again through retarded spiritual beings, as explained—those beings that belong to our present plant kingdom. On the *Sun* there was as yet no plant kingdom, but only a human and an animal kingdom: the plant kingdom was added on the *Moon*. A mineral kingdom, such as today constitutes the solid foundation upon which all else stands, had not yet come into existence on the

Moon. In this way the kingdoms evolved one after another, with the human kingdom, highest of these, as the first one. Something in the nature of an outcast, something of the human kingdom that remained behind, is the animal kingdom; and what lagged one step farther still became the plant kingdom.

When the old *Moon* evolution was accomplished, that of the *Earth* commenced; and in connection with the latter we described the splitting off of the sun and moon. During this period all the germs of the former kingdoms reappeared: the animal kingdom, the plant kingdom, and finally—when the moon, as to its substance, was still united with the earth— the mineral kingdom. The appearance of the mineral kingdom as the solid foundation was what caused the hardening and desiccation that rendered the earth so barren; for the mineral kingdom that surrounds us today is nothing but what was sloughed off by the higher kingdoms. I have drawn attention in the past to the fact that you need only consider thoughtfully what modern science recognizes, and you will be able to imagine how the mineral kingdom was gradually ejected. Consider that coal, a mineral product proper, is taken out of the earth. What was this coal long, long ago? Trees that grew on the earth, plants that perished and petrified and became minerals. What you now dig out as coal was once a quantity of plants, hence it is a product that was first discarded: originally there were plant beings where now there is coal.

You can now readily imagine that everything else forming the solid foundation of our earth is also matter that was cast off by the higher kingdoms. Think, for example, of certain mineral products that even today remain the secretions of animal beings, such as the shells of snails and mussels. Formerly nothing of a mineral nature existed; only in the course of time has it come about through elimination. Not until the earth evolution was in progress did the mineral kingdom join the others; and the reason for its formation was that beings like those on *Saturn* were still present and active on the earth. It was only through the activity of the Spirits of Personality that the mineral kingdom came into being; in fact, those beings are active in all the higher stages. Yet if evolution had proceeded in this manner there would have been so many mineral influences, so much hardening and densification, that gradually the whole earth would have become a desert waste.

This brings us to an important moment in the evolution of our earth. We visualize the sun as having split off, and we think of those beings who are now spiritual beings on the sun as having withdrawn as well, along with the finest substances. We behold the earth with its increasing desolation, becoming ever denser as mineral; and we see as well the growing desiccation of the forms it harbors—even the human forms. Already at that time a certain change came over the conditions under which human beings lived; and an illustration from the growth of the plant will clarify what then confronted men as well.

From the insignificant seed the plant sprouts forth in the spring, unfolds into blossom and fruit, and withers again during autumn. All that gladdens the eye in spring and summer disappears in the fall, and outwardly, physically, only an unpretentious remnant remains. But if you imagined that during winter nothing of the real being of the plant persisted, or if you looked for it only in the physical seed, you would not comprehend the plant. True, as constituted today the plant consists of physical body and etheric body, but observed clairvoyantly its upper part is seen to be surrounded by an astral being, as by a border; and this astral being is animated by a force that streams to earth from the sun, from the spiritual element of the sun. For clairvoyant consciousness every blossom is surrounded as though by a cloud, and this cloud breathes the life that is exchanged between sun and earth. While the plants are sprouting and burgeoning during spring and summer, something of the sun being approaches and hovers over the surface of the plant; and with the coming of autumn the astral being withdraws and unites with the life of the sun. It can be put this way: In spring the plant astrality seeks its physical plant body on the earth and embodies itself—not in it, but at least around it; and in the fall it returns to the sun, leaving behind the seed as a sort of pledge that it will find its way back to its physical expression.

Similarly, a sort of exchange took place between the physical human beings and the sun beings, although the human forms were still primitive and simple. And there was a time when the sun spirits surrounded human bodies with astrality, just as today the plant astrality hovers over plants from spring to fall. We can therefore say that during certain epochs the astral principle of man united, to a certain extent, with his physical body on earth, that it then withdrew to the sun, and again returned; and only the seed was left behind in the physical principle. But the earth kept on hardening; and then something of great importance occurred, something I shall ask you to keep well in mind. While formerly, when the sun had first withdrawn from the earth, it was still possible for the astral beings to reunite with the physical body when they returned after the separation, this body, which the descending beings sought to occupy, had now become so hard under the ever increasing influence of the moon that they could no longer use it.

That is a more accurate description of what I characterized yesterday somewhat abstractly. I said: The sun forces had lost the power of forming the substances on earth; but expressing it more concretely one can say: The substances dried up, and the beings no longer found suitable bodies.

This resulted in the desolation of the earth, and human souls wanting to descend again realized that the bodies were no longer suitable. They had to abandon them to their fate, and only the bodies possessing the strongest forces could prevail through this period of desolation. The latter reached its climax at the time when the moon was about to withdraw from the earth. The souls who during that time yearned to be human souls were unable to make use of such bodies, with the result that only a handful of people still inhabited the earth. This desolation appeared to forecast a gradual extinction of life on the earth, and the situation is described quite accurately by saying that when the moon withdrew, only very few human beings had survived these conditions: there were very few cases in which a union had come about between souls craving embodiment and the physical forms with which they wished to unite.

Now I must describe these conditions more in detail. Let us go back once more to the point in time at which the *Moon* evolution had run its course and the *Earth* re-emerged from the womb of the cosmos. It did not come into being as did the old *Saturn*, for what here appeared comprised within it the after-effects of all that had occurred previously; nor was it physical matter only that was connected with it, but also all the beings who had been active before. The fact that the Thrones united with *Saturn* means that they remained connected with the entire evolution; and they came forward again when the *Earth* emerged once more from the obscurity of the cosmic womb. In like manner there appeared again the Spirits of Personality, the Spirits of Motion, and so on, as well as the germs of human beings, animals, and plants, for all this was contained in the earth.

Our physical science sets up hypotheses that are pure fancy. In connection with cosmogony, for example, a theory is proffered to the effect that once there was a great cosmic fog reaching out past Saturn. Now, a cosmic nebula of that kind, consisting of mere mists and vapors, is a fantastic conception; there never was any such thing. If one had been able to see only with external, physical eyes, something of the sort could indeed have been perceived; a vast fog mass would have been visible. But this fog mass contained something that physical eyes could *not* have seen, namely, all the beings associated with this evolution. The fact that later all this became organized and formed was not brought about by a mere rotary motion, but rather, because of the needs of those beings that were linked with it all. You will arrive at a sensible view of these matters only after you have completely emancipated yourselves from all that represents the official view of today, from what is inculcated into our children from the beginning of their school days. The children are told that in olden times only childish views and conceptions prevailed: those misguided ancient Indians believed in a Brahma who filled out all cosmic space! And people such as the old Persians believed in Ormuzd, the good God, and Ahriman, who opposed him! Worse yet: the old Greeks, who had a lot of divinities—Zeus, Pallas Athene, and so forth! We know today, of course—so the children are told—that all those beings originated in popular imagination and childish conceptions. Think of the old Germanic Gods—Wotan, Thor—we've long since known them for mythological figures; nowadays we know that such Gods had nothing to do with the development of the world. No: In the beginning there was a primeval fog in space, and it began to rotate. It cast a sphere out of its mass and kept on rotating. In time a second sphere split off, then a third, and so on.

As a matter of fact, these conceptions are but the form of a modern, physico-Copernican mythology which in time will be supplanted by some other mythology; but the earlier mythologies have one point of superiority over the present form: they come nearer the truth than do the later ones which have extracted merely what is abstract and pertains wholly to outward matter. We should ever keep in mind how easy it is to present, for the children's benefit, this most plausible way for a cosmic system to come into being. You take a drop of oil, cut a little card into the shape of a disk, insert this horizontally into the drop, stick a pin through the disk from above, and place it in water, where it floats. Now you begin to turn the whole thing, explaining, "just the way the cosmic fog once revolved." First the oil drop flattens out, then a smaller drop is thrown off, then a second and a third, while a big drop remains in the middle—and lo, a little cosmic system has come into being! Then it is quite easy to explain plausibly that what here appeared on a small scale is analogous to what took place on a large scale. But people who perform this experiment forget one thing—something which in other circumstances may be a very good thing to forget: themselves. They forget that they are doing the turning. The whole analogy could have validity only if some worthy professor deigned to add something like the following: Just as I stand here and turn the pin, so there is a gigantic professor somewhere out there, seeing to it that the whole comes into rotation and that the planets split off, as did the drops of oil on a small scale. In that case it might pass.

We know that there is no giant professor out there twirling the pin, but that beings of all ranks are there, and that it is these spiritual beings who attract appropriate matter to themselves. The beings that needed certain conditions for their life drew to themselves the requisite matter when they proceeded to the sun, appropriated it, and fashioned a sphere of action by means of their spiritual forces; and other beings took for themselves of the earth substance. That which acts right into the tiniest particle of matter—into the atom, if we chose to call it that—is spirit. It is erroneous to ascribe any

70

sort of activity to mere matter. Men will learn what takes place in the smallest confines only when they understand that spirit acts throughout the greatest spaces. And by this is not meant spirit in general, of which people say, "in general, matter simply contains spirit"—a universal or primordial spirit. That sort of thing opens the way for concocting almost anything. No, we must learn to know the spirits in their concrete reality, in detail, and in their various vital requirements.

Now I will supplement a point we touched upon yesterday: the separation of the sun from the earth-plus-moon, and the subsequent division of the moon and the earth. In its main outline that is a correct picture, but it must be completed. Before the sun could withdraw, it became necessary for certain beings to segregate special fields of action for themselves, and these spheres figure today as the outer planets, Saturn, Jupiter, and Mars. It can therefore be said that overall matter, which contained sun and moon, comprised Saturn, Jupiter, and so forth, as well; and certain beings withdrew from the beginning with these heavenly bodies, beings requiring for their life precisely what these planets could offer. Then the sun split off, together with the highest beings, and what remained was earth-plus-moon. This evolution proceeded until the moon was cast out in the manner described. But of the beings who had gone with the sun, not all were able to keep pace with the sun development. Speaking figuratively—it is difficult to find words in our prosaic language, hence it is occasionally necessary to use images— we can say that when the sun withdrew, certain beings believed they would be able to travel with the sun; but in reality only the most exalted beings could accomplish this, and the rest had to withdraw later. And the fact that the latter created special spheres for themselves accounts for the genesis of Venus and Mercury. So the separation of Saturn, Jupiter, and Mars occurred before the division of sun and earth, while later Venus and Mercury split off from the sun, and finally the moon from the earth.

There we have a spiritual picture of this evolution. We have comprehended the development of our solar system to the extent of visualizing the various beings dwelling on the different heavenly bodies. With this in mind we can now answer the question, What happened to those spirit-astral beings who wished to descend as human beings, but found hardened bodies they could not enter? Not all of these beings could unite with the sun spirits for lack of sufficient maturity, and so the following occurred: Those beings who had to abandon the bodies on earth withdrew temporarily to Saturn, Jupiter, and Mars. While down below, the earth was becoming desolate, producing only bodies incapable of harboring human soul beings, we find the souls betaking themselves to these planetary worlds, there to await the time when they should again be able to find appropriate human bodies. Only vew few, only the most tenacious human bodies, were capable of receiving souls in order to preserve life during the moon crisis. The other souls ascended to other cosmic bodies.

Then the moon was cast out of the earth, and in consequence the sun forces were enabled once again to work upon human forms. The human form received a new impetus and once more became soft, pliable, plastic; and the souls who had waited on Saturn, Jupiter, and so forth, could now occupy these pliant human bodies. While formerly they had been compelled to quit the earth, they now gradually returned —after the expulsion of the moon—and populated the rejuvenated human bodies. So the casting out of the moon was followed by a period in which more and more new bodies kept emerging. During the moon crisis the number of human beings extant was very small. These never lacked descendants; but when the souls came down they could make no use of the bodies, and they left them to perish. The human race was headed for extinction; but after the rejuvenation had set in the descendants of those human beings who had survived the moon crisis were again able to receive the souls from Saturn, Jupiter, and Mars. The earth was gradually peopled with souls. Now you will understand what a significant, deeply incisive event this exit of the moon was: really everything was changed by it.

Let us return once more to the development preceding the moon's withdrawal. We found that man must be designated the first-born of our creation, for he came into being on *Saturn*. On the *Sun* was added the animal kingdom, on the *Moon*, the plant kingdom, and on the *Earth*, the mineral kingdom. But now, beginning with the splitting off of the moon, matters assume a different aspect. Had the moon not withdrawn, everything on the earth would have perished: first the human beings, then the animals, and finally the plants; and the earth would have become mummified. But it was rescued from this fate by the withdrawal of the moon; everything revived and experienced a recovery.

How did this regeneration come about? The lowest kingdom, the mineral, required the least aid; the plant kingdom, though in a way withered, could also revive rapidly; and the animal kingdom as well was able gradually to resume its upward development in certain respects. The human forms took longest to come into their own, to be able to receive the souls flowing toward them out of the highest regions of the world. The world development is thus reversed after the moon's withdrawal: while originally the human kingdom was the first to come into being, followed by the animal, plant, and mineral kingdoms in this order, it is now the mineral kingdom that is first capable of exploiting the revivifying forces. That is followed by the plant kingdom, then by the animal and the human kingdoms, each in turn developing upward to its highest forms. After the moon's withdrawal the entire plan of evolution appears in reverse; and the beings that had been able to wait longest, so to speak, to unite their spirit with matter, these are the ones who, after the moon's departure, ascended to a more spiritual sphere in the highest sense of the word. Those whose spiritual development stopped earlier remained behind in a less perfect stage.

After the exit of the moon those who had remained behind reappeared first, and you will readily understand the reason for this. Consider a human soul, or any soul-endowed being, that had previously been unwilling to incarnate because of the condition of solidification. Such a soul might have reflected—again expressed in our human language—Shall I incarnate now or shall I wait still longer? Let us assume that the moon had not been gone very long, and that consequently all substance was still very hard; but the being desiring to incarnate is impatient, descends whether or no, and makes the best of an inadequately developed body. This means that it must remain at a lower level. Another being reflects, I would better wait longer, remaining in cosmic space until such time as the earth shall have further lightened and rarefied its physical being. Such a being, by awaiting a later point in time, succeeds in physically molding the being in which it embodies, making it into its own image.

All the beings that incarnated too soon came to a standstill on a lower plane, while those who were willing to wait advanced to a higher one. Our higher animals stopped at the animal level because they did not wait long enough after the secession of the moon: they put up with whatever bodies they could find. Those descending somewhat later could form the bodies only into those of the lower human races, which were dying out or about to do so. Then came a point in time that was just right for the union of souls and bodies, and this period produced what was capable of genuine human development.

What we have, then, is desolation on earth up to the moon's withdrawal, after this a regeneration of earthly conditions, and from then on the reappearance of those beings who had left the earth because it had too far deteriorated for their purposes. And this refers not only to those who develop the higher human beings but also to others who descended for quite different reasons. Here again it is a matter of awaiting the right moment to enable such a being to enter a body on the earth. Going back to the time of ancient India, we find human beings in a very high stage of development. Just as the souls descending from Mars, Saturn, and Jupiter sought their bodies, so more exalted beings sought bodies of a higher type in order to carry on their activity in man's inner nature. Consider the great and holy teachers of the ancient Indians, the Rishis; a portion of their being they placed at the disposal of certain higher beings who took up their dwelling there. But other higher beings said, No, we shall wait until other beings appear down there, beings who themselves are undergoing a higher development. We have no desire to descend yet. We will remain above until men have reached a greater inner maturity; then we will descend, for at present we would find the inner nature of man ill prepared to receive us.

Then, during the Persian cultural epoch, certain higher beings said to themselves, Now we can descend into man's inner nature as it has thus far developed. And again in Egyptian times this occurred in the same way. But the loftiest one among the sun beings still waited. He sent His forces down to the holy Rishis from without; and when these gazed up to the Being they called Vishva Karman they said, He is beyond our sphere. He waited, for He knew that the inner nature of man was not sufficiently prepared to receive Him.

Then came the Persian epoch in which Zarathustra gazed up to the sun and saw there Ahura Mazdao; but still this exalted Being did not descend to the earthly sphere.

There followed the Egyptian epoch and then the civilization of that people which had waited longest. And there appeared the man who had waited longest and had already developed his inner nature through many incarnations. Then the Sun Being gazed down and beheld the inner nature of this man who lived in Jesus of Nazareth and who had perfected his inner nature. The loftiest of the sun beings gazed down and said, As the lower beings once descended to build up bodies, so I now descend to occupy the inner nature of this man who has waited longest. Beings of a high order, to be sure, had united with men in the past; but the one who had waited longest—he it was who received into himself the Christ: he was so far advanced at the Baptism in the Jordan that the Spirit Who hitherto had remained in cosmic spheres could now descend and unite with his inner nature. Ever since the Baptism the Christ had dwelt in the body of Jesus of Nazareth, because the individuality that permeated Jesus of Nazareth had attained, through many incarnations, to the degree of maturity which enabled it to receive this lofty Spirit in its own spirit-permeated body.

This Christ Spirit had always existed; but after the withdrawal of the moon it was necessary that all beings attain to a certain degree of maturity. First there gradually emerged the lowest beings, those who in respect of their spiritual principle had been least able to wait; then progressively the higher ones. And when man had achieved an ever higher development of his inner nature, and the time had come when Jesus of Nazareth had attained to the stage that enabled him to receive the Christ, then he who enjoyed the gift of higher vision could say:

76

I saw the Spirit descending upon him.

And what could he say, he upon whom the Spirit had descended, if he voiced what now lived within him? It was the same Being the Rishis knew as Vishva Karman. What would Vishva Karman have had to say of Himself—not if the Rishis had spoken, but if He Himself had spoken? This lofty Sun Spirit, active in light as spirit, would have had to say, *I am the light of the world.* What would Ahura Mazdao have had to say of Himself? *I am the light of the world.* And what did the same Spirit say when a human being had become ripe to receive Him into himself? How does that which heretofore had dwelt in cosmic space, on the sun, now speak out of a human being? What does it now say from within a human being? *I am the light of the world.*

The utterance of heavenly choirs—innermost self-revelation of the leading cosmic Spirit—we hear intoned again out of the inner being of a man when the Being Itself had come to dwell in a human principle. Inevitably there sound forth from Jesus of Nazareth, when the Christ is within him, the words:

I am the Light of the World.

V

If we observe with clairvoyant consciousness the present form of a human being, composed as it is of physical body, etheric body, astral body, and ego, there emerges most clearly the important fact that as regards size and shape—at least in the upper portions—the physical and etheric bodies are approximately equal. The head in particular, if we think of it as it appears physically, coincides almost completely with its etheric counterpart: the latter protrudes only slightly beyond the physical head. This is by no means the case in animals. Even in the higher animals there is a tremendous difference between the shape and size of the etheric head and the physical head. If you observe, for example, a horse clairvoyantly, you see that the etheric head extends far beyond the physical head and has a decidedly different shape. If I were to draw a picture of what hovers above the trunk and head of an elephant you would be greatly astonished at the true being of that animal; for all that physical perception sees of such an animal is merely the solidified part in the center.

Let us examine this fact. The degree of man's perfection on our physical plane is basically due to the fact that his etheric body so nearly coincides with his physical body. But that was not always the case. There have been periods in the evolution of our *Earth*, treated in the foregoing lectures, in which man's etheric body by no means thus coincided with his physical body, as it does today. In fact, man's progress during the course of his development is due to the circumstance that gradually his protruding etheric body crept into his physical body, as it were, until in time the two came to coincide. Here it is essential to keep in mind that this interpenetration of the etheric and physical bodies had to take place at a very special moment in *Earth* evolution if mankind was to achieve its development in the right way. Had it occurred earlier, man would have reached a certain stage of development too soon: he would have hardened there, and remained fixed in it. But a possibility for him to develop resulted from the fact that his etheric and physical bodies came to coincide at just the right time.

In order to understand this, let us examine more closely evolution as we viewed it in its larger outlines yesterday and the day before. Visualize once more how, at the beginning of our *Earth* evolution, the earth was united with the sun and the moon. At that time man had arisen again out of the potential germ that comprised the physical, etheric, and astral bodies. He existed, so to speak, in his first earth form, that is, the only form possible for him at a time when the *Earth* still contained both sun and moon. In spiritual-scientific literature this period of *Earth* evolution which man passed through, together with his planet, is usually called the *Polarian* period. It would lead too far afield today to explain this name, so let us simply accept it. Then came the time when the sun prepared to withdraw from the *Earth*, when the beings that could not continue, so to speak, with the denser and constantly solidifying substances of the Earth departed with the finer substances of the sun. This period we call the *Hyperborean* period. Then followed an epoch in which only the moon remained united with the Earth, a time in which increasing barrenness spread over our Earth life. Yesterday we learned how human souls abandoned this Earth and only withered human forms remained. In spiritual-scientific literature this is called the *Lemurian* period. It is the time in which the splitting off of the moon occurred, result-

79

ing in a revival on earth of all the kingdoms established there. The mineral kingdom stood least in need of reanimation, the plant kingdom more, and still more, the animal kingdom, while the further development of the human race called for the most outstanding and powerful forces.

This revival commenced with the moon's exit. As mentioned yesterday, only a handful of human beings were left, and these consisted of the three principles acquired during the *Saturn*, *Sun* and *Moon* evolutions, to which the potential ego was added on the *Earth*. But at the time of the moon's exit the human being did not bear the fleshy substance in which we encounter him later: he was composed of the most tenuous matter of that time. In the Lemurian period the solid minerals of today were still liquid, dissolved in the other substances that nowadays are segregated as aqueous matter, like water. The air was still saturated with dense vapors composed of a great variety of substances. Pure air and pure water, as we know them today, did not exist at that time except in very limited areas of the earth.

It was out of the purest substances of the period, then, that man molded his evanescent, tenuous body. Had he employed coarser substances his body would have acquired a form with definite outline, with sharply defined contours. These contours would have been inherited by the descendants, and the human race would there have come to a standstill. But it was not intended that man should create his form in matter of that sort; rather had he to see to it that he could freely move his corporeal substance according to the impulses of his soul. The matter forming his body was at that time so soft that it obeyed the impulses of will in all directions. Nowadays you can stretch out your hand, but by no effort of the will can you make it ten feet long. You cannot coerce matter because form, as it is today, is bequeathed. At the time of which we are speaking that was not the case. The human being could be shaped at will, could build the form according to the dictates of his soul. His further development demanded, so to speak, that he incorporate himself, after the withdrawal of the moon, in the softest possible substances, leaving his body plastic and flexible, capable of obeying the soul's every wish.

Then came the time when certain elements, indispensable for our present-day life—air and water—were purged of all they contained in the way of dense matter; what had formerly been dissolved in the water was now precipitated. Just as dissolved substances precipitate in cooling water, so the dissolved matter sank, as it were. The water became pure water and the air was rid of denser matter; air and water came into existence. Man was able to use this rarefied matter for his physical development.

From this third age human beings gradually passed over into an evolutionary epoch we call the *Atlantean*, because during that time the greater part of the human race inhabited a continent, now submerged, situated in the area now occupied by the Atlantic Ocean—between America, and Europe-Africa. So after the Lemurian age had continued yet a while, the human race carried on its evolution on the Atlantean continent; and that was the scene of all that I shall now describe, as well as of much that was mentioned yesterday.

At the time the moon withdrew from the earth, only a small number of human souls that were to incarnate later were on the earth. Most of them were distributed over the various cosmic bodies; but during the last part of the Lemurian and the first part of the Atlantean age these souls descended to the earth. Only few human beings, as I told you, had been able to experience the crisis of the Lemurian epoch, for only the most robust—those capable of living in the ever hardening substance prior to the moon's exit—had survived the moon crisis of the earth. But when everything that had solidified during the moon crisis began to soften again, when descendants appeared who were no longer compressed within fixed outlines through hereditary necessity, but were mobile, then the souls gradually descended from the various planets and moved into these bodies. Those forms, however, that incorporated physically very soon after the withdrawal of the moon retained their rigid form through heredity, and could not receive human souls even after the separation.

We can visualize the process accurately by imagining the craving of these souls to return to earth. Down there, forms came into being in the greatest variety, descendants of those that had been left over after the separation; and among these, many different degrees of solidification obtained. Those human souls—in fact, all soul beings—that in a certain respect felt as yet the least urge to unite completely with a physical substance now selected the softest forms for occupation, and soon abandoned them again. But the others, those that united at this early stage with the hardened forms, were imprisoned in them and consequently were compelled to remain behind in evolution. In fact, the animals ranking closest to man came into being as a consequence of this impatience on the part of certain souls descending from cosmic space. These souls sought earth bodies prematurely and made definitely bounded forms of them before they could be wholly permeated by etheric bodies. The human form remained plastic until such time as it could adapt itself completely to the etheric body; and it was thus that the physical and etheric bodies came to coincide, as explained, approximately during the last third of the Atlantean age. Previously, the human soul principle that descended kept the earthly body in a fluid state and guarded against a complete amalgamation of the etheric body with any part of the physical body. This interpenetration of the etheric and physical bodies came about at a definite point in time. Only during the

82

Atlantean epoch the physical human body assumed a definite form and began to harden.

Had nothing else occurred at this point in the Atlantean development, had no other factor intervened, evolution would have taken a different course. Man would have passed rather rapidly from an earlier to a later state of consciousness. Before he became a complete unit as regards the principles of body and soul he was a clairvoyant being, but his clairvoyance was dim and dull. He was able to see into the spiritual world but he could not address himself as "I," could not distinguish himself from his surroundings. He lacked self-consciousness, for this only entered during the period of evolution in which the physical body united with the etheric body.

If nothing else had intervened, the following would have occurred in a comparatively short time: Hitherto man had had a consciousness of the spiritual world. Plants, animals, and so on, he could not see distinctly, but what he did see was spirit enveloping them. He would not have seen the form of an elephant, for instance, very clearly, but he would have seen the etheric principle extended over its physical body. This form of human consciousness would have gradually disappeared, the ego would have evolved along with the coincidence of the physical and etheric bodies, and man would have seen the world confronting him as though from another side. While previously he had beheld clairvoyant pictures he would thenceforth have perceived an outer world; but at the same time he would have perceived as well the spiritual beings and spiritual forces underlying this outer world. He would not have seen the physical image of the plant as we see it today: he would have perceived the spiritual being of the plant coincident with the physical image.

Why, in the course of evolution, was the dim, clairvoyant form of consciousness not simply superseded by a consciousness of objects which at the same time would have provided perception and knowledge of spirit? That is because precisely during the moon crisis, when man was reviving, he began to be influenced by beings that must be characterized as retarded, although they are on a higher plane than man. We have already acquainted ourselves with a number of such higher beings and we know that some of them ascended to the sun, others to various planets. But there were also spiritual beings that had failed to complete the tasks they were obligated to perform on the moon. These beings, ranking lower than the Gods and higher than man, we designate Luciferic beings after their leader, Lucifer, the highest and most powerful among them.

At the time of the moon crisis man had evolved to the point of possessing a physical body, etheric body, astral body, and ego. For his ego, he was indebted to the influence of the Spirits of Form; for his astral body, to the Spirits of Motion; for his etheric body, to the Spirits of Wisdom; and for his physical body, to the Thrones. The Spirits of Form—Exusiai, or Mights, in Christian esotericism—were those who made it possible for the germinal ego to join the other principles. Now, if man had been involved only in the normal stream of development, and if all the beings surrounding him had properly performed their tasks, certain beings would have worked on his physical body, others on his etheric body, others on his astral body, and still others on his ego—as they should have done, to put it that way—each being working on the principle assigned to it. But here were those beings that had lagged behind on the *Moon*, the Luciferic beings. If they had been able to carry on their work in the right way they would have been appointed to work on the ego; but on the *Moon* they had only learned to work on the astral body, and that entailed a significant consequence. Had it not been for these Luciferic spirits man would have received his ego principle; and his further development would have taken a course, in the last third of the Atlantean age, involving the exchange of his dim, clairvoyant consciousness for the consciousness of outer objects. As it was, however, the effects of the Luciferic spirits penetrated his astral body like powerful rays.

And the nature of these effects? Well, the astral body is the vehicle of impulses, desires, passions, instincts, and so forth; and in the constitution of his astral body man would have developed quite differently had he not been affected by the Luciferic spirits. He would have developed only such impulses as would have guided him surely and advanced him unfailingly. The spirits would have led him to see the world as consisting of objects behind which the spiritual beings revealed themselves. But what would have been lacking is freedom, enthusiasm, the sense of independence—a passion for these loftier considerations. Man would have lost his former clairvoyant consciousness and would have regarded the glories of the world as a sort of God, for he would have become a component part of divinity. Furthermore, such a view of the world would have induced a perfect reflection of itself in his mind, but in all his perfection man would have remained a reflection of the universe.

But before this could occur the Luciferic spirits filled his astral body with passions, instincts, desires which merged with all that man absorbed into himself in the course of his evolution. This meant that he was able not only to perceive the stars, but at the same time to warm to a rapturous enthusiasm in beholding them; not merely to follow the divinely inspired instincts of his astral body, but to unfold impulses of his own through freedom. That is what the Luciferic spirits had infused into man's astral body; but it implied another factor, something else that they had given him as well: the potentiality of evil, of sin. This he would not have possessed had he been led forward step by step by the more sublime Gods. The Luciferic spirits made man free and endowed him with the capacity for enthusiasm; but at the same time they bestowed on him the potential for base desires. Given a normal course of development, man would in every case have associated the normal sensations with whatever he encountered. As it was, however, he derived greater pleasure from things of the sense world than he should, he clung to these with undue interest. And the result was that the process of physical solidification set in at an earlier stage than it would have done otherwise.

So man attained to a solid form sooner than the divine-spiritual beings had intended, so to speak. It was in the last third of the Atlantean age that he really should have descended from a gaseous to a solid form; as it was, however, he descended prematurely and became a solid being. That is what the Bible describes as the "fall of man"; that is the Luciferic influence which makes itself felt.

But during the period just considered there were also lofty spiritual beings at work on the ego with which they had endowed man. In the same measure as these human beings descend again and unite with human bodies, the spiritual beings infuse the forces that advance man on his cosmic path; they hold a protecting hand over him. But on the other hand we have the activity of those beings who failed to learn to work on the ego, who now work on the human astral body, and there develop quite special instincts.

Observing the physical life of man in this period we see an image of these two mutually antagonistic powers: the divine-spiritual powers at work upon the ego, and the Luciferic beings. Let us now trace something of the spiritual side of this process. During the time of desolation on earth the human souls ascended to the various cosmic bodies belonging to our solar system. Now they returned in as far as they were able to find bodies in the line of physical heredity. Remembering that the earth was most sparsely populated precisely at the time of the moon's withdrawal, you can imagine that the expansion of the human race started from a mere handful of people. Gradually the number increased, more and more souls descended and occupied the bodies coming into being on earth. Throughout a long period there were descendants only of the few who were present at the time of the moon's exit, and upon these the lofty sun forces themselves acted: these human beings had retained sufficient vigor to present to the sun forces a point of contact, even during the moon crisis. They and their descendants felt themselves to be sun men, so to say.

Let us understand this clearly. For simplicity's sake, imagine that during the moon crisis there existed all told but one human couple. (I do not wish to decide whether this was actually the case.*) This couple has descendants, these in turn have descendants, and so on; and thus the human race branched out. Now, as long as there existed only the progeny, in the narrower sense, of the old sun men, all these enjoyed a quite special form of consciousness by reason of their ancient clairvoyance. At that time human memory included not only experiences that had occurred since birth, or as is the case today, since a certain point of time after birth, but everything that the father, grandfather, and even early progenitors, had experienced. Memory reached back to the ancestors, to all with whom a man was related by blood. That was because in a certain sense the sun forces held a protecting hand over those of blood relationship, those who traced their descent to the human beings who had

---

*In the ninth lecture of his remarkable cycle *Genesis: the Biblical Secrets of Creation* (Munich, 1910) Dr. Steiner made clear, with many details, that there *was* such a single primeval couple.

survived the moon crisis. The sun forces had engendered the ego consciousness and maintained it throughout the line of blood generation.

Now the human race multiplied and the souls that had ascended into cosmic space returned to earth. Those souls, however, in whom the sun forces were strong enough still felt these forces, although they had descended and become related to spheres quite different from those of the sun. But then came the time when these souls, as later descendants, lost that connection, and with it the common ancestral memory. The more the human race multiplied, the dimmer became this living consciousness that was connected with blood heredity. This was because the powers that led men forward and implanted the ego in them were opposed by the Luciferic powers that influenced the astral body. The Luciferic powers obstructed everything that cemented men into a unit. What they wanted to teach them was freedom, self-consciousness.

So the oldest survivors of the moon's withdrawal thought of the word "I" as referring not only to what they experienced themselves, but to what their ancestors had experienced. They felt the common sun being that worked in their blood. And even after this state, too, had passed, those who had come down, for instance from Mars felt the bond that united them with the protecting Spirit of Mars. Having been recruited from Mars souls, the descendants of those who had come down from Mars felt the protecting hand of the Mars Spirit.

It was against this group feeling, in which love held sway, that the Luciferic spirits attempted their attack. They learned how to cultivate the individual human ego, as opposed to the common ego developed by such groups. The farther back we seek, the more firmly we find the community consciousness bound up with consanguinity, and passing on in

88

time we see it decreasing; man's feeling of independence becomes ever stronger, and he senses the necessity for developing an individual ego, as opposed to the common ego.

Thus two realms were at work in the human being, the realm of the Luciferic spirits and that of the divine-spiritual beings. The divine-spiritual powers brought men together, but did so by means of blood ties, while the Luciferic beings sought to separate them, to segregate them individually. These two forces were active throughout the Atlantean age, and they remained so even after the Atlantean continent perished through the great catastrophies, and Europe, Asia, and Africa on one side, and America on the other, had assumed their present form. They are still active in the fifth earth epoch, right into our own time.

Thus we have described five earth epochs: the Polarian, in which the earth was still united with the sun, the Hyperborean, in which the moon was still united with the earth, and the Lemurian; then the Atlantean; and finally, the post-Atlantean, our own age. We learned how the Luciferic spirits intervened and worked against the divine-spiritual powers that drew men together, and we have come to understand that something very different would have occurred had the Luciferic spirits not taken a hand in human evolution. In the last third of the Atlantean epoch the old form of clairvoyant consciousness would have been exchanged for a consciousness of objects—but an object consciousness permeated by spirit. As it was, however, the Luciferic spirits brought about a premature hardening of the physical body, enabling man to get his bearing in the physical world at an earlier stage than would otherwise have been the case; and the result of all this was that man entered upon the last third of the Atlantean age in a totally different state than he would have done if the divine-spiritual beings alone had guided

89

him. Instead of an outer world aglow and spiritualized by higher beings, he now beheld a physical world only, for the divine world had withdrawn from him.

The Luciferic spirits had taken a hand in the shaping of man's astral body; and now, because he had united with the physical world, Zarathustra's "Ahrimanic spirits"—we can also call them "Mephistophelian" spirits—interfered with his outer perception, with the relation of his ego to the outer world, with his ability to distinguish his ego from the outer world. The constitution of his physical, etheric, and astral bodies is not as it would have been had only the superior Gods worked on them. Beings we term Luciferic gained access to his astral body and expelled him from Paradise sooner than was intended; and the consequence of this Luciferic activity was the interference of the Ahrimanic, or Mephistophelian, spirits in his perception of the outer world, which they now showed him in its physical form only, not as it is in reality. That is why these spirits that dupe mankind with what is spurious are called by the Hebrew people *mephiztopel: mephiz*, the corrupter, and *topel*, the liar. This eventually became Mephistopheles; and it is merely another name for Ahriman.

Now, what did Ahriman effect in man, as opposed to Lucifer? Lucifer brought about a deterioration of the forces of the astral body greater than it should have been, as well as the premature solidification of man's physical substance— though it must be kept in mind that thereby the attainment of freedom was made possible. The Mephistophelian spirits, on the other hand, prevented man from discerning the spiritual basis of the world, tricking him instead with a mere illusion of it. Mephistopheles induced in men the belief that the outer world is nothing but a material existence, that there is no such thing as spirit underlying and permeating

90

all material substance. The scene so beautifully portrayed in Goethe's *Faust* has been enacted by mankind throughout the ages. On the one hand we see Faust seeking the path into the spiritual world; on the other, Mephistopheles, who calls that spiritual world "nothingness," because it is to his interest to represent the sense world as being all that exists. Faust replies, as would every spiritual scientist in this case, "In what is nothingness to thee I hope to find my all." Only when we know that in every tiniest particle of matter there is spirit and that the idea of matter is a lie; only when we recognize Mephistopheles as that spirit in the world who distorts our conceptions—only then can the outer world appear to us as it really is.

What was needed to carry mankind onward, to prevent its succumbing to the fate prepared for it by Lucifer, by Ahriman? As early as in the Atlantean age the influence of the Luciferic beings had to be checked. Even then there were men who worked on themselves in such a way as to counteract the Luciferic influence in their astral bodies, who were on the alert for what emanated from Lucifer, who examined their own souls for Luciferic passions, instincts, and desires. And as a result of eradicating these Luciferic qualities they recaptured the capacity for seeing in its pure form what all men would have seen had they not been exposed to the influence of the Luciferic, and later of the Ahrimanic, spirits. By means of pure living and conscientious self-knowledge certain human beings of the old Atlantean epoch sought to rid themselves of this Luciferic influence; and this enabled them, at a time when remnants of the old clairvoyance still survived, to see into the spiritual world and discern loftier things than could the others, whose physical substance had hardened as a result of the Luciferic influence. Such men—those that cast out the Luciferic influence by means of strong-minded self-knowledge—became the leaders of the Atlantean age. We can call them the Atlantean initiates.

Now what, exactly, was the nature of Lucifer's activity? In the main, Lucifer directed his attack against everything that united human beings, against blood ties that expressed themselves in love. But the leaders just mentioned knew how to resist Lucifer's influence, and by doing so they acquired the ability to envision this connection spiritually: they came to realize that the factor conditioning man's progress lies not in separation, in segregation, but in that which unites men. Hence these initiates endeavored to restore, as it were, the ancient state of affairs in which the upper spiritual world was not yet threatened by Lucifer's power. They aimed at eradicating the personal element: Kill that which endows you with a personal ego! Gaze back to olden times when the ties of blood spoke so eloquently that a descendant experienced his ego as reaching back to his earliest forebearer; when the first ancestor, long since dead, was still held sacred! The age of the primeval human community—that is the age into which the Atlantean leaders endeavored to lead men back. Throughout this whole period of evolution there appeared such leaders of mankind again and again, proclaiming, Endeavor to resist the influences that would drive you to a personal ego; try to learn what it was that bound men together in olden times! Then you will find the way to the divine spirit.

This attitude had retained its purest form among those we know as the ancient Hebew people. Just recall and try to understand the exhortations of the leaders of this old Hebrew nation. They stood before their people and proclaimed: You have reached a state in which each of you stresses the personal ego in him—each of you seeks his being within himself alone. But development will be furthered only by subduing the personal ego and exerting all those forces that guide you to the consciousness of being all connected, of having descended one and all from Abraham, of being members of a great organism reaching back to Abraham. If you are told, "I and Father Abraham are one," and you take these words to heart, ignoring all that is personal, then you have the right consciousness that will lead you to the divine; for the path to the divine leads by way of the original ancestor. The vital impulse determining the leadership of those who contended against the Luciferic influence was preserved longest by the Hebrew people. But man had been entrusted with the mission to develop and cultivate the ego, not to destroy it. The old initiates had no quarrel with the personal ego, but they maintained that the ascent to the old Gods should be made by way of the early forbears.

With the coming to earth of the great impulse, as we characterized it yesterday—the Christ impulse—a new utterance resounded for the first time clearly and distinctly; and it was among the Hebrew people that it could be heard with special clarity and distinctness, because this was the people that had longest preserved what we may consider an echo of the old Atlantean initiate teaching.

Christ transmuted that teaching of the old initiates, and said: It is possible for man to cultivate his own personality. He need not obey the physical bonds of blood brotherhood alone; he can look into his own ego and there seek, and find, the divine. What we have characterized as the Christ impulse bears within it the force which, if we unite with it, offers us the possibility of establishing a spiritual bond of brotherhood among human beings, in spite of the individuality of the ego. Thus the Christ force was very different from the one prevailing in the community into which He was placed. There the idea was, I and Father Abraham are one. That is what I must know if I am to find the way back to the divine.

But Christ said: There is another Father through Whom the ego will find the way to the divine; for the ego, or the *I am*, is one with the divine. There is something eternal thou canst find if thou remainest within thyself.

That is why Christ could characterize the force He would transmit to men with the words we find in the Gospel of St. John. *Before Abraham was, was the I am.* And the "I am" was nothing other than the name which Christ called Himself. If men can enkindle the thought within them: Within me there dwells something that existed long before Abraham; I have no need to go back to Abraham, for I find the divine Father Spirit within me—then they can turn into good all that Lucifer contributed to the cultivation and fostering of the ego, which had proved an obstacle in the path of humanity. The transformation of Lucifer's influence into good—that was the deed of Christ.

Supposing that only the high divine-spiritual beings had been at work, those who had restricted love to blood ties, who kept demanding of men that they go back through the whole line of descent if they would find the way to the Gods. Had that occurred, mankind would have been herded together into one human community without enjoying full consciousness; and never would men have risen to a complete awareness of their freedom and independence. But that is what the Luciferic spirits implanted in man's astral body before the advent of Christ. They segregated men, tried to make them independent of each other. But Christ turned to good the evil that would inevitably have resulted had the Luciferic influence become extreme. If the latter had run its full course mankind would have lost its capacity for love. Lucifer endowed man with freedom and independence; Christ transmuted this freedom into love. And the bond Christ brought mankind is what will lead men to spiritual love.

This point of view throws a different light on the deeds

94

of the Luciferic spirits. Are we still justified in thinking of their once having lagged behind as due to indolence and laziness? No indeed, for it was done in order to fulfill a definite mission in *Earth* evolution: to prevent men from becoming fused into a mere mass through purely natural ties, as well as to prepare the way to Christ. It is as though they had said to themselves on the *Moon*: We will renounce our present goal in order to be able to work on the *Earth* in conformity with progressive development. This is one of the examples that show how an ostensible evil, a seeming error, can turn out for the best in the whole context of world events. To enable the Christ to intervene in *Earth* evolution at the right moment, certain *Moon* spirits had to sacrifice their *Moon* mission and prepare for Him. This shows us that Lucifer's retardation on the *Moon* can also be regarded in the light of a sacrifice.

In this way we come ever closer to a truth which should be engraved in the human soul as a lofty moral maxim: When you see something evil in the world, do not say, Here is evil —that is, imperfection; ask, rather, How can I attain to the enlightenment which will show me that on a higher plane this evil is transformed into good by the wisdom of the cosmos? How can I learn to tell myself: Here you see naught but imperfection because you are as yet unable to grasp the perfection of this imperfect thing?

Whenever man sees evil he should look into his own soul and ask himself, Why am I not yet able to recognize the good in this evil that confronts me?

VI

Yesterday we drew attention to the existence of great leaders of mankind as far back as the epoch we call the Atlantean period of human evolution. We know from what was brought forth yesterday that this epoch ran its course on a continent we call the Old Atlantis, lying between Europe-Africa, and America. We also mentioned that human life at that time was very different from what it is today, particularly with regard to the nature of human consciousness. We learned from yesterday's lecture that the consciousness with which man is endowed today developed only gradually, and that he started from a sort of dim clairvoyance. We know further that the human beings of the Atlantean period possessed a body consisting of a substance far softer, more flexible, more plastic, than that of the human body today. Clairvoyant consciousness reveals the fact that at that time men were not yet able, for example, to perceive solid objects such as our eyes see today in sharp outline. The Atlantean could distinguish the objects of the outer world—the mineral, plant, and animal kingdoms—but only indistinctly, blurred. Just as nowadays on a foggy autumn evening the street lights show a fringe of color, so people of that time saw objects surrounded by a colored border—an *aura*, as the term is. The auras were the indications of the spiritual beings belonging to the objects. At certain times in the course of the day the perception of these spiritual beings was very indistinct, but at other times very clear, especially in the intermediate states between waking and sleeping.

If we want to imagine the consciousness of an ancient Atlantean vividly, we must say to ourselves: He did not see a rose, for example, so sharply outlined as we do today. It was blurred, hazy, and surrounded by colored borders. Already by day it was indistinct, but it became more so and disappeared entirely in the interval between waking and sleeping. On the other hand, however, he discerned quite clearly what we must term the rose spirit, the rose soul. And the same was true of all other objects in his environment. In the progress of evolution outer objects became ever clearer, while perception of the spiritual beings associated with them grew ever dimmer. But in place of it, man kept developing his self consciousness; he learned to be aware of himself.

Yesterday we mentioned the point in time when a distinct sense of the ego emerged, adding that the etheric body came to coincide with the physical body as the last third of the Atlantean age approached. You can imagine that previously the nature of leadership as well was quite different, for at that time there existed nothing like a mutual understanding among men resting on an appeal to reason. In those days of dim clairvoyance mutual understanding was based upon a subconscious influence passing from one to the other. Especially was there still present to a high degree something we know today only in its last misinterpreted and misunderstood surviving form, namely, a kind of suggestion, a subconscious influence from man to man, appealing but little to the active cooperation of the other's soul. Looking back to early Atlantean times we see that a powerful effect was exercised on the other's soul the moment any image, any sensation, arose in a man's soul, and he directed his will upon the other person. All influences were powerful, as was also the will to receive them. Only traces of all this still exist today.

Picture to yourself a man of that time passing another while executing certain gestures. If the observer were even slightly the weaker of the two, he would have felt impelled to imitate and mimic all the gestures. The only surviving remnant of this sort of thing is our inclination to yawn when we see another person yawning. Formerly a far closer tie prevailed between human beings, based on the fact that they lived in an atmosphere totally different from that of today. Only during a heavy rain do we nowadays live in water-soaked air. In that time, however, the air was constantly saturated with dense moisture. In the early Atlantean age, man was composed of a substance no more dense than that of certain jellyfish now living in the sea and scarcely distinguishable from the surrounding water. That was the way man was constituted at that time, and he solidified only gradually. Nevertheless we know that even then he was exposed to influences not only of the regular guiding higher spiritual beings, who either dwelt on the sun or were distributed among the various planets of our solar system, but also of the Luciferic spirits that influenced his astral body. We have also characterized the manner in which these influences took effect. But we found further that those who were to be the leaders of the Atlantean people had to combat these Luciferic influences in their own astral body. By reason of the spiritual and clairvoyant nature of their consciousness all men of that time could perceive whatever spiritual influences were exerted on them. Nowadays one who knows nothing of spiritual science laughs when you tell him his astral body shows the effects of Luciferic spirits; but then, he does not know that the influence of these spirits is far stronger than it would be if he took note of them.

"The Devil your good-folk ne'er scent,
E'en though he have them by the collar."

That is a very profound utterance in Goethe's *Faust*; and many a materialistic influence of today would not exist if people knew that man is by no means rid of all the Luciferic influences even yet.

In Atlantis, the leaders and their disciples kept a careful watch over everything that excited passions, instincts, and desires from that direction, which aroused in man a deeper interest in his physical-sensible surroundings than was beneficial for his progressive development in the world. One who aspired to become a leader had first of all to practice this self-knowledge and watch himself carefully for anything that might arise through Lucifer's influence. He had to observe these Luciferic spiritual beings in his own astral body most accurately, for by so doing he could keep them at a distance. This also enabled him to perceive the other divine-spiritual beings, the higher, guiding ones, and particularly those who had transferred their own sphere of action from the earth to the sun, or to other planets; and the regions beheld by men corresponded to the one from which they had descended. There were human souls, for instance, that had come down from Mars; and when these, in keeping with their development, combatted the Luciferic influences in their own astral body, they attained to a higher degree of clairvoyance, to a pure and good seership, and they beheld the higher spiritual beings of the region from which they themselves had descended, from the Mars region. Souls that had come down from Saturn learned to see the Saturn beings, those from Jupiter or Venus, the Jupiter or Venus beings; each beheld his own region.

But the most advanced among men, those who had survived the moon crisis, were able gradually to prepare themselves to envision not only the spiritual beings of Mars, Jupiter, or Venus, but those of the sun itself, the exalted sun beings. The fact that the persons who had become initiated had descended from the various planets made the spiritual nature of these planetary worlds visible to them once again. From this it is clear why, in ancient Atlantis, there were institutions, schools, where those who had descended, for example, from Mars were accepted, when sufficiently mature, for the purpose of studying the mysteries of Mars. There were other sanctuaries where those who had come from Venus became acquainted with Venus mysteries. Applying the later term "oracle" to these institutions, we have in Atlantis a Mars Oracle, where the mysteries of Mars were studied, a Saturn Oracle, a Jupiter Oracle, a Venus Oracle, and so on. The most exalted was the Sun Oracle; and the loftiest of all the initiates was the ranking initiate of the Sun Oracle.

Because suggestion and the influences of will played so important a part, the whole method of instruction was very different. Let us try to imagine how teacher and pupil conversed with each other. Assuming the presence of spiritual teachers who had achieved initiation as by an act of grace, we ask, How did the later neophytes arrive at initiation in the Atlantean age? Here we must picture first of all the mighty impression exercised by those already initiated—through their whole conduct, their mere presence—upon those predestined to become their pupils. The very sight of an Atlantean initiate was enough to start sympathetic vibrations in the souls of those who were destined to become pupils, thus disclosing their fitness for discipleship. The influences that passed between men at that time were entirely remote from objective day-consciousness, and the type of instruction we know today was then unnecessary. All intercourse with the teacher, everything the teacher did, worked hand in hand with men's imitative faculty. A great deal passed unconsciously from teacher to pupil; hence the most important factor, for those sufficiently matured through their previous life conditions, was that in the beginning they should merely be admitted to the sanctuaries and remain in proximity to their teachers. Then, by observing what the teachers did and by impressions made on their feelings and sensations,

100

they were trained—prepared, indeed, over a very long period of time. Eventually, the harmonious accord between the soul of the teacher and the soul of the pupil reached the point where everything the teacher possessed in the way of deeper spiritual secrets passed to the disciple. Such were the conditions in those ancient times.

Now, what was the situation after the union of the etheric and physical bodies had become established? Although the two bodies had achieved complete coincidence during the Atlantean epoch, the union was as yet not very firm, so that by an effort of will the teacher could, in a certain sense, withdraw the pupil's etheric body from the physical. It was no longer possible, even when the right moment had come, for the teacher's wisdom to pass over into the pupil as of its own accord; but the teacher could easily withdraw the pupil's etheric body and then the pupil could see whatever the teacher saw. So the slight or loose connection between the etheric and physical bodies made it possible to lift out the pupil's etheric body, and the wisdom, the clairvoyant vision, of the master passed over into the disciple.

Then there occurred the great cataclysm that swept away the Atlantean continent. Mighty elemental disturbances in air and water, terrific upheavals in the earth, gradually altered the entire face of the globe. Europe, Asia, and Africa, which had been dry land only to a very slight extent, arose out of the water, as did likewise America. Atlantis disappeared. Men migrated eastward and westward, and a great variety of settlements came into being. But after the mighty catastrophe mankind had advanced another step. Again a change had taken place in the relationship between the etheric and physical bodies: in the post-Atlantean time, the union of the two became much firmer. The teacher could now no longer detach the pupil's etheric body by an impulse of will and thereby transmit his observations as he had formerly done. Hence, initiation, leading to vision of the spiritual world, had to take another form which can be described somewhat as follows.

The instruction, which had been based largely upon direct psychic influence from teacher to pupil, had gradually to be superseded by a form slowly approaching what we know as instruction today; and the farther the post-Atlantean age advanced, the greater grew the resemblance to our modern method of instruction. Correspondingly to the Atlantean oracles, institutions were now established by the great leaders of mankind exhibiting similarities to the old Atlantean oracles. Mysteries, initiation temples, came into being in the post-Atlantean epoch; and just as formerly those fitted for it were received into the oracles, so now they were admitted to the Mysteries. There, the neophytes were carefully trained by means of exacting instruction, because they could no longer be influenced as they were formerly. In all civilizations, over a long period of time, we find such Mysteries. Whether you seek in the culture we know as the first post-Atlantean, which ran its course in ancient India, or in that of Zarathustra, or among the Egyptians or Chaldeans, you will invariably find neophytes being admitted to the Mysteries, which were something part-way between church and school. There, they underwent a severe training calculated to promote thinking and feeling as these apply to events of the invisible, spiritual world, not merely as related to things of the sense world.

And what was taught there can now be accurately defined: to a great extent it was the same as what we have come to know today as anthroposophy. That was the subject of study in the Mysteries. It differed only in that it was adapted to the customs of that time and was imparted according to strict rules. Today, people who in a certain sense are mature can be told of the mysteries of the higher worlds in a more

102

or less free way and comparatively rapidly. Formerly, however, instruction was strictly regulated. In the first grade, for instance, only a certain sum of knowledge was imparted and all else kept completely secret. Not until the pupil had digested this was he apprised of anything pertaining to a higher grade. Through this sort of preparation, concepts, ideas, sensations, and feelings referring to the spiritual world were implanted in his astral body, a procedure tending at the same time to combat the influences of Lucifer; for all that is imparted in the way of spiritual-scientific concepts refers to the higher worlds, not to the world in which Lucifer aims to stimulate man's interest, not to the sense world alone.

Eventually, when the neophyte had been prepared in this way, the time approached for him to be guided to independent vision. He himself was to see into the spiritual world. This necessitated the ability to reflect in his etheric body everything he had accumulated in his astral body; for vision of the spiritual world is achieved only when the fruits of study stored in the astral body are experienced so intensely, through certain feelings and sensations connected with the knowledge acquired, that not only the astral body, but the denser etheric body as well, is thereby influenced. If the pupil was to rise from learning to seeing, all that had been taught him had to have borne fruit.

That is why, throughout the Indian, Persian, Egyptian, and Greek epochs, the training period closed with the following act. First the pupil was again prepared for a long time, now not through learning, but by means of what we call meditation and other exercises designed to develop inner concentration, inner tranquility, inner equanimity. He was prepared to make his astral body in every respect a citizen of the spiritual worlds; and when the right time had come, the conclusion of this development consisted in his being placed in a deathlike state lasting three and a half days. While in Atlantean times the etheric and physical bodies were so loosely joined that the former could be withdrawn more easily than in later periods, it had now become necessary in the Mysteries to place the neophyte into a deathlike sleep. While this lasted, he was either placed in a coffinlike box or bound to a sort of cross, something of that sort. The initiator, known as the hierophant, possessed the power to work upon the astral, and particularly upon the etheric body, for during this procedure, the etheric left the physical body. That is something differing from sleep. In sleep, the physical and etheric bodies remain in bed while the astral body and ego withdraw. In this final act of initiation, however, only the physical body remained in place. The etheric body was withdrawn from the greater part of the physical body, only the lower portions remained, the upper portions were lifted out; and this left the candidate in a deathlike state. Everything that had been learned through meditation and other exercises was now impressed into the etheric body while in this condition. During these three and a half days, the human being really traversed the spiritual worlds wherein the higher beings dwell. After the three and a half days had passed, the hierophant called him back, meaning that he had the power to awaken him; and the candidate brought with him a knowledge of the spiritual world. Now he could see into this spiritual world and could proclaim its truths to his fellow men who as yet did not possess the maturity to behold it themselves.

Thus, the ancient teachers of pre-Christian time had been initiated into the profound secrets of the Mysteries. There, they had been guided by the hierophant during the three-and-a-half-day period; they were living witnesses to the existence of a spiritual life and to the fact that behind the physical there is a spiritual world to which man belongs with his higher principles and into which he must find his way. But evolution proceeded. What I have just described to you as an initiation existed most intensively in the first epoch after the Atlantean catastrophe. The union of the etheric and physical bodies, however, grew ever firmer; hence, the procedure became more and more dangerous, because man's whole consciousness accustomed itself increasingly to the physical sense world. This, after all, was the purpose of human evolution: men were to become used to living in this physical world with all their inclinations and propensities. It implied great progress for mankind that human beings truly developed this love for the physical world.

In the early part of the post-Atlantean civilization there still remained a living recollection of the existence of a spiritual world. People said: We, the late descendants, can still see into the spiritual world of our ancestors. They still retained their dim, dull, clairvoyant consciousness and they knew where lay the world of truth, which was their true home. They said, All that surrounds us in our day-consciousness is like a veil spread over truth, it hides the spiritual world from us, it is *maya*, illusion. They did not accustom themselves at once to what they now could see. They could not readily understand that it was intended that they lose their awareness of the old spiritual world. That was the characteristic feature of the first post-Atlantean civilization; hence that was the time in which men could most easily be guided to the spirit, for they still felt a lively interest in the spiritual world. Naturally, matters could not remain thus, because the *Earth's* mission consists in man's becoming fond of the forces of the earth and conquering the physical plane. Were you able to envision ancient India, you would discover the spiritual life to be on a tremendously lofty level.

A comprehension of what the original teachers revealed to mankind is possible for the human being in this day and age only after a study of spiritual science. For everybody else, the teachings of the great holy Rishis are nonsense, foolishness, for he can make no sense out of what is told him in them about the mysteries of the spiritual world. From his standpoint, he is naturally quite right, everyone is always right from his own standpoint.

In ancient India, spiritual vision was enormously developed, but the use of even the simplest implements was nonexistent. People provided for themselves in the most primitive ways. There was nothing like a natural science of any kind, or what is so called today, because everything that could be observed on the physical plane was looked upon as *maya*, the great illusion. The real, the true, was found only by elevation to the great sun being or similar beings. But again, matters could not remain there. Human beings had to gradually learn to love this earth. Among the post-Atlanteans, there had to be those as well with the will to conquer the kingdom of earth; and the first attempt to this end was made in the time of Zarathustra. In the transition from the old Indians to the ancient Persians, we see a mighty step forwards. In Zarathustra's view, the outer world ceased to be mere *maya* or illusion. He showed men that what surrounds them is of value, though he emphasized the presence of spirit underlying all. While the ancient Indian saw a flower as *maya* and sought the spirit behind it, Zarathustra said, The flower is something we must value, for it is an integral part of the universal spirit existing in all things; matter grows out of spirit.

We have already mentioned that Zarathustra drew attention to the physical sun as the field of action of spiritual beings. But initiation was difficult; and for those who wanted not merely to be told of the spiritual world by the initiates but to see for themselves into the great sun aura, more severe measures were required in connection with their initiation.

Furthermore, all human life gradually changed. In the next cultural epoch, the Egypto-Chaldean, the physical world was conquered to a still greater extent. Man was no longer bent upon a purely spiritual science which studies the realm that underlies the physical. He observed the course of the stars; and in their position and movement, in what is outwardly visible, he sought to perceive a script of divine-spiritual beings. In this script co-ordinating visible objects he recognized the will of the Gods. That is the way cosmic inter-relationships were studied in the Egypto-Chaldean time. And in Egypt we see arising a geometry applied to external things. Such is the story of man's conquest of the outer world.

In Greece, even greater progress was made in this direction. There, we see how the union of soul experiences and external matter comes about. If a statue of Pallas Athene or Zeus confronts us, we see that what first lived in the human soul has been communicated to material substance. It is as though everything which man had conquered had flowed out into the sense world. But as man became ever more powerful in the sense world and his soul grew more and more attached to it, his alienation from the spiritual world increased correspondingly in the life between death and a new birth. When the soul left an ancient Indian body and entered the spiritual world, there to pass through the requisite development before the next birth, it retained a feeling for the living spirit. Through his whole life the man of that time yearned for a spiritual environment; and all his sensations were stimulated by the revelations he had heard concerning life in the spiritual world, even if he was not an initiate himself. So, when he passed the portal of death, the spiritual world lay open before him, as it were, in light and radiance.

But as the physical world became more and more congenial and men adapted themselves to it ever more readily, the periods between death and birth were proportionately obscured. In the Egyptian epoch, this had progressed so far that one can establish by clairvoyant consciousness that, in passing from the body into the spiritual world, the soul was enveloped in darkness and gloom. The soul experienced a sense of loneliness, of segregation from other souls; and when a soul feels loneliness and can hold no converse with other souls, it experiences a frosty chill. And while the Greeks lived in an age in which, by means of a civilization of such glorious external beauty, men had made the earth into something quite special, this period was darkest, gloomiest, most chilling, for the souls living between death and rebirth. A noble Greek, questioned as to his sojourn in the nether world, replied, "Better a beggar in the upper world than a king in the realm of shades." That is not a legend, but an utterance actually in accord with the attitude of that time.

It can therefore be said that with the advance of civilization men became more and more alienated from the spiritual world. The initiates, who could see into the higher regions of the spiritual world, became increasingly rare because of the growing dangers connected with the initiation procedure. It became more and more difficult to preserve life for three and a half days in a cataleptic state, with the etheric body withdrawn.

Then, a regeneration of the whole life of humanity took place through the impulse already mentioned in the foregoing lectures, the Christ-Impulse. We have already described how Christ, the exalted Sun Spirit, gradually approached the earth. We have learned how in Zarathustra's time He still had to be sought in the sun as *Ahura Mazdao*, and how Moses beheld Him already in the burning bush and in the fire on Mount Sinai. He gradually entered the sphere of the earth, which thereby was destined to be changed. To begin with this Spirit was concerned that men should become acquainted with Him on this earth.

The outstanding feature of all the old initiations was the necessity for withdrawing the etheric out of the physical body. Even in the post-Atlantean initiations, the candidate had to be reduced to a death-like state of sleep, that is, a state in which he was devoid of physical consciousness. This implied coming under the control of another ego. This was invariably the case. The candidate's ego was wholly controlled by his initiator, his hierophant. He abandoned his physical body completely; he did not dwell in it, nor did his own ego exercise any influence upon it. But the great aim of the Christ-Impulse is that man shall undergo a wholly self-contained ego development and not descend to a state of consciousness beneath that of the ego in order to attain to the higher worlds. In order to achieve this, someone had first to offer himself in sacrifice so that the Christ Spirit itself might be received into a human body. We have already pointed out that a certain initiate who had prepared himself through a great many incarnations had become able, beginning with a definite period in his life, to yield up his own ego and receive the Christ within himself. This is indicated by the Baptism in the Jordan, as told in the Gospel of St. John.

Now, what was the real significance of this baptism? We know that John the Baptist, the Forerunner, who told of the coming of Christ Jesus, carried it out among those whom he had prepared to receive the Christ in the right way. We will understand what the St. John Gospel tells us of the Baptism only if we bear in mind that John's purpose in baptizing was the true preparation for the coming of Christ. If you picture a modern baptism, which is but an imitation of the original symbol, you will gain no understanding of what it once signified. It was not a mere sprinkling with water, but a complete immersion. The candidate was submerged under water for a certain length of time, varying according to circumstances. What this signified we shall now learn by delving into the mystery of the being of man.

Recall to mind that the human being consists of physical body, etheric body, astral body, and ego. In the waking state during the daytime, these four principles are firmly knit together, but in sleep the physical and etheric bodies remain in bed, while the astral body and the ego are outside. In death, on the other hand, the physical body remains as a corpse: the etheric body withdraws, and for a short time, the ego, the astral body, and the etheric body remain united. To those of you who have heard even a few of my lectures it must be clear that in this moment a quite definite experience appears first: the deceased sees his past life spread out before him like a magnificent tableau. Side by side, in space, all the situations of his life surround him. That is because one of the functions of the etheric body is that of memory bearer, and even during life only the physical body prevents all this from appearing before him. After death, with the physical body laid aside, everything man has experienced during his lifetime can enter his consciousness.

Now, I have mentioned as well that such a review of life also results from being in peril of death, or from any severe fright or shock. You know, of course, from reports that when a man is in danger of drowning or of falling from a mountain height, he experiences his whole past life as in a great tableau, provided he does not lose consciousness. Well, what a man thus experiences as the result of some danger, such as drowning, was experienced by nearly all who were baptized by John. The baptism consisted in keeping a person under water until he had experienced his past life. But what he experienced in this way was, of course, experienced as a spiritual picture. It became apparent that in this abnormal state the spiritual experiences linked up, as it were, with the spiritual world in general, so that after being lifted out of the water again, after the baptism by John, a man knew: There is a spiritual world! In truth, what I bear within myself is something that can live without the body. After baptism a man was convinced of the existence of a world to which he belonged in respect of his spirit.

What, then, had John the Baptist brought about by baptizing in this way? People had become more and more attached to the physical world as a means of mutual contact, and believed the physical element to be the true reality. But those who came to the Baptist experienced their own lives as spiritual. After being baptized, they knew that they were something over and above what their physical body made them. The human mind* had gradually developed in the direction of the physical world; but John evoked in those he baptized the awareness of the existence of a spiritual world to which their higher selves belonged. You need only clothe John's utterance in other words and you have: "Transform your mind* that is now directed toward the physical world." And that is what they did—those who received the baptism in the right way. They knew, then, that spirit dwelt in them, that their ego belonged to the spiritual world.

Man gained this conviction in the physical body. No special procedure had taken place, as in initiation; what occurred was experienced in the physical body. In addition, the whole experience of the baptism by John acquired a special meaning as a result of the manner in which the whole doctrine of

---

*The German has "Sinn" here. Where, in Matthew 3:2, it says in English: "Repent ye . . ," the German has "Andert euren Sinn . . " ("Transform-change- your mind (or attitude)"). This is also the correct meaning of the Greek metanoite.

111

the time was received and merged with the soul—the doctrine that existed since Moses' proclamation. After baptism, a man not only was aware of his union with the spiritual world, he also recognized the particular spiritual world which was approaching the earth. He knew that what now pervaded the earth was identical with what had revealed itself to Moses as *ehjeh asher ehjeh* in the burning bush and in the fire on Sinai; and he knew that the word Jahve or Jehovah, or *ehjeh asher ehjeh*, or *I am the I AM*, truly expressed the nature of this spiritual world. So through the baptism by John, man knew not only that he was one with the spiritual world, but that in this spiritual world there dwelt the *I AM* out of which the spirit in him was born. That was the preparation John imparted through his baptisms; that was the feeling, the sensation, he aroused in those whom he baptized. Their number, of course, was necessarily small, since few of them were mature enough to experience all this when submerged; but some discerned the approach of the Spirit later to be called the Christ.

Try now to compare all this with what was set forth yesterday. What the ancient spiritual beings had brought about was love based on blood ties, on physical communion. The aim of the Luciferic spirits on the other hand was to render each individual dependent solely upon his own personality, his own individuality. Lucifer and the lofty spiritual beings had been working simultaneously. Gradually the old blood ties had loosened, as can be established even historically. Think of the conglomeration of peoples in the great Roman Empire! That was a result of the loosening of the blood ties and of the universal desire, in varying degrees, to find the center of gravity in one's own personality. But another result was that people had lost contact with the spiritual world: they had identified themselves with the physical world and developed a love for the physical plane. To the degree that ego-consciousness had increased through Lucifer's agency, man had grown together with the physical world and rendered barren his life between death and a new birth.

Now, the Baptist had indeed prepared something that was of great significance for mankind: he had prepared the way for man to remain within his personality and at the same time find there, after the submersion, exactly what once he had experienced as the "gods" at the time when he himself still lived in water, when the atmosphere was saturated with moisture and fog. That experience in the divine worlds was now repeated. In spite of possessing an ego, man, as a human being, could now be reunited with his fellowmen, could be led back to a love that was now spiritualized.

That is the mainspring of the Christ event characterized from another aspect. Christ represents the descent to our earth of the spiritual power of love, though even today its mission is only beginning to take effect. If we trace this idea by means of the John and the Luke Gospels we find spiritual love to be the very core of the Christ impulse through which the egos that had been sundered are increasingly brought together again, but now in respect of their innermost souls. From the beginning, men have been able to surmise but dimly what Christ had come to mean for the world; and today very little of it has been realized, because the sundering force, the after-effect of the Luciferic powers, is still present and the Christ principle has been active only for a short time. And though nowadays people seek to co-operate in certain external activities, they have not so much as an inkling of what is meant by harmony and accord between souls where the most intimate and important matters are concerned—or at best they vaguely sense it with their thoughts, their intellect, which counts for little.

Truly, Christianity is only at the beginning of its activity. It

113

will penetrate ever deeper into the souls of men and will increasingly ennoble their ego. This has been felt particularly strongly by people of the younger nations: they feel the need of identifying themselves with the Christ force, to steep themselves in it, if they are to get on. One of our contemporaries in eastern Europe, the executor of the great Russian philosopher Solovyev,* once said: "Christianity must unite us as a nation, otherwise we shall lose our ego, and with it, all possibility of being a people." A mighty utterance, emanating as from an intense interest in Christianity. But that again proves the need for Christianity to penetrate into the depths of the human soul.

Let us examine a certain rather drastic case. It will show us that precisely in respect of the innermost life of the soul even the most highminded and noble men are still far from possessing what will one day lay hold on them, when Christianity shall have filled man's innermost thoughts, his innermost ideas and feelings. Think of Tolstoi and of his work during the last decades which seeks to reveal in its own way the true meaning of Christianity. A thinker of his caliber should arouse enormous respect, especially in the West where whole libraries are cluttered up with lengthy philosophical hairsplitting speculations saying no more than a Tolstoi can say in a few great and powerful words as in his book *On Life*. There are pages in Tolstoi's writings in which a certain extensive understanding of theosophical truths is expounded with elemental grandeur, truths, to be sure, which a philosopher of western Europe cannot hit upon so accurately—or at best he must write volumes about them, because what they reveal is mighty. It can be said that in Tolstoi's works there is an undertone we can call the Christ

---

*As yet no one has been able to identify this "executor" with certainty.

impulse. Engross yourselves in his books, and you will see that what pervades him is the Christ impulse.

Now turn to Tolstoi's great contemporary, interesting if for no other reason than that he expanded his comprehensive philosophical world view to the very gates of a life of such genuine vision as enabled him to survey an epoch in full perspective—apocalyptically, so to speak. While his visions themselves become distorted, due to an inadequate foundation, Solovyev nevertheless rises to a clairvoyant perception of the future. He places before us future perspectives of the 20th Century. And if we study his writings with sympathetic understanding, we find there much that is great and highminded, especially in connection with Christianity. Yet he speaks of Tolstoi as of an enemy of Christianity, as of the Antichrist! This goes to show that two men today can be profoundly convinced they are giving their age the best there is, can act out of the very depths of their souls, and yet fail to understand each other: for each of them the other is "anti." Nowadays people do not reflect that if outer harmony, a life permeated by love, is to become a possibility, the Christ impulse must first have penetrated to the profoundest depths; love of mankind must be something very different from what it is today, even in the noblest spirits.

The impulse that was foretold and then entered the world is only at the beginning of its work, and it must be ever better understood. What is it that is lacking, particularly in our time, among all those who cry for Christianity and declare it a necessity, yet cannot bring it within reach? Anthroposophy, spiritual science, that is what they lack, the *present-day way* of understanding Christ. For Christ is so great that each successive epoch will have to find new means of comprehending Him. In former centuries, other ways and forms were employed in the search for wisdom. Today we need anthroposophy. What anthroposophy offers today for an understanding of Christ will hold good through long ages to come, for anthroposophy will prove to be something capable of stimulating every human capacity for knowledge. Man will in time grow into a comprehension of the Christ.

But even the anthroposophical conception is a transient one. We are aware of this; and the time will come when so great a subject, now framed in ephemeral terms, will call for still loftier conceptions.

VII

Yesterday's discussion brought us to a comprehension of the real nature of the baptism by John, the forerunner of Christ Jesus, so that it will now be comparatively easy to understand the difference between this baptism and what we may call the baptism by Christ. Precisely by striving to comprehend this difference will the very essence of the Christ impulse and its influence in the world become clear and distinct in our minds.

We must first of all remind ourselves that the condition to which men were subjected by the baptism in the Jordan was, after all, an abnormal one as compared with the ordinary, every-day state of consciousness. We learned that the old initiation, for instance, was based upon the withdrawal, in a certain respect, of the etheric body, which normally is firmly joined to the physical body, and that this enabled the astral body to imprint its experiences into the etheric body. Such was the procedure in ancient initiation, and an abnormal condition had to occur in the baptism by John as well. The disciple was submerged in water, resulting in a certain separation of the etheric from the physical body; and thus he could attain to a survey of his life and become aware of the connection of this individual life with the regions of the divine-spiritual world. To make it a little clearer, we can say that when the submersion was successful it produced in the disciple the conviction: I have spirit within me; I am not just a being in this physical-material body; and this spirit within me is one with the spirit underlying all things. And he knew in addition that the Spirit Whom he thus confronted

117

was the same that Moses had perceived in the fire of the burning bush and in the lightning on Sinai as Jahve, as *I am the I AM*, as *ehjeh asher ehjeh*. All this was revealed to him through the baptism by John.*

Now, in what way did this sort of consciousness differ from that of an initiate of olden times? The latter perceived, when in the abnormal state I described yesterday, those divine-spiritual beings that had already been connected with the earth before Zarathustra's Ahura Mazdao—the Jahve of Moses—had united with the earth. So what men perceived by means of the ancient wisdom was the old spiritual world out of which man was engendered, in which he still dwelt in the old Atlantean age, and for which the people of ancient India longed: the old Gods. Unknown, however, to the old initiate was the God Who had long remained remote from the earth in order ultimately to appear on it, that much more effectively—He Who throughout long ages influenced the earth only from without and Who then approached it gradually, so that Moses was able to perceive the approach. Not until men underwent initiation in the form customary in the times of the Old Testament did they discern anything of the unity of all that is divine.

Let us consider the frame of mind of an initiate who had not only experienced what the Persian or the later Egyptian Mysteries offered, but who in addition had passed through all that could result from Hebrew occult research. Let us suppose, for example, that such an initiate had also received initiation on Mount Sinai of old, possibly in an incarnation occurring during the ancient Hebrew evolution, or even earlier. There he had been guided to cognition of the old

---

*In the first lecture of his cycle *Christ and the Human Soul* (Norrkoping, 1914) Rudolf Steiner tells us that it was in fact Christ Whom Moses saw in the burning bush, but Moses did not recognize Him.

divine world out of which mankind had evolved. Equipped with this primordial wisdom and its capacity for observing the primordial divine world, he came to the Hebrew Mystery teaching. There he learned what could be put somewhat as follows: The Gods I learned to know in former times were connected with the earth before the Divinity Jahve-Christ came to unite with it; now I know that the first and foremost Spirit among them, the Leading Spirit, is He Who approached the earth only gradually.

Thus an initiate of this sort recognized that the spiritual world he knew was identical with the world in which the approaching Christ reigns. One, who was immersed in water by John the Baptist, did not have to be an initiate, but through this act he learned to know the connection between his own individuality, and what he was as a personality, and the great Father-Spirit of the world. Only few, to be sure, could achieve this result. Most of them only needed to take the baptism as a symbol, as something that served, so to speak, under the powerful influence of John's teaching, to consolidate their faith in the existence of Jahve-God. But among them were some, who, in earlier incarnations, had already developed themselves so far that they were now able to learn to know some matters through their own observation. It was, nevertheless, an abnormal state into which the human being was placed by John's baptism.

John baptized with water, with the result that the etheric body was separated for a short time from the physical body. But John the Baptist wanted to be the forerunner of Him "Who baptizes with fire and with the Holy Spirit." The baptism with fire and the spirit came to our earth through Christ. Now, what is the difference between John's baptism with water and Christ's baptism with fire and the spirit? That can be understood only by one, who acquires such understanding from its very beginnings, for, in regard to a comprehension of the Christ, we today are really still dependent on the beginnings. This comprehension will become greater and greater, but as yet men can assimilate only just the beginnings. I ask your patience in following me along this path, beginning with the A B C.

First we must recall that spiritual processes really underlie all physical processes, including those that pertain to the human being. For people of our day this is hard to believe, but in time the world will learn to recognize the fact; and only then will a full understanding of the Christ be reached. Today, even those who like to talk about spirit do not seriously believe that everything taking place in man in a physical way is ultimately controlled by spirit. They disbelieve it unconsciously, if I may put it that way, even when they consider themselves idealists. There is a certain American,* for example, who systematically assembles facts intended to prove that in abnormal states man attains the ability to ascend to a spiritual world, and thereby he endeavors to establish a certain basis for a variety of phenomena. This American, William James by name, goes to work most exhaustively; but even the best of men are powerless to oppose the influential spirit of the time. They claim not to be materialists, but they are. The philosophy of William James has influenced a number of European scholars; and for this reason we shall point out several grotesque statements of his that will confirm what has just been said. He maintains, among other things, that a man does not weep because he is sad, but is sad because he weeps. Well, hitherto people have always believed that one must first be sad; that is, that a psycho-spiritual process must occur, which only then can penetrate the physical principle of the human body. When

---

*Footnote: William James, 1842-1910; the quote mentioned here is from his *Principles of Psychology*.

the tears flow there must be present a psychic process underlying the secretion of the tear fluid.

Even today, when everything of a spiritual nature lies as though buried under a veil of matter and awaits rediscovery by a spiritual conception of the world, there remain processes within us which are a heritage of primeval times when the spiritual element was more powerful, and which can reveal most significantly the manner in which spirit acts. There are two phenomena to which I like to draw attention in this connection: the sensation of shame, and that of fear, or fright. Let it be said in advance that it would be easy to enumerate all the hypothetical attempts to explain these two kinds of experience; but they do not concern us here, and in connection with any objection of that sort it would be a grave mistake to imagine that the spiritual scientist would be unacquainted with these hypotheses. Of the sensation of shame it can be said that when a person is ashamed it is as though he were trying to prevent his environment from seeing something that is taking place in him. Inherent in the sensation of shame is a feeling akin to a wish to conceal something. And what is the physical effect of this psychic experience? It causes him to blush: the blood rushes to his face. This means that under the influence of some psycho-spiritual event, such as a sensation of shame, a transformation, a change, results in the blood circulation. The blood is driven from within outward, toward the periphery. Its course is altered as the result of a psycho-spiritual event— this is a physical fact.

When a person is frightened his impulse is to protect himself from something he considers threatening: he pales, the blood withdraws from the outer surface. Here again is an external process called forth by a psycho-spiritual one, by fear, fright. Remember that the blood is the expression of the ego. What would a man want to do when he sees some

121

peril approaching? He would assemble his forces and consolidate them in the center of his being. The ego, with the intention of making a stand, draws the blood back into the center of its being.

There you have physical processes resulting from psychospiritual processes. Similarly, the flow of tears is a physical process brought about by soul and spirit. It is not a case of some mysterious physical influences joining forces and squeezing out the tears, and of the person then becoming sad when he feels the tears flow. That is an example of the way a materialistic view turns the simplest things upside-down. Were we to go into the matter of various physical ills which can affect human beings and which are connected with psycho-spiritual processes, we could multiply such instances indefinitely. But what concerns us at the moment is to understand that physical processes are effects of psycho-spiritual processes. Whenever this does not appear to be the case, we must realize that we have simply not yet recognized the underlying psycho-spiritual principle. Present-day man is not at all inclined to recognize this principle offhand. The modern scientist sees how the human being develops, beginning with the moment of conception, from the very first embryonic stages in the mother's womb, then outside the maternal body. He sees the outer physical form grow and expand. And because he observes this by means of present-day research, he concludes that the genesis of a human being starts with the development of the physical form as he sees it at conception and he is averse to considering the fact that spiritual processes underlie the physical ones. He does not believe that back of the physical human embryo there is something spiritual, that this unites with the physical and then develops what derives from a former incarnation.

One who lays store by theory but ignores practical life

might here object: Well, it may be possible that some higher form of cognition can discern spirit underlying matter, but we human beings simply cannot recognize it. That is one attitude. Others say: But we don't want to make the effort which we are told is necessary for attaining to a knowledge of the divine-spiritual! What difference does it make in the world whether we know that or not? But it is a grave error, indeed a dire superstition, to imagine that in practical life such knowledge is of no consequence. On the contrary, we shall proceed to show as clearly as possible how very much depends upon it.

Suppose we have a man who refuses to consider the idea that a psycho-spiritual principle underlies all that is physical in the human being, who fails to understand, for instance, that the enlargement of a physical liver is the expression of something spiritual. Another man—stimulated by spiritual science, if you like—readily accepts the possibility that by penetrating into the realm of spirit one may arrive first at an inkling, then at faith, and finally at cognition and vision of spirit. Thus we have two men, one of whom rejects spirit, being satisfied with sense observation, while the other follows what we may call the will to achieve cognition of spirit. The one who refuses spiritual enlightenment will grow ever weaker, for he will be letting his spirit starve, wilt, and perish for lack of adequate nourishment which such enlightenment alone can provide. His spirit will lose strength—it cannot gain it; and everything that functions apart from this spirit will gain the upper hand and overpower him. He will become weak in regard to all that takes place independently of him in his physical and etheric bodies. But the other, he who has the will to cognition, furnishes nourishment for his spirit, which consequently gains strength and mastery over all that occurs independently in his etheric and physical bodies. That is the most important point. We shall presently be able to apply it to a prominent case of our own day.

We know that the human being enters the world from two directions. His physical body is inherited from his ancestors, from his father and mother and their forbears. He inherits certain traits, good or bad, that are simply inherent in the blood, in the line of descent. But in every case of this sort, the forces a child brings along from his previous incarnation unite with these inherited qualities. Now, you know that today a great deal is said about "hereditary tendencies," whenever some disease or other makes its appearance. How this term is abused nowadays—though it is quite justified within narrow limits! Whenever anything crops up that can be proved to have been an attribute of some ancestor, hereditary tendencies are invoked; and because people know nothing of active spiritual forces derived from the previous incarnation, they endow these inherited tendencies with overwhelming power. If they knew that a spiritual factor accompanied us from our previous incarnation they would say, Well and good: we do believe in hereditary tendencies, but we know as well what stems from the previous incarnation in the way of inner, central soul forces, and that if sufficiently strengthened and invigorated these will gain the upper hand over matter—that is, over hereditary tendencies. And such a man, capable of rising to a knowledge of spirit, would continue: No matter how powerfully the inherited tendencies affect me, I shall provide nourishment for the spirit in me; for in this way I shall master them. But anyone who does not work upon his spiritual nature, upon that which is not inherited, will positively fall a prey to inherited tendencies as a result of such lack of knowledge. In this way, materialistic superstition will actually bring about a steady increase in their power over us. Men will be engulfed

124

in the quagmire of hereditary tendencies unless they fortify their spirit and, by means of a strong spirit, vanquish each time anew whatever is inherited.

In our time, when the consequences of materialism are so formidable, you must naturally still guard against overestimating the power of spirit. It would be a mistake to object: If that were the case, all anthroposophists would be bursting with health, for they believe in the spirit. Man's position on the earth is not only that of an individual being, he is a part of the whole world; and spirit, like all else, must grow in strength. But once spirit has become debilitated, as at present, it will not at once affect even the most anthroposophical of men—no matter how much nourishment he furnishes the spirit—to such an extent that he can overcome what derives from the material realm; yet all the more surely will this tell in his next incarnation, as expressed in his health and strength. Men will grow weaker and weaker unless they believe in the spirit, for otherwise they deliver themselves over to their inherited tendencies. They themselves have after all effected this weakening of the spiritual element, because everything here concerned depends upon their attitude toward spirit.

Nor should one imagine it an easy matter to correlate all the conditions here involved. I will give you a grotesque instance of the extent to which a man who judges only by externals may be in error. He might say: There was a man who had been an ardent adherent of the anthroposophical world view. Now it is precisely the anthroposophists who maintain that anthroposophy invariably improves the health and even prolongs life. A fine doctrine, that: the man dies at the age of forty-three! That much people know: the man died at forty-three—they witnessed it. But what is it that they do not know? They do not know when he would have died without anthroposophy. Maybe he would have lived to be only

125

forty; if a man's life span were forty years lacking anthroposophy, it might well reach forty-three with its aid. When anthroposophy will have come to permeate life in general, its effects will not fail to become manifest. True, if a man wants to see all its fruits in one life between birth and death he is simply an egotist: he wants everything for his own selfish purposes. But if he attains to anthroposophy for the benefit of mankind, he will have it through all his future incarnations.

Thus we see that by influencing his spiritual being, by yielding himself to what really derives from the spirit, man can at least provide new strength for his spirit, can make it strong and vigorous. That is what we must understand: it is possible to let ourselves be influenced by the spiritual element and thereby become ever more completely master within ourselves.

Now let us seek the most efficacious means for receiving the influence of spirit in our present stage of evolution. We have already pointed out that spiritual science, by means of spiritual research, nourishes our spirit. We might say, what man can thus receive in the way of spiritual nourishment is as yet but little; but we also understand that it can keep growing and growing in subsequent incarnations. This, however, presupposes one condition and in order to become acquainted with it we will turn to the anthroposophical world view itself.

The anthroposophical world outlook teaches us what kind of components make up the being of man. It teaches us what remains invisible in a visible man we confront. It then shows us how, as regards the core of his being, man passes on from one life to another, how all that he brings along from his last life in the way of soul and spirit is organically introduced into the physical, material elements inherited from his ancestors. Anthroposophy further discloses the way in which mankind has developed on the earth and describes its life in the Atlantean time, the preceding periods, and the post-Atlantean cultural epochs. It also tells us of the transformations undergone by the *Earth* itself: of its earlier embodiment which we called the old *Moon* phase, of the still earlier *Sun* phase, the *Saturn* phase, and so forth. In this way the spiritual-scientific world view leads us from clinging to what is nearest at hand—what our eyes see, our hands touch, and what our present science investigates—out into the vast, comprehensive phenomena of the world and particularly into the supersensible realm. By doing this it provides man with spiritual nourishment.

Those of you who have accompanied us more extensively into this anthroposophical world view know that during the past seven years we have elaborated the evolution of man in detail, described in detail the various transformations of the *Earth* and the life of man in the different cultural stages. It really is possible in our time to give such subtle and detailed descriptions; and if the opportunity arises we shall enter still more fully into these matters.

A tableau of supersensible facts must be painted for the eye of our soul. But a certain peculiarity is connected with this tableau. Among other things, we learned that our sun split off at a given time, together with the beings destined there to pursue their immediate further development. Now, the Leader of these sun beings is the Christ; and as their Leader He withdrew with the sun when it separated from the earth. For a time He then sent His force down to earth from the sun; but He kept gradually approaching the earth. In Zarathustra's time He could still be seen only as Ahura Mazdao, but Moses already perceived Him in the outer elements; and when this Christ *force* finally appeared on earth, it appeared in a human body, in Jesus of Nazareth.

That is why the anthroposophical point of view sees the Christ Being as a sort of central point in the whole panorama of reincarnation, of the being of man, of our contemplation of the cosmos, and so forth and so on. And whoever studies this anthroposophical world view in its true sense will say to himself: I can contemplate all that, but I can comprehend it only when the whole immense picture focuses at the great central point, at the Christ. I have pictured in different ways the doctrine of reincarnation, of the various human races, of planetary evolution, and so forth; but the Being of Christ is here painted from a single point of view, and this sheds light on all else. It is a picture with a central figure to which everything else is related, and I can fathom the significance and expression of the other figures only if I understand the main figure.

That is the way the anthroposophical world view goes about it. We project a great picture of the various phenomena of the spiritual world; but then we concentrate upon the principal figure, upon the Christ, and only then do the details of the picture become intelligible.

All those who have participated in our development of spiritual science will feel how everything can be comprehended thereby. Spiritual science itself will become more perfect in the future, and our present comprehension of Christ will be superseded by a far loftier one. The power of anthroposophy will thereby become greater and greater, and so will the human being develop, who accepts this power of anthroposophy into himself; and the mastery of his spirit over his material nature will gain ever greater strength. Burdened as he is with today's inherited body, a man can call forth only such processes as blushing, paling, and phenomena like laughing and crying, but in time he will gain ever greater power over them: out of his soul he will spiritualize his bodily functions and thus take his place in the outer world as a mighty ruler of soul and spirit. That will be the Christ power, the Christ impulse acting through the agency of mankind. This is the impulse which even today, if sufficiently intensified, can lead to the same results as did the ancient initiation.

The procedure of the old initiation was as follows: The candidate first learned comprehensively all that today we are taught by anthroposophy. That was the preparation for the old initiation. Then, all this was directed to a certain culmination which was achieved by having him lie in a grave for three and a half days, as though dead. When his etheric body was withdrawn and, in his etheric body, he moved about in the spiritual world, he became a witness of this spiritual world. In order that in the sphere of his etheric forces he might behold the spiritual world, thus achieving initiation, it was necessary at that time to withdraw the etheric body. Formerly these forces were not available in the normal state of waking consciousness: the neophyte had to be brought into an abnormal condition. Christ brought this force to the earth for initiation also; for today, it is possible for man to become clairvoyant without the withdrawal of the etheric body.

When a person attains the maturity to receive so strong an impulse from the Christ, even for a short time, as to affect the circulation of his blood—this Christ influence expressing itself in a special form of circulation, an influence penetrating even the physical principle—then he is in a position to be initiated within the physical body. The Christ-Impulse has the power to bring this about. Anyone who can become so profoundly absorbed in what occurred as a result of the Event of Palestine and the Mystery of Golgotha as to live completely in it and to see it objectively, see it so spiritually alive that it acts as a force communicating itself even to his circulation, such a man achieves through this experience the same result that was formerly brought about by the withdrawal of the etheric body.

129

You see, then, that through the Christ impulse something has come to earth which enables the human being to influence the force that causes his blood to pulsate through his body. What is here active is no abnormal event, no submersion in water, but solely the mighty influence of the Christ-Individuality. No physical substance is involved in this baptism—nothing but a spiritual influence; and the ordinary, every-day consciousness undergoes no change. Through the spirit that streams forth as the Christ impulse something flows into the body, something that can otherwise be induced only by way of psycho-physiological development through fire—an inner fire expressing itself in the circulation of the blood. John still baptized by submersion with the result that the etheric body withdrew and man could see into the spiritual world. But if a man opens his soul to the Christ impulse, this impulse acts in such a way that the experiences of the astral body flow over into the etheric body, and clairvoyance results.

There you have the explanation of the phrase, "to baptize with the spirit and with fire," and those are the facts concerning the difference between the John baptism and the Christ baptism. The Christ impulse made it possible for an order of new initiates to come into being. Formerly there existed among mankind a mere handful who were disciples of the great teachers and were inducted into the Mysteries. Their etheric body was withdrawn to enable them to become witnesses of the spirit, and then to step forth and proclaim, There is a spiritual world! We have seen it for ourselves. Just as you see the plants and the stones, so we have seen the spiritual world. Those were the "eye witnesses"; and those who thus emerged from the obscurity of the Mysteries proclaimed the gospel of the spirit, though only out of primeval wisdom.

But while the old initiates guided humanity back to a

wisdom out of which man had originally come forth, Christ opened the way for initiates capable of arriving at an observation of the spiritual world within the confines of the physical body and within the every-day state of consciousness. These new initiates learned through the Christ impulse the same fact that had revealed itself to the old ones, namely, that there is a spiritual world; and then they, in their turn, could proclaim its gospel. What was therefore needed to become an initiate and to proclaim the gospel of the spiritual world in a new sense, in the Christ sense, was that the force which was in the Christ should stream over as an impulse into the disciple, who had then to disseminate it.

When did a Christ initiate of this kind first arise? In all evolution the old must be merged with the new, and thus even Christ had to lead the old initiation into the new one gradually. He had to create a transition, so to speak; He had to take into account certain procedures of the old initiation, but in such a way that everything deriving from the old gods should be suffused by the Christ Being. Christ undertook the initiation of that one among His disciples who was then to communicate to the world the Gospel of the Christ in the most profound way. An initiation of this sort lies concealed behind one of the narratives in the Gospel of St. John, behind the story of Lazarus (Chapter 11).

Much has been written about this story of Lazarus—an incredible amount; but only those have comprehended it who have known, either through esoteric schooling or from their own contemplation, what it conceals. For the moment I shall only quote you one characteristic utterance from this story. When Christ Jesus was told that Lazarus lay sick, He replied:

This sickness is not unto death, but that the God may be manifest in him.

His sickness is for the purpose of manifesting the God in

131

him. It was only due to a lack of understanding that the word *doxa*, given in the Greek text, was translated with "for the glory of God." Not for the glory of God was this ordained, but that the God in him might emerge and become manifest. That is the true meaning of this utterance: the divine that is in Christ is to flow over into the individuality of Lazarus; the divine, the Christ Divinity, is to be revealed in and through him.

Only by understanding the resurrection of Lazarus in this sense does it become wholly clear. Do not imagine for a moment, however, that in communicating spiritual-scientific truths it is possible to speak so openly that everything can be made obvious to all and sundry. What is concealed behind a spiritual-scientific fact of that sort is communicated under many a veil of reservation. That is inevitable; for anyone who would attain to an understanding of such a mystery should first work his way through seeming difficulties in order to strengthen and invigorate his spirit. And precisely because it is laborious to find his way through the maze of words will he arrive at the underlying spirit.

Recall the passage dealing with the "life" which was supposed to have left Lazarus and which his sisters Martha and Mary longed to have back. Christ Jesus said unto them: *I am the resurrection, and the life.* Life is to reappear in Lazarus. Do take everything literally, especially in the Gospels, and you will see how much comes to light! Do not speculate or interpret, but take in its literal meaning the sentence, "I am the resurrection, and the life." When Christ appears and raises Lazarus, what does He bring to bear? What is it that passes over into Lazarus? It is the Christ impulse, the force flowing forth from the Christ. What Christ gave Lazarus was the *life*. Indeed, Christ had said, "This sickness is not unto death, but that the God may be manifest in him." Just as all the old initiates lay as dead for three and a half days, and then the God became manifest in them, so Lazarus lay in a deathlike state for the same period; but Christ Jesus was well aware that with this act the old initiations would come to an end. He knew that this ostensible death led to something higher, to a higher life: that during this period Lazarus had beheld the spiritual world; and because the Leader of this spiritual world is the Christ, Lazarus received into himself the Christ force, the vision of the Christ. Christ pours his force into Lazarus, and Lazarus arises another man.*

There is one particularly noteworthy word in the St. John Gospel: in the story of the Lazarus mystery it is said that the Lord "loved" Lazarus; and the word is again applied to the disciple "whom the Lord loved." What does that mean? Only the *Akasha Chronicle* can tell us. Who is Lazarus after his resurrection? He is himself the writer of the John Gospel, Lazarus, who had been initiated by Christ. Christ had poured the message of His own being into the being of Lazarus in order that the message of the Fourth Gospel, the Gospel of St. John, might resound through the world as the portrayal of the being of Christ. That is why no disciple John is mentioned in this Gospel before the story of Lazarus. But you must read carefully and not be misled by those curious theologians who have discovered that at a certain spot in the Gospel of St. John—namely, in the thirty-fifth verse of the first chapter—the name John is supposed to appear as an indication of the presence of the disciple John. It says there:

Again the next day after John stood, and two of his disciples. There is nothing in this passage, nothing whatever, to sug-

---

*You will find this subject treated in detail in my book, *Christianity as Mystical Fact*, where a separate chapter is devoted to an attempt to clarify particularly the Lazarus miracle in the sense of spiritual science.

gest that the disciple who later is called the one "whom the Lord loved" is meant here. That disciple does not appear in the John Gospel before the resurrection of Lazarus. Why? Because he who remained hidden behind "the disciple whom the Lord loved" was the one whom the Lord had already loved previously. He loved him so greatly because He had already recognized him—invisibly, in his soul—as the disciple who was to be awakened and carry the message of the Christ out into the world. That is why the disciple, the apostle, "whom the Lord loved" appears on the scene only beginning with the description of the resurrection of Lazarus. Only then had he become what he was thenceforth. Now the individuality of Lazarus had been so completely transformed that it became the individuality of John in the Christian sense. Thus we see that in its loftiest meaning a baptism through the Christ impulse itself had been performed upon Lazarus; Lazarus became an initiate in the new sense of the word, while at the same time the old form, the old deathlike sleep, had been retained in a certain way and a transition thus created from the old to the new initiation.

This will show you the profundity with which the Gospels reflect spiritual truths that can be brought to light through research, independently of any documents. The spiritual scientist knows that he can find beforehand anything the Gospels contain, without reference to documents. But when he finds again in the John Gospel what he had previously discovered by spiritual means, this Gospel becomes for him a document revealed by Christ Jesus' own initiate. That is why the Gospel of St. John is so profound a text.

Nowadays it is specially emphasized that the other Gospels differ in certain respects from that of St. John. There must be a reason for this; but we shall find it only when we penetrate to the core of the other Gospels as we have now done in the case of St. John. And what we discover by doing so is that the difference could arise only from the fact that the author of the John Gospel was initiated by Christ Jesus Himself. Because of this was it possible to portray the Christ impulse as John did. And we must examine in like manner the relation of the other Gospel writers to Christ and discover to what extent they received the baptism by fire and by the spirit. Then only will we find the inner connections between the Gospel of St. John and the other Gospels, and so penetrate ever deeper into the spirit of the New Testament.

VIII

As the fruit of yesterday's enquiries we learned that the Christ-Impulse, once it had worked through the person of Jesus of Nazareth, united with the evolution of the earth; and now its power within the earthly development of mankind is such that in our time it affects man in the same way as did formerly the procedure which is becoming ever more dangerous for human life—that of withdrawing the etheric from the physical body during the three and a half days of initiation. The Christ-Impulse actually affects human consciousness as powerfully as does an abnormal process of the above sort.

Now you must realize that such a radical change needed time to take root in human evolution, that it could not appear from the start with such intensity. It was therefore necessary to create a sort of transition in the resurrection of Lazarus. The deathlike state lasting three and a half days was still retained in the case of Lazarus, but you should clearly understand that this state differed from the one undergone by the old initiates. Lazarus' condition was not brought about artificially by the initiator, as was the case in former times, by withdrawing the etheric from the physical body through processes I am not at liberty to describe here. We may say that it came about in a more natural way. From the Gospel itself you can gather that Christ had associated with Lazarus and his sisters Martha and Mary before, for we read, "The Lord loved him." This means that for a long time Christ Jesus had been exercising a great and powerful influence on Lazarus, who had thereby been adequately prepared and developed. And the consequence was that in

136

his case the initiation did not call for the artificial inducing of a three-and-a-half day trance, but that this came about of itself under the mighty impression of the Christ-Impulse. So, for the outer world, Lazarus was as though dead, so to speak, for three and a half days, even though during this time he experienced what was of the utmost importance; and thus only the last act, the resurrection, was undertaken by Christ.

Anyone who is familiar with what there occurred recognizes an echo of the old initiation process in the words employed by Christ Jesus:

Lazarus, come forth.

The resurrected Lazarus, as we have seen, was John—or better, the writer of the John Gospel. It was he who could introduce the Gospel of the Christ Being into the world because he was, so to say, the first initiate in the Christian sense. For this reason we may safely assume that this Gospel of St. John, so badly abused by present-day research of a purely historical, critical, theological nature, and represented as a mere lyrical hymn, as a subjective expression of this author, will prove the means of insight into the profoundest mysteries of the Christ-Impulse.

Nowadays, this Gospel of St. John constitutes a stumbling block for the materialists who carry on Bible research when they compare it with the other three, the so-called synoptic Gospels. The picture of Christ that arises before them out of the first three is so flattering to the learned gentlemen of our time! The pronouncement has gone forth, even from theological quarters, that what we are dealing with is the "simple man of Nazareth." Again and again it is emphasized that one can gain a picture of Christ as perhaps one of the noblest of men who have walked the earth; but the picture remains merely that of a *human being*. There is even a tendency to simplify this picture as far as possible; and in this connection one hears it mentioned that after all, there have been other great ones as well, such as Plato and Socrates. The most that is admitted are differences in degree.

The picture of Christ yielded by the John Gospel is indeed a very different one. At the very beginning it is stated that what lived in the body of Jesus of Nazareth for three years was the *Logos*, the primordial, eternal Word, for which there is also the term "eternal, creating wisdom." Our epoch cannot understand that in the thirtieth year of his life a man could be sufficiently developed to be able to sacrifice his own ego and receive into himself another being, a Being of wholly superhuman nature: the Christ, Whom Zarathustra addressed as Ahura Mazdao. That is why theological critics of this type imagine that the writer of the John Gospel had set out merely to describe his attitude to his Christ in a sort of lyrical hymn—nothing more. On the other hand, so they maintain, we have the John Gospel, and on the other, the other three; but by taking the average one can compound a picture of Christ as the "simple man," while granting His historical eminence. Modern Bible critics resent the idea of a divine being dwelling in Jesus of Nazareth.

The *Akasha Chronicle* discloses the fact that in his thirtieth year the personality we know as Jesus of Nazareth had, as a result of all he had experienced in former incarnations, achieved a degree of maturity that enabled him to sacrifice his own ego; for that is what took place when, at the Baptism by John, this Jesus of Nazareth could make the resolution to withdraw—as an ego, the fourth principle of the human being—from his physical, etheric, and astral bodies. And what remained was a noble sheath, a lofty physical, etheric, and astral body which had been saturated with the purest, most highly developed ego. This was in the nature of a pure vessel which at the Baptism could receive the Christ, the primordial, eternal *Logos*, the "creating wis-

138

dom." That is what the *Akasha Chronicle* reveals to us; and we can recognize it, if we only will, in the narrative of the John Gospel.

But clearly it behooves us to consider what our materialistic age believes. Some of you may be surprised to hear me speak of theologians as materialistic thinkers, for after all, they are occupied with spiritual matters. But it is not a question of what a man believes or what he studies, but rather, of *how* he performs his research, regardless of its content. Anyone who rejects our present subject or repudiates a spiritual world, who considers only what exists in the outer world in the way of documents and the like, is a materialist. The *means* of research is the important thing. But at the same time we must come to terms with the opinions of our age.

In reading the Gospels you will find certain contradictions. As to the essentials, to be sure—that is, as to what the *Akasha Chronicle* discloses as essential—it can be said that the agreement among them is striking. They agree, first of all, in the matter of the Baptism itself; and it is made clear in all four Gospels that their authors saw in this Baptism the greatest imaginable import for Jesus of Nazareth. The four Gospels further agree on the fact of the Crucifixion and the fact of the Resurrection. Now, these are precisely the facts that seem most miraculous to the materialistic thinker of today—and no contradiction exists here.

But in the other cases, how are we to come to terms with the seeming contradictions? Taking first the Evangelists, Mark and John, we find their narratives commencing with the Baptism: they describe the last three years of Christ Jesus' activity—that is, only what occurred after the Christ Spirit had taken possession of his threefold sheath, his physical, etheric, and astral bodies. Then consider the Gospels according to St. Matthew and St. Luke. In a certain respect

139

these trace the earlier history as well, the section which, within our meaning, the *Akasha Chronicle* discloses as the story of Jesus of Nazareth before sacrificing himself for the Christ. But at this point the contradiction seekers notice at once that Matthew tells of a genealogy reaching to Abraham,, whereas Luke traces the line of descent back to Adam, and from Adam to Adam's Father: to God Himself. A further contradiction could be found in the following: According to Matthew, three Wise Men, or Magi, guided by a star, come to do homage at the birth of Jesus; while Luke relates the vision of the shepherds, their adoration of the Child, the presentation in the Temple—in contrast with which Matthew narrates the persecution by Herod, the flight into Egypt, and the return. These points and many others could be focused upon as single contradictions; but by examining more closely the facts gleaned from the *Akasha Chronicle* without reference to the Gospels, we can come to terms with them.

The *Akasha Chronicle* informs us that at about the time stated in the Bible—the difference of a few years is immaterial—Jesus of Nazareth was born, and that in the body of Jesus of Nazareth there dwelt an individuality that in former incarnations had experienced lofty stages of initiation, had gained deep insight into the spiritual world. And it tells us something more, with which for the present I shall deal only in outline. The *Akasha Chronicle*, which provides the only true history, reveals the circumstance that he who appeared in this Jesus of Nazareth had, in former incarnations, passed through manifold initiations in all sorts of localities; and it leads us back to the fact that the later bearer of the name of Jesus of Nazareth had originally attained to a lofty and significant stage of initiation in the Persian world and had exercised an exalted, far-reaching activity. This individuality dwelling in the body of Jesus of Nazareth had al-

140

ready been active in the spiritual life of ancient Persia, had gazed up at the sun, and had addressed the great Sun Spirit as "Ahura Mazdao."

We must clearly understand that the Christ entered the bodies of this same individuality which had passed through the sort of incarnations mentioned. What does that mean: the Christ entered into the bodies of this individuality? It means none other than that the Christ made use of these three bodies—the astral, etheric, and physical bodies of Jesus of Nazareth—for fulfilling His mission. Everything we think, all that we express in words, that we feel or sense, is connected with our astral body. The astral body is the vehicle of all this. Jesus of Nazareth, as an ego, had lived for thirty years in this astral body, had communicated to it all that he had experienced within himself and assimilated during former incarnations. In what way, then, did this astral body form its thoughts? It had to conform and amalgamate with the individuality that lived in it for thirty years.

When in ancient Persia Zarathustra lifted his gaze to the sun and told of Ahura Mazdao, this stamped itself into his astral body; and into this astral body there entered the Christ. Was it not natural, then, that Christ, when choosing a metaphor or an expression of feeling, should turn to what His astral body offered—of whatever nature? When you wear a grey coat you appear to the outer world in a grey coat. Christ appeared to the outer world in the body of Jesus of Nazareth—in his physical, etheric, and astral bodies—and consequently His thoughts and feelings were colored by the images of the thoughts and feelings living in the body of Jesus of Nazareth. No wonder, then, that many an old Persian expression is reflected in His utterances, or that in John's Gospel we find an echo of terms used in the ancient Persian initiation; for the impulse that dwelt in the Christ passed over, of course, into His disciple, into the resurrected

141

Lazarus. So it can be said that the astral body of Jesus of Nazareth speaks to us through John, in his Gospel.

No, it is not surprising that expressions should appear which recall the ancient Persian initiation and the form in which its ideas were presented. In Persia, "Ahura Mazdao" was not the only name for the spirits united in the sun: in a certain connection the term *"vohumanu"* was used, meaning the "creative Word," or the "creative spirit." The *Logos*, in its meaning of "creative force," was first employed in the Persian initiation, and we meet it again in the very first verse of the John Gospel. There is much besides in this Gospel which we may understand through knowing that the Christ Himself spoke through an astral body which for thirty years had served Jesus of Nazareth, and that this individuality was the re-embodiment of an ancient Persian initiate. Similarly I could point to a great deal more in the John Gospel that would show how this most intimate of the Gospels, when using words associated with the mysteries of initiation, employs phrases reminiscent of Persia, and how this old mode of expression has persisted into later times.

If we now wish to understand the position of the other Evangelists in this matter we must recall various points that have already been established in the previous lectures. We learned, for example, that there existed certain lofty spiritual beings who transferred their sphere of action to the sun when the latter detached itself from the earth. It was pointed out that their outer astral form was in a sense the counterpart of certain animal forms here on earth. There was first, the form of the Bull spirit, the spiritual counterpart of those animal natures the essence of whose development lies in what could be called the nutritional and digestive organization. The spiritual counterpart is naturally of a lofty spiritual nature, however inferior the earthly image may appear. So we have certain exalted spiritual beings who transferred their sphere to the sun whence they influenced the earth sphere, appearing there as the Bull spirits. Others appear as the Lion spirits, whose counterpart lives in animal natures pre-eminently developed as to their heart and organs of circulation. Then we have spiritual beings who are the counterparts of what we meet in the animal kingdom as eagle natures, the Eagle spirits. And finally there are those that harmoniously unite, as it were, the other natures as in a great synthesis, the Man spirits. These were in a sense the most advanced.

Passing now to the old initiation, we find that this offered the possibility of beholding, face to face, the exalted spiritual beings that had advanced ahead of man. But the manner in which men of old had to be initiated, in accord with the demands of those ancient times, depended upon the origin of their descent—that is, whether from Mars, Jupiter, Saturn, Venus. This is why, in Atlantis, there existed oracles in manifold variety. Some had adjusted their spiritual vision primarily to the beholding of what we have described as the Eagle spirits, while others saw the Lion spirits, the Bull spirits, or the Man spirits. The initiation depended on the specific traits of the candidate. This differentiation was one of the characteristics of the Atlantean age, and certain after-effects of it have persisted into our own post-Atlantean time. Thus, you could find Mystery temples in Asia Minor, or in Egypt, where the initiation took a form that brought about the vision of the lofty spiritual beings as Bull spirits, or as Eagle spirits. And it was in the Mysteries that outer culture had its source.

The initiates who saw the Lion form in the exalted spiritual beings conjured up in the Lion body a sort of image of what they had beheld; but they saw as well that these spirits take part in the evolution of man. That is why they assigned a human head to the lion body, a concept that later became

143

the sphinx. Those who saw the spiritual counterparts as Bull spirits bore testimony to the spiritual world by introducing a Bull worship, which led on the one hand to the Apis Bull worship in Egypt, and on the other, to the worship of the Persian Mithras Bull; for everything we find in the way of outer cult usages among the different peoples derived from the initiation rites. There were initiates everywhere whose spiritual vision was focussed principally on the Bull spirits, others attuned primarily to the Eagle spirits, and so on. To a certain extent, we can even indicate the differences in the various modes of initiation. Those initiated, for example, in such a way that the spiritual beings appeared to them in the form of Bull spirits were informed principally concerning the secrets connected with man's glandular system, with what pertains to the etheric principle. And they were initiated into still another branch of the nature of man: the human properties that are firmly attached to the earth—welded to it, as it were. All this was grasped by those initiated in the Bull Mysteries.

Let us try to experience the soul mood of such an initiate. These initiates had in effect received the following teaching from their great teachers: Man has descended from divine heights; the primordial human beings were the descendants of divine-spiritual beings. Therefore, they traced the first man back to his Father-God. Thus man came down to earth and passed from one earthly form to another. These men were primarily interested in what was bound to the earth, as well as in all that men had experienced when they had thought of divine-spiritual beings as their ancestors. That was the attitude of the Bull initiates. The Eagle initiates constituted a different case. These perceived those spiritual beings who bear a most peculiar relation to the human being; but in order to understand this a few words must be said concerning the spiritual character of the bird nature.

144

Animals rank below human beings by reason of their inferior functions, and they represent, as you know, beings that solidified too early, having failed to retain the softness and flexibility of their body substance until the moment when they might have been absorbed into the human form. But in the bird nature we have beings that did not assume the lowest functions; instead they overshot the mark in the opposite direction. They failed to descend far enough, as it were; they remained in unduly soft substances, while the others lived in substances that were too hard. But as evolution continued, outer conditions compelled them to solidify; hence they hardened in a manner compatible with a nature that had not descended far enough to the earth, being too soft. That is a rough description in untechnical terms, but it gives the facts. The archetypes of these bird natures are those spiritual beings who likewise overshot the mark, who remained in too soft a substance, and who consequently were carried, as it were, beyond what they might have become at a certain point of their development. They deviate from the normal development in an upward direction, while the rest diverge downwards. The middle position is in a certain sense occupied by the Lion spirits, as well as by the harmonious ones, the Man spirits, who grasped the right moment to incorporate.

We have already seen how the Christ event was received by those in whom there lived something of the old initiation.* According to the nature of their specific initiation they had been able in the past to see into the spiritual world. Those who had received the Bull initiation—the initiates of a great

*There is a very valuable lecture on the subject of the initiations of the different evangelists in the booklet entitled *Deeper Secrets of Human History in the Light of the Gospel of St. Matthew* (London, 1957). The lecture in question was given on November 1, 1909, and is the first one included in the booklet.

part of Egypt, for example—were aware of the following: We can gaze up into the spiritual world, and therefore the lofty spiritual beings appear to us as the counterparts of the Bull nature in man. But now—so said those who had come in contact with the Christ impulse—now there has appeared to us in His true form the Ruler of the spiritual realm. What we have formerly always seen, what we had attained through the stages of our initiation presented us with an antecedent form of the Christ. Into what was earlier beheld by us we must now place the Christ. Remembering all that we saw, all that the spiritual worlds gradually disclosed to us, we can ask, Whither would it all have led us if at that time we had already attained to the requisite heights? It would have led us to the Christ. An initiate of that type described the journey into the spiritual world in line with the Bull initiation; but he added: The truth it harbors is the Christ. And a Lion or an Eagle initiate would have spoken similarly.

It was definitely prescribed in each of these initiation Mysteries how the candidate should be led up into the spiritual world, and the rites varied according to the manner in which he was to enter it. There were Mysteries of many different shades, especially in Asia Minor and in Egypt, where it was customary to guide the initiates in such a way as to bring them eventually to the Bull nature, or to a vision of the Lion spirits, as the case might have been. With this in mind let us now consider those who, as a result of many different kinds of initiations in the past, had become capable of sensing the Christ impulse, of comprehending Christ in the right way. Let us observe an initiate who had passed through the stages enabling him to behold the Man spirit. Such a one could say, The true Ruler in the spiritual world has appeared to me, Christ, Who lived in Jesus of Nazareth. And what led me to this? My ancient initiation. He knew the path that leads to the vision of the Man spirit; so he describes what a man experiences in order to attain to initiation and to understand the Christ nature at all. He knew initiation in the form prescribed in those Mysteries that led to the Man initiation. That is why the lofty initiate who dwelt in the body of Jesus of Nazareth appeared to him in the image of the Mysteries he had gone through and knew, and he described him as he himself saw the whole matter.

That is the case in the narrative according to Matthew; and an old tradition hit upon the truth when it connected the Matthew Gospel with that one of the four symbols recognizable as the symbol of the Man spirit, and that form the capitals of the columns you see in this hall on the left and the right.* An ancient tradition associates the writer of the Gospel according to St. Matthew with the Man spirit. This is because this writer knew, so to speak, the Man Mystery initiation as his own point of departure, for in the time when the Gospels were written it was not customary to write biographies as is done today. What seemed essential to those people was the presence of an exalted initiate who had received the Christ into himself. The manner of becoming an initiate, the experiences he had to undergo, that was what they considered important. That is why they ignored the external every-day happenings that appear so important to biographers of today. The modern biographer will go to any lengths to collect enough material. Once, when Friedrich Theodor Vischer ("Schwaben-Vischer") was indulging in a bit of sarcasm at the expense of modern biographies, he hit on an excellent illustration. A young scholar set about writing his doctor's thesis, which was to be on Goethe. As a preparation he first assembled all the material he could use; but as there was not enough to satisfy him, he poked about

---

*These two columns decorated the lecture hall in Kassel, together with a statue representing the Archangel Michael, by Professor Bernewitz.

in all the rooms and attics of the various towns where Goethe had lived. He swept out all the corners, and even emptied the dustbins in an effort to find whatever might chance to be there, which would then enable him to write a thesis on *The Connection between Frau Christiane von Goethe's Chilbains and the Mythologico-allegorico-symbolical Figures in the Second Part of Faust*. Well, that is laying it on rather thick, but it is after all quite in the spirit of modern biographers. People who plan to write on Goethe sniff about in all sorts of rubbish, hunting material. The meaning of the word "discretion" is no longer known to them today.

But those who portrayed Jesus of Nazareth in their Gospels went about their descriptions quite differently. Everything in the way of external occurrences appeared to them negligible as compared with the various stages which Jesus of Nazareth, as an initiate, had to undergo. That is what they described; but each one did so in his own way, as he himself saw the matter. Matthew described it in the manner of those initiated in the Man spirit. This initiation was closely akin to the wisdom of Egypt.

And now we can also understand how the writer of the Luke Gospel arrived at his unusual representation. He was one of those who in former incarnations had achieved initiations leading to the Bull spirit, and he could describe what accorded with such an initiation. He could say, A great initiate must have passed through such and such stages—and he portrayed him in the colors he knew. He was one of those who formerly had lived principally within the Egyptian Mysteries, so it is not surprising that he should stress the trait which represents, let us say, primarily the Egyptian character of initiation. Let us consider the author of the Luke Gospel in the light of what we have thus learned. He reasoned as follows: A lofty initiate lived in the individuality that dwelt in the body of Jesus of Nazareth. I have learned

148

how one penetrates to the Bull initiation through the Egyptian Mysteries. That I know. This special form of initiation was vividly before him. And now he continued: He who has become so exalted an initiate as Jesus of Nazareth must have passed through an Egyptian initiation, as well as through all the others—so in Jesus of Nazareth we have an initiate who had undergone the Egyptian initiation. Naturally, the other Evangelists knew that, too; but it did not appear to them as of any special importance, because they had not known initiation from this aspect so intimately.

For this reason, a certain characteristic of Jesus of Nazareth did not strike them as in any way noteworthy. I said in one of the first lectures that if a man has undergone an initiation in the past, something special happens to him when he reappears. Definite events occur resembling, in the outer world, repetitions of former experiences. Let us assume a man had been initiated in ancient Ireland; he would now have to be reminded, by some experience in his life, of this old Irish initiation. This could come about, for instance, by some outer event impelling him to travel to Ireland. Now, someone familiar with the Irish initiation would be struck by the fact that it was Ireland of all places that the man visited; but no one else would see anything unusual in this. The individuality that dwelt in Jesus of Nazareth was an initiate of the Egyptian Mysteries, among others—hence the journey to Egypt. Who would be particularly struck by this flight into Egypt? One who knew it from his own life; and such a one did describe this particular point because he knew its significance. It is narrated in the Matthew Gospel because the writer knew from his own initiation what a "journey to Egypt" meant to a great many initiates in ancient times.

And when we know that in the writer of the Luke Gospel we are dealing with a man who was specifically conversant,

149

through his knowledge of the Egyptian Mysteries, with the initiation that led to the Bull cult, we shall find truth in the old tradition that couples him with the Bull symbol. For good reasons—which we lack the time to explain at the moment—the Luke Gospel does not mention the journey to Egypt; but typical events are cited whose significance can be rightly judged only by one in close contact with the Egyptian initiation. The author of the Matthew Gospel indicates this connection of Jesus of Nazareth with the Egyptian Mysteries in a more external way, by means of the journey to Egypt. The writer of the Luke Gospel sees all the events he describes in the spirit provided by an Egyptian initiation.

Now let us turn to the writer of the Mark Gospel. This Evangelist omits all the early history and describes particularly the activity of the Christ in the body of Jesus of Nazareth during three years. In this respect his Gospel tallies completely with that of St. John. This writer passed through an initiation strongly resembling those of Asia Minor, even those of Greece—we can call them European-Asiatic-pagan initiations—and at that time these were the most up-to-date. Reflected in the outer world, they all imply that one who is a lofty personality, initiated in a certain manner, owes his origin not merely to a natural but to a supernatural event.

Consider that Plato's followers, those who were anxious to form the right conception of him, did not care particularly who his bodily father was. For them, Plato's spirituality outshone all else. Hence they said, That which lived in the Plato body as the Plato soul, that is the Plato who was born for us as a lofty spiritual being that fructifies the lower nature of man. That is why they ascribed to the God Apollo the birth of the Plato who meant so much to them, the awakened Plato. In their sight Plato was a son of Apollo. Especially in these Mysteries it was customary to pay no particular attention to the earlier life of the personality in question, but to focus on the moment at which he became what is so often mentioned in the Gospels: a "divine son," a "son of god." *Plato, a son of god!* Thus was he described by his noblest devotees, by those who understood him best. Here, we must clearly understand the significance that such a characterization bore for the human life of such sons of the gods on earth. It was particularly in this fourth epoch that men adapted themselves the most to the physical sense world that they came to love this earth. The old gods were dear to them because they could symbolize the fact that precisely the leading sons of the earth were sons of the gods. What moved about on earth was to be represented in this manner.

Such a one was the author of the Gospel of St. Mark, hence he describes only what occurred after the Baptism by John. The initiation this Evangelist had undergone was the one that led to a knowledge of the higher world in the sign of the Lion spirit. Therefore, ancient tradition links him with the symbol of the Lion.

Now we turn back once again to what we already touched on today, the Gospel according to St. John. We said that he who wrote the John Gospel was initiated by Christ Jesus Himself, hence he had something to give which contains the germ, so to say, of the efficacy of the Christ-Impulse, not only for that time, but for the far distant future. He proclaims something that will remain valid for all time. This Evangelist was one of the Eagle initiates, who had skipped the normal evolutionary stage. What is normal for that time is set down by the author of the Mark Gospel. All that reaches out beyond that period, showing the nature of Christ's activity in the distant future, all that transcends earthbound matters, we find in St. John. That is why tradition connects John with the symbol of the Eagle.

This shows us that ancient tradition associating the Evangelists with what may be called the essence of their own ini-

151

tiation is by no means based on mere fancy, but is born out of the depths of Christian evolution. This is how deeply one must penetrate into the events. Then, one comprehends that the greatest, the most transcendent events in the life of Christ are all described in the same way, but that each of the Evangelists portrays Christ Jesus as he understands Him according to the type of his initiation. I indicated this in my book, *Christianity as a Mystical Fact*, but only in such a way as could be done for readers as yet unprepared, for it was written in the beginning of our spiritual-scientific development. Allowance was made for the lack of understanding, in our time, of occult facts proper.

We now understand that Christ is illuminated for us from four sides, each Evangelist throwing light upon Him from the aspect he knew most intimately. In view of the mighty impulse He gave, you will readily believe that he had many sides. But, I said this: all the Gospels agreed on the following points. The Christ-Being Himself descended from divine-spiritual heights at the Baptism by John, this Christ-Being dwelt in the body of Jesus of Nazareth, He suffered death on the Cross, and He vanquished this death. Later we shall have occasion to examine this Mystery more closely. Today let us look at the death on the Cross in the light of the question: What feature of it is characteristic in the case of the Christ-Being? The answer is, we find it to be an event that created no distinction between the life that went before and the life that followed. The most characteristic feature of the death of Christ is that He passed through death unchanged, that He remained the same, that it was He Who exemplified the insignificance of death. For this reason all who could know the true nature of the Christ death have ever clung to the living Christ.

Considered from this point of view, what was the nature of the event of Damascus, where he who had been Saul became Paul? From what he had previously learned Paul knew that the Spirit first sought by Zarathustra in the sun as Ahura Mazdao, the Spirit later beheld by Moses in the burning bush and in the fire on Sinai, had gradually been approaching the earth. He also knew that the spirit would have to enter a human body. What Paul could not grasp, however, while he was still Saul, was that the man destined to be the Christ bearer should have to suffer the disgrace of death on the cross. He could only imagine that when Christ came He would triumph, that once He had approached the earth He would have to remain in all that pertained to it. Paul could not think of Him Who had hung upon the Cross as the bearer of the Christ. That is the substance of Paul's attitude as Saul—before he became Paul. The death on the Cross, this humiliating death and all that it implied, was primarily what prevented him from recognizing the fact that Christ had really been present on the earth. What, then, had to occur? Something had to take place in Paul which at a certain moment would create in him the conviction: The individuality that hung upon the Cross in the body of Jesus of Nazareth was indeed the Christ. Christ has been here on earth! Paul became clairvoyant through the event of Damascus. Then he could convince himself.

After the event on Golgotha, when a clairvoyant seer looked into the spiritual world, it appeared changed to him. Earlier, he had found the Christ in the spiritual worlds. Since the event on Golgotha, he could find the Christ in the earth's aura. Prior to the event on Golgotha, Christ could not be perceived there; following it, He could be beheld in the earth-aura. That is the difference; and Saul reasoned: With clairvoyant perception I can verify the fact that He Who hung upon the Cross and lived as Jesus of Nazareth was the Christ Who is now in the earth aura. In the aura of the earth he saw the same Being first beheld in the sun by

153

Zarathustra, Ahura Mazdao; and now he knew that He Who had been crucified had arisen. Now he could proclaim that Christ had arisen and had appeared to him, as He had appeared to Cephas, to the other brethren, and to the five hundred at one time. Thenceforth he was the apostle of the *living* Christ for Whom death has not the same meaning as for other men.

Whenever the Death on the Cross is doubted—that is, this particular manner in which the Christ died—anyone who is really informed on the subject will agree with another* Swabian who, in his *Urchristentum*, has assembled with the greatest historical accuracy everything that is indisputably related to what we know about it. In that connection Gfrörer —for he it was—rightly emphasized specifically the Death on the Cross; and in a certain sense we can agree with him when he says, in his rather sarcastic mode of expression, that when anyone contradicted him in this matter he would look him critically in the eye and ask whether there might perhaps be something wrong in his upper story.

Among the most indubitably established elements of Christianity are this Death on the Cross and what we shall elucidate tomorrow: the Resurrection and the effect of the words: *"I am with you always, even unto the end of the world."* And these were the substance of Paul's message, hence he could say, *"If Christ be not risen, then is our preaching vain, and your faith is also vain."* He ties Christianity to the Resurrection of Christ. Not until our time have people begun again to reflect, so to speak, upon such things—not in circles where they are made the subject of theological disputes, but where the actual life of Christianity is involved. The great philosopher Solovyev really takes entirely the Pauline stand-

---

*The reference is to "Schwaben-Vischer," mentioned earlier in this lecture.

point in emphasizing that everything in Christianity rests upon the idea of the Resurrection, and that a Christianity of the future is impossible unless the concept of the Resurrection be believed and grasped. And after his own fashion he repeats Paul's utterance, *"If Christ be not risen, then is our preaching vain, and your faith is also vain."* In that case the Christ impulse would be an impossible thing. There could be no Christianity without the risen Christ, the living Christ.

It is characteristic, and therefore worthy of emphasis, that certain deep thinkers have come to recognize the truth of Paul's message solely by means of their philosophy, without benefit of occultism. If we devote some attention to such thinkers we realize that men are beginning to appear in our time who have a concept of what the future conviction and world view of mankind will have to be, namely that which spiritual science must provide. But those who do not have spiritual science achieve no more than an empty conceptual form. This is the case also in the profound thinker Solovyev. His philosophical systems resemble vessels for containing concepts; and what must be poured into them is something they indeed crave and for which they form the molds, but something they lack—and this can come only out of the anthroposophical current. It will fill the molds with that living water which is the revelation of facts conerning the spiritual world, the occult. That is what this spiritual-scientific world outlook will offer these finest minds, who already today show that they need it, and whose tragedy lies in their not having been able to obtain it. We can say of such minds that they positively yearn for anthroposophy. But they have not been able to find it.

It is the task of the anthroposophical movement to pour into these vessels, prepared by such minds, all that can contribute to clear, distinct, true conceptions of the most significant events, such as the Christ event and the Mystery of

155

Golgotha. By means of its revelations concerning the realms of the spiritual world, anthroposophy or spiritual research alone can throw light on these events. Verily, it is *only* through anthroposophy, through spiritual research, that the Mystery of Golgotha can be comprehended in our time.

IX

At the close of yesterday's exposition we indicated the intention to consider next the cardinal issue within the Christ impulse: the death and its significance. But before turning to a description of the death of Christ, and thus to the climax of this study cycle, we must discuss today the true meaning and significance of much that we find in the John Gospel itself and its relation to what the other Gospels offer. In the last few days we have been endeavoring to comprehend the Christ impulse and to establish it as an actual event in human evolution by means of quite a different source: by clairvoyant reading of the *Akasha Chronicle*. In a sense, we referred only to those passages in the Gospels which appear to confirm what clairvoyant research justifies us in stating as truths.

Today, in order to follow up our studies, we shall consider the John Gospel itself and characterize this important document of mankind from a certain aspect. We said yesterday that the theological research of our time, in as far as it is affected by materialism, can find no points of contact with this John Gospel, is unable to see its historical value; but regarded with the vision of spiritual science this Gospel proves to be one of the most marvelous documents possessed by the human race. It is not too much to say that not only as a religious document but, to use a profane expression, among all purely literary works in existence, it is one of the greatest. Let us now approach it from this literary angle.

From the very first chapters—if rightly understood and if one knows all that lies concealed in the words—this Gospel of St. John shows a rounded beauty of style equal to any in the world, although a superficial study does not reveal this fact. What superficial observation discloses first is that in enumerating the miracles the writer of the John Gospel, whose background we now know, mentions precisely seven up to the Lazarus event proper. (The significance of the number seven will be treated in the following lectures.) What were these seven miracles or signs?

1. The sign in connection with the Marriage in Cana in Galilee.
2. The sign given in the healing of the nobleman's son.
3. The one given in the healing of the man who had lain sick for thirty-eight years by the Pool of Bethesda.
4. The Feeding of the Five Thousand.
5. The sign given in the vision of Christ walking on the sea.
6. The sign given in the healing of the man born blind. And finally:
7. The greatest sign, the initiation of Lazarus, the transformation of Lazarus into the writer of the John Gospel.

These are the seven signs. But now we must ask ourselves, What about these signs, this question of miracles? If you listened attentively to a number of things that were told you in the previous lectures you will remember having heard that the state of human consciousness has changed throughout the course of our evolution. We cast our gaze back to remote times and found that men did not issue from a merely animalistic stage of development, but from a form in which they possessed the power of clairvoyance as a congenital endowment. People of that time were clairvoyant, even though their consciousness still lacked the ability to say "I am." The capacity for self-consciousness was something they had to acquire gradually, and for this they had to forfeit their old clairvoyance. In the future, a time will come again when all men are clairvoyant, but they will have retained self-consciousness, the "I am." Those are the three stages which humanity has in part passed through, in part still has ahead of it.

In Atlantis men still lived in a sort of dream consciousness, but this was clairvoyant. Then they gradually achieved self-consciousness, outer objective consciousness, in exchange for which, however, they had to give up the old gift of dim clairvoyance. And finally, what man will have in the future is clairvoyant consciousness coupled with self-consciousness. Thus man traverses the path from an ancient dim clairvoyance through an opaque objective consciousness, finally ascending to conscious clairvoyance.

But in addition to consciousness, everything else about man has changed as well. The belief that conditions must always have been as they are today is due to nothing but human shortsightedness. Everything has evolved. Nothing has always been as it is today, not even men's relation to each other. You have already gathered from intimations in the last lectures that in older epochs—up to the time when the Christ impulse entered human evolution—the influence of soul upon soul was much stronger. Such was human disposition at that time. A man did not merely hear what was told him in externally audible words: in a certain way he could feel and know what the other felt and thought vividly, livingly. Love was something quite different from what it is today, albeit in those times it was largely a matter of blood ties. Nowadays it has taken on more of a psychic character, but it has lost its strength. Nor will it regain this until the Christ impulse shall have entered all human hearts. In olden times, active love possessed at the same time a healing property, a powerful balm, for the soul of its recipient.

Coincident with the development of the intellect and of cleverness, qualities that came into being only gradually, these ancient direct influences of soul upon soul dwindled away. The ability to act upon the other's soul, to cause one's own soul force to stream into it, was a gift possessed by ancient peoples. You must therefore imagine the force that one soul could receive from another as much greater, the influence one soul could exert upon another as much stronger, than is the case today. Although external historical documents report nothing of all this, and tablets and monuments do not mention it, clairvoyant study of the *Akasha Chronicle* nevertheless discloses the fact that in these ancient times the healing of the sick, for example, was extensively accomplished through a psychic influence passing from the one to the other. And the soul was capable of much else as well. Though today it sounds like a fairy tale, it is a fact that in those times a man's will, if he so desired and had specially trained himself for the purpose, had the power to act soothingly upon the growth of a plant, to accelerate or retard it. Today but scanty remnants of all this are left.

Human life, then, was very different at that time. No one would have been surprised—given the right mutual relationship—at the passing over of a psychic influence from one person to the other. It must be kept in mind, however, that two or more were needed if the exercise of a psychic influence of that sort was to take effect. We could imagine the possibility of a man imbued with the power of Christ entering our midst nowadays; but those with the requisite faith in him would be very few in number, so that he would not be able to achieve all that can be accomplished by the influence of one soul upon another. For not only must the influence be exerted, someone must be present who is sufficiently developed to receive it. Remembering that formerly those who could receive such influences were more numerous, we should not be surprised to learn that for the healing of the sick there indeed existed the means by which psychic influences could take effect, but also, that influences which today can be transmitted only by mechanical means were at that time applied psychically.

We must keep in mind that the Christ event entered human evolution at a very special point in time. Only the very last remnants, so to say, of those soul currents that flowed from man to man were left as a heritage of the old Atlantean age. Humanity was about to descend ever deeper into matter, and the possibility for such psychic currents to be effective constantly diminished. That was the moment when the Christ impulse had to enter, the impulse that by its very nature could accomplish so very much for those who were still sufficiently receptive.

He who is really familiar with mankind's evolution will therefore find it quite natural that the Christ Being, having once entered the body of Jesus of Nazareth in about the thirtieth year of his life, could unfold very special powers in this sheath, for the latter had been developing since time immemorial. We mentioned yesterday that this individuality of Jesus of Nazareth had in one former life been incarnated in ancient Persia, and then, through one incarnation after another, had continued to rise in its spiritual development. That is why the Christ could dwell in such a body, and why this body could be sacrificed to Him. This the Evangelists knew well, hence they presented the entire narrative in such a way as to be wholly comprehensible for spiritual research. Only, we must take everything in the Gospels literally—that is, we must first learn to read them. As has been said, the deeper significance of the miracles we shall learn in due time; but here we can ask, for example, why, precisely in the first of the signs [John 2:1-11] it is specially emphasized in dealing with the Marriage in Cana of Galilee that this took place in Cana "of Galilee." Seek as you will, you can find in old Palestine within the radius then known no second Cana;

161

and in such a case it would seem superfluous to specify the locality. Why, then, does the Evangelist tell us that this miracle occurred in Cana "of Galilee"? Because the important point to be stressed was that something occurred which had to take place in Galilee. It means that nowhere else but in Galilee could Christ have found just those people whose presence was indispensable. As I said, an influence implies not only the one who exerts it, but the others as well who are appropriately fitted to receive it. Christ's first appearance would not have been possible within the Jewish community proper, but it was possible in Galilee with its mixture of many different tribes and groups. Just because members of so many peoples from various parts of the world were assembled in one spot, there was far less blood relationship, and above all, far less faith in it, than in Judea, in the narrow circle of the Hebrew people. Galilee was a heterogeneous racial mixture.

But what was it to which Christ, in view of His impulse, felt Himself particularly called? We have said that one of His most significant utterances was, *Before Abraham was, was the I am*; and the other, *I and the Father are one.* By this He meant: among those who cling to the old forms of life, the ego is entrenched in a system of blood relationships. The words *I and Father Abraham are one* aroused a very special feeling in the true believer in the Old Testament, a feeling nowadays very difficult to share. What a man calls his own self, circumscribed by birth and death, he sees as transitory. But one who had true faith in the Old Testament, who was influenced by the widespread teachings of that time, asserted, not allegorically, but as a fact: As regards myself I am isolated; but I am a member of a great organism, of a great life-relationship reaching back to Father Abraham. Just as my finger can remain a living member only as long as it is part of my body, so my memory is contingent upon my feeling

162

myself a member of the great folk organism that goes back to Father Abraham. I am part of the great folk complex, exactly as my finger is part of my body. Cut off my finger and it ceases to be a finger. It is safe only as long as it is part of my hand, my hand part of my arm, and my arm part of my body; it ceases to have meaning if severed from my hand. And in like manner, I myself have meaning only when I feel myself a member of all the generations through which the blood flows down from Father Abraham. Then I feel sheltered. My individual ego is transient and fleeting, but not so this whole great folk organism way back to Father Abraham. When I sense and feel myself wholly embraced by it I conquer my temporally transient ego: I am sheltered in one great ego, the ego of my people that has come down to me from Father Abraham through the blood of the generations.

That represents the conviction of the Old Testament adherents. All the great events narrated in the Old Testament, everything that even today seems marvelous, occurred through the power of the inner experience contained in the words, *I and Father Abraham are one*. But the time came when men were destined to relinquish this state of consciousness for another, hence it gradually disappeared. That is why Christ could not address those who, on the one hand, had lost the magic power of being effective by means of blood ties, and on the other, still believed only in the common bond with Father Abraham. Clearly, among these Christ could not find the faith necessary to effect what could flow from His soul into the other souls. For this purpose, He had to turn to those who, owing to their mixed blood, no longer clung to this old belief: to the Galileans. That is where His mission had to commence. Even though the old state of consciousness was generally on the wane, still He found in Galilee a medley of peoples that stood at the beginning of the era in which blood became mixed. From all quarters tribes as-

163

sembled here that had previously been governed solely by the forces of the old blood ties. They were on the point of finding the transition. They vividly retained the feeling that their fathers were still endowed with the consciousness of former times, that they possessed the magic powers which act from soul to soul. Among these people Christ could be effective with His new mission, which consisted in endowing man with an ego consciousness no longer bound to blood relationship; an ego consciousness which could say, Within myself I find the connection with the spiritual Father Who, instead of letting His blood flow down through the generations, radiates His spiritual force into each individual soul. The ego which is within me, and which is in direct communion with the spiritual Father, was before Abraham was. It is for me, then, to infuse into this ego a force that will be strengthened through my being aware of my connection with the spiritual Father force of the world. *I and the Father are one.* No longer I and Father Abraham—that is, a physical ancestor.

Such were the people to whom Christ turned, people who had just arrived at the point of understanding this, people who, having broken away from the blood ties by intermarriage, needed to find the strong force—not in consanguinity, but in the individual soul; the force that can lead man gradually to express the spiritual in the physical. Do not ask, Why do we not see things happening today as they happened then? Aside from the fact that he who has the will to see them can see them, we must remember that mankind has emerged from that state of consciousness and has descended into the world of matter; that the period in question represented the boundary line, and that Christ used the last representatives of the previous epoch of evolving humanity in whom to demonstrate the power of spirit over matter. The signs that were done while the old state of consciousness was still present, but disappearing, were intended as an example and a symbol—a symbol of faith.

Now let us turn to this Marriage in Cana of Galilee itself. If I were to develop in detail all the implications indicated in the John Gospel, in the entire Gospel content, fourteen lectures would certainly not suffice: several years would be needed. But such a literal development of the subject would only serve to confirm what I can suggest in brief elucidations.

The first thing we are told in connection with this *first sign* is: *There was a marriage in Cana of Galilee*. Here we must stop to realize that the John Gospel contains not one word that has not a definite meaning. Well, then: why "a marriage"? Because the marriage for one thing brings about what the Christ mission effects in such an eminent way: it brings human beings together. And then, a marriage "in Galilee"? It was in Galilee that the ancient blood ties were severed, that mutually alien bloods came to mingle. Now, Christ's task was intimately connected with this mixing of blood. So, we are here dealing with a union having the object of creating progeny among people who are no longer related by blood.

What I am now about to say will seem very strange to you. What would people have felt in such a case in very old times when there still prevailed the close or endogamous marriage, as one is inclined to call it in the spiritual-scientific sense? For the transformation of this close marriage into a distant or exogamous marriage is very much a part of human evolution, and what I have already said explains what an endogamous marriage implies. Among all people of ancient times it was contrary to law to marry outside of the tribe, away from consanguinity. People related by blood, members of the same tribe, intermarried; and this custom of marrying within the tribe, within blood relationship, resulted in the marvel of engendering intense magical force. This can be verified at any time by means of spiritual-scientific research. The descendants of a blood-related tribe possessed, as a consequence of such intermarriage of relatives, magical powers that worked from one soul to another.

Let us imagine that in ancient times we had been asked to attend a wedding, and that the customary drink—in this case, wine—had given out. What would have happened? Provided the right relations had existed among the blood-related members of this wedding party, it would have been possible, through the magical power of love arising out of consanguinity, for the water—or whatever was offered later in place of wine—to be sensed by the others as wine as a result of the psychic influence of these persons. Wine is what they would have been drinking if the right magical relationship had existed between the one person and the others. Do not say: This wine would still have been only water! A sensible person would reply to that: For the human being, things are of the nature in which they communicate themselves to his organism, they are what they become for him, not what they look like. I believe that even today many a wine lover would like water if, by means of some influence or other, it appeared to be changed into wine; that is, if it tasted like wine and produced the same effect in his organism. Nothing else is necessary than that a man should take water for wine. What, then, was required in olden times to render possible such a sign as that of the water in the vessels becoming wine when it was drunk? The magical power deriving from blood relationship, that is what was required. And furthermore, those assembled at the Marriage in Cana of Galilee possessed the psychic capacity for sensing that sort of thing. Only, a transition had to be brought about.

The story continues in the John Gospel:

And the mother of Jesus was there: and both Jesus was called, and his disciples, to the marriage.

And since they lacked wine, the mother of Jesus drew attention to this, and said to Him:

They have no wine.

I said that a transition had to be effected if such an event was to take place; the psychic force had to be assisted by something. By what, then? Here we come to the utterance which, as it is usually translated, is really a blasphemy; for I believe it will strike any sensitive person as offensive when, to the statement "they have no wine," Jesus replies: "Woman, what have I to do with you? My hour has not yet come."* It is quite impossible to accept that in a document of this sort. Imagine the ideal of love, as the Gospels describe the relations between Jesus of Nazareth and his mother, and then try to imagine Him using the expression, "Woman, what have I to do with you!" It is not necessary to say more, the rest must be felt. But the point is, these words are not in the text. Examine this passage in the John Gospel and then look up the Greek text. This contains nothing more than the words employed by Jesus of Nazareth in indicating a certain event:

Oh Woman, that passes here from me to you!

What He refers to is this subtle, intimate force from soul to soul, that passes from Him to His mother; and this is what He needs at this moment. Greater signs He is as yet unable to perform, for this, his time has to gradually ripen. Therefore He says: My time, the time when I shall merely work

---

*The four Greek words translated this way have in fact no clear meaning in the Greek. It cannot even be said with certainty whether or not Christ asked a question or made a statement because the marks of interrogation did not exist at the time the Gospel was written. Since none of the words is a verb, a verb has to be supplied, and if one supplies "passes" as Steiner does here the Greek words can certainly bear the meaning he gives it, the first word ti becoming a relative pronoun rather than an interrogative—what?

through *my* force has not yet come. For the present, the magnetic psychic bond that passes from the soul of Jesus of Nazareth to the mother is still indispensable.

"Oh Woman, that passes here from me to you!" Otherwise, after an utterance like "Woman, what have I to do with you?" why would she turn to the servants and say, "Whatsoever he says to you, do it?" She had to possess the old forces of which nowadays people can have no conception; and she knew that He referred to the blood tie between son and mother, to the bond that should then pass to the others. Then she knew that something like an invisible spiritual force held sway, capable of effectuating something. And here let me beg you to read the Gospel—really to read it. I ask how anyone can come to terms with the Gospel who believes that something happened at that wedding—I really don't know what—that six ordinary jars stood there "for the Jewish purification," as we are told; and that according to ordinary observation—without reference to anything such as we have just been considering—the water turned into wine. How could such a thing have come about externally?

What is the meaning of this? And what is the faith in this miracle held by him who speaks before you—in fact, the only faith anybody can have in a miracle—that here one substance transformed itself into another for the benefit of those present?! No ordinary interpretation will get us far. We must assume that the jars which stood there contained no water, for nothing is said about their being emptied. But it says they were filled, so if they have been emptied and then re-filled—assuming the water had really been changed to wine as by a sleight of hand trick—one would really have to believe that the water which had previously been in the jars had been turned into wine. You see, this does not help, nothing squares.

We must understand that the jars must obviously have

been empty, because a special significance attached to the filling of them. "Whatsoever he says to you, do it," the mother had told the servants. What sort of water did Christ need? He needed water fresh from the sources of nature. That is why it was necessary to specify that the water had just been drawn. The only water suitable for Christ's purpose was such as had not yet lost the inner forces that are inherent in any element so long as it is united with nature. As has been said, the John Gospel contains not one word that is not fraught with deep meaning. Freshly drawn water had to be used because Christ is the Being Who had but recently approached the earth and become associated with the forces that work in the earth itself. Now, when the living forces of the water work, in turn, with what flows "from me to you," it becomes possible for the event described in the Gospel to take place. The steward of the feast is called, and he is under the impression that something unusual has occurred. He does not know what this was; it is specifically stated that he had not seen what happened, only the servants had seen it, but under the influence of what has taken place he now takes the water for wine. That is stated clearly and distinctly, so we know that through psychic force even an outer element—that is, the physical component of the human body—was affected.

And what had to be present in the mother of Jesus of Nazareth herself in order that at this moment her faith might be strong enough to produce such an effect? She needed just what she did indeed possess, namely the realization that he who was called her son had become the Spirit of the Earth. Then her strong force combined with His, with that which acted from him upon her, developed so mighty an influence as to produce the effect described.

Thus we have shown, through the whole constellation of conditions surrounding this first sign, how the unison of souls which results from blood ties produces an effect even in the physical world. It was the first sign, and the Christ force is shown at its minimum. It still needed the intensification resulting from contact with the mother's psychic forces; and she needed the additional support of forces still united with nature in water, which remain present in the freshly drawn water. The active force of the Christ Being is here shown at its minimum: but special emphasis is made of the fact that the Christ-force passes over to and affects the other soul, and, the latter being particularly suited for it, evokes reaction from it. The essential point is that the Christ force has the power to render the other soul capable of exerting influences. It engenders in the wedding guests as well the ability to taste the water as wine. But every real force increases through its own exercise, and the second time it is called upon it is already stronger. Just as any ordinary force increases with exercise, so is especially a spiritual force strengthened when it has once been successfully applied.

The second of the signs, as you know from the John Gospel, is the healing of the nobleman's son. By what means was he healed? Here again the right answer will be found only by reading the Gospel in the right way and by concentrating on the crucial words of the chapter in question. In the fiftieth verse of the fourth chapter, after the nobleman had told Jesus of Nazareth his story of distress, we read:

Jesus saith unto him, Go thy way, thy son liveth.
And the man believed the word that Jesus had spoken
unto him, and he went his way.

Again we have two souls in accord, the soul of the Christ and that of the boy's father. And when Christ said, *Go thy way, thy son liveth*, what effect did this have? It enkindled in the other soul the force to believe all that Christ's words implied. These two forces worked together. Christ's utterance had the power so to kindle the other soul that the nobleman believed. Had he not believed, his son would not have recovered. That is the way one force acts upon another: two are needed. And already here we find a greater measure of the Christ force. At the Marriage in Cana it still required the support of the mother's force in order to function at all. Now it has progressed to the point of being able to impart the kindling word to the nobleman's soul. We behold an intensification of the Christ force.

Passing to the third sign, the healing at the Pool of Bethesda of the man who had lain sick for thirty-eight years, we must again seek the most important words that throw light on the whole subject. They are these: (John 5:1-9)

Jesus saith unto him, Rise, take up thy bed, and walk.
Speaking of his being forced to remain prone, the sick man had previously said that he could not move:

> *Sir, I have no man, when the water is troubled, to put me into the pool: but while I am coming, another steppeth down before me.*

But Christ spoke to him—and it is important that it was on the Sabbath, a day of general rejoicing and great brotherly love—clothing His injunction in the words, *Rise, take up thy bed, and walk.* This utterance we must take in conjunction with the other equally important one in which He tells him:

> *Behold, thou art made whole: sin no more, lest a worse thing come unto thee.*

What does that mean? It means that there was a connection between the man's sickness that had persisted for thirty-eight years, and his sin. We need not enquire at the moment whether the sin had been committed in this life or in a former one. The point is that Christ infused into the other's soul the force to accomplish something that reached right down into his psycho-moral nature. Here again we see an intensification of the Christ force. Previously, all that was involved was something intended to produce only a physical effect;

171

but here it is a question of a sickness of which Christ Himself said that it had to do with the man's sin. At this moment Christ was able to intervene in the sick man's very soul. The previous sign still required the presence of the boy's father, but here the Christ force acts directly on the sick man's soul.

A special magic is lent this event by reason of its having been enacted on the Sabbath. Present-day man no longer has any feeling for such things, but the fact that this happened on the Sabbath meant something to a believer in the Old Testament. It was something very special; that is why the Jews were so indignant at the sick man when he carried his bed on the Sabbath. That is an extraordinarily significant detail—people should learn to think when they read the Gospels. They should not consider it a matter of course that the sick man could be cured, that one now walked who for thirty-eight years had not been able to walk. What they should do is ponder a passage such as the following:

> The Jews therefore said unto him that was cured, it is the sabbath day: it is not lawful for thee to carry thy bed.

What struck them was not that the man had been cured, but that he carried his bed on the Sabbath.

So the whole scene was an integral part of the healing of this sick man, which had to take effect particularly on the hallowed day. Christ Himself harbored the thought, If the Sabbath is indeed to be dedicated to God, the souls of men must enjoy special strength on this day by virtue of the divine force. And it was by means of this force that He worked upon the man before Him; that is, it was transmitted to the sick man's own soul. Hitherto the latter had not found in his soul the force that would overcome the consequences of his sin, but now he has it as an effect of the Christ force. Once again, an intensification of the Christ-force. As I have said, the essential nature of the miracles will be dealt with later, and for the moment we will continue on.

172

The fourth sign is the Feeding of the Five Thousand. Again, we must seek for the most significant passage and we must bear in mind that an event of this sort should not be viewed in the light of present-day consciousness. Had those who wrote about Christ at the time the John Gospel was written believed what our materialistic age believes today, their narratives would have been very different, for quite other things would have struck them as important. In this case they were not particularly surprised even at the phenomenon of five thousand being fed from so small a supply; but what is most important and specially emphasized is the following passage:

> And Jesus took the loaves; and when he had
> given thanks, he distributed them to the disciples,
> and the disciples to them that were set down;
> and likewise of the fishes as much as they
> would. [John 6:11]

Just what is it that Christ Jesus does here? In order to bring about what was to take place He makes use of the souls of His disciples, of those who had been with Him and had by degrees matured to the level of His stature. They are a part of the procedure. They surround Him; in their souls He can now evoke a power of charity. His force flows forth into that of the disciples. Of the manner in which this event could take place we will speak later, but here we must again observe an increase in the Christ force. Previously, He infused His force into the man who had lain sick for thirty-eight years. Here, His force acts upon the force of the disciples' souls. What is active here is the intensification of forces that proceeds from the soul of the master to the souls of the disciples. The force has expanded from the one soul to the souls of others. It has become stronger.

Already at this point, then, there dwells in the disciples' souls the same principle that dwells in the soul of Christ. Anyone inclined to ask what happens as a result of such an

173

influence should observe the facts, should consider what actually occurred when Christ's powerful force acted not alone but kindled the force in other souls, so that it then worked on. There are none today with such living faith; they may believe theoretically, but not with sufficient strength. But not until they do so will they be able to observe what occurred there. Spiritual research knows very well what occurred.

So we observe a step-by-step increase of the Christ force. The fifth sign, told in the same chapter, begins:

> *And when even was now come, his disciples went down unto the sea, and entered into a ship, and went over the sea toward Capernaum. And it was now dark, and Jesus was not come to them. And the sea arose by reason of a great wind that blew. So when they had rowed about five and twenty or thirty furlongs, they see Jesus walking* on the sea, and drawing nigh unto the ship: and they were afraid.* [John 6:16–19]

Modern publishers of the Gospels assign to this chapter the highly superfluous title, "Jesus walks on the sea"—as though that were stated anywhere in this chapter! Where does it say, "Jesus walks on the sea?" It says, "The disciples saw Jesus approaching on the sea." That is the point. The Gospels must be taken literally. It is simply a case of the Christ force having again increased in strength. So powerful had it become as a natural result of its exercise in the previous deeds that not only could it now act from one soul upon

---

*The translators who have used the word "walk," here criticized by Dr. Steiner, were giving an English equivalent for the Greek word peripatein, which does indeed mean to walk around, or stroll, and not to approach. Steiner is saying here what should have been written, not what all the MSS say was written. Steiner's word was "dahergehen," meaning "approaching."

another—not only could the soul of Christ communicate itself, in its force, to other souls—but the Christ could live in His own form before the soul of another who was ripe for it.

The event, then, occurred as follows: Someone who is absent possesses so great a force that it acts upon men at a distance, far away. But the influence of the Christ force is now so powerful that it does more than set free a force in the disciples, as had been the case with those who had sat with Him on the mountain. There, the force had merely passed over into the disciples in order that the miracle might be performed. Now, although their physical sight could not reach the Christ, they had the power to see Him, to behold His very form. Christ could become visible at a distance to those with whose souls His own had united. His own form is now sufficiently advanced to be seen spiritually. At the moment when the possibility of physical vision disappears, there arises in the disciples all the more intensely the ability to see spiritually—and they see the Christ. But the nature of this seeing at a distance is such that the image of the object in question appears in the immediate vicinity.—Again an increase of the Christ power.

The next sign is the healing of the man born blind. This narrative, as it appears in the John Gospel, is again particularly distorted. Doubtless you have often read the story:

> And as Jesus passed by, he saw a man which
> was blind from his birth. And his disciples asked
> him, saying, Master, who did this sin, this
> man, or his parents, that he was born blind?
> Jesus answered, Neither hath this man sinned,
> nor his parents; but that the works of God should
> be made manifest in him. [John 9:1–3]

We need only ask if it is a Christian attitude to interpret the matter as follows: Here is a man born blind. His blindness is not a result of his parents' sin, nor of his own; but he

175

was rendered blind by God in order that Christ might come and perform a miracle for the glory of God. In other words, in order that a miraculous act might be ascribed to God, God had first to make the man blind.

The original passage was simply not read correctly. It does not say at all that "the works of God should be made manifest in him." If we would understand this sign we must examine the old usage of the word "God." You can do this most readily by turning to another chapter in which Christ is positively accused of asserting of himself that He and God were one. How does He reply?

Is it not written in your law, I said, Ye are Gods?
[John 10:34]

What Christ meant by this answer was that in the innermost soul of man there is the potential nucleus of a God: something divine. Hows often have we not pointed out that the fourth principle of the human being is the potential human capacity for the divine! "Ye are Gods." That is, something divine dwells in you. It is not the human being but something different, not the person of a man as he lives on earth between birth and death; and it is different also from what man inherits from his parents. Whence derives this element of divinity, this human individuality? It passes through repeated earth lives from incarnation to incarnation. This individuality comes over from an earlier earth life, from a previous incarnation. Hence we read, not the man's parents have sinned, nor has his own personality—the personality one ordinarily addresses as "I"; but in a previous incarnation he created the cause of his blindness in this life. He became blind because out of a former life the works of the God within him revealed themselves in his blindness. Christ Jesus here points clearly and distinctly to karma, the law of cause and effect.

What principle in man had to be worked upon if this

176

kind of sickness was to be healed? Not upon what lives as a transitory ego between birth and death: the forces must penetrate deeper, must enter the ego that continues from one life to another. Again the Christ force has increased. Hitherto we have seen it influencing only what is directly before it; now it acts upon the principle that survives human life between birth and death, that continues from life to life. Christ feels Himself the representative of the I Am. As He pours His force into the I Am—as thus the exalted divinity of Christ communicates Himself to the divinity in man—the human being receives the force enabling him to heal himself from within. Now Christ has penetrated to the innermost being of the soul. His force has acted upon the eternal individuality of the sick man and strengthened it by causing His own force to appear in the individuality, thereby influencing even the consequences of former incarnations.

What intensification still remains for the Christ force to achieve? None but the ability to approach another and awaken in him the capacity for enkindling the Christ impulse in himself, so that his whole being is saturated with it and he becomes another, a Christ-permeated man. And that is what occurred in the Raising of Lazarus, where we find still another increase in the Christ force. It has progressed step by step throughout.

Where else in the world could you find a lyrical document of such glorious composition? No other authors have mastered composition on such a plane. Who would not bow down in reverence when reading the marvellous building up, step by step, in the narrative of these events! Even contemplating the John Gospel only as an artistic composition we cannot but feel deep reverence. It all grows step by step and rises steadily.

One point remains to be elucidated. We have pointed out a number of isolated features tending to show the intensification in the sequence of signs, of miracles; but the narrative embraces a great deal in between, and we must examine the organization of the whole. Tomorrow it will be our task to show that, in addition to the admirable intensification in the miracles, there is definite purpose in the way all the connecting links are embodied; we realize that these could not possibly have been filled in better than was done by the writer of the John Gospel. Today we have considered its artistic composition and found it unthinkable that a work of art could be more perfectly or beautifully composed than is the John Gospel up to the description of the Raising of Lazarus; but only one who can read aright and knows what is essential senses its great and mighty meaning. It is the mission of anthroposophy in our time to bring this meaning before our souls. But this John Gospel contains more. Our expositions of it will be followed by others imbued with a wisdom loftier than ours; but this wisdom will in turn serve to find fresh truths, just as during the past seven years our wisdom has served to find what cannot be found without anthroposophy.

X

Among the events that occurred in Palestine at the beginning of our era there is one in particular to which repeated reference has been made: the Baptism of Jesus of Nazareth by John. The fact was emphasized that regarding its essentials all four Gospels are in agreement. What we shall do today is once again to consider this Baptism from one particular aspect.

From the manner of its presentation in the Gospels we gather that the Baptism points to an event of the utmost import—an event also explicable by means of the *Akasha Chronicle*—which had to be characterized somewhat as follows: In about the thirtieth year of Jesus of Nazareth's life there entered into his three sheaths that divine Being Whom we call the Christ. We must distinguish, then—and this is revealed through a study of the *Akasha Chronicle*—between two stages in the life of Christianity's founder. In the first place we have the life of the great initiate whom we call Jesus of Nazareth. In this Jesus of Nazareth there dwelt an ego-being which we showed to have passed through many previous incarnations, to have lived repeatedly on earth, to have ascended ever higher in these succeeding lives, and to have risen by degrees to the capacity for the great sacrifice. This sacrifice meant that toward Jesus of Nazareth's thirtieth year his ego was able to renounce his physical, etheric, and astral bodies, which hitherto he had purified, cleansed and ennobled, thus providing a threefold human sheath of incomparable purity and perfection. When the ego of Jesus of Nazareth abandoned these sheaths at the Baptism, these received the Being Who had never previously dwelt on earth, Whom we cannot think of as having passed through previous incarnations. The Christ Being could formerly be found only in the world existing outside our earth. Not until this moment of the Baptism by John did this Individuality unite with a human body, in order to accomplish, in the three years following, what we must endeavor to set forth in ever greater detail.

What I have just told you was acquired by means of clairvoyant observation. The Evangelists clothe this event in their descriptions of the Baptism; and what they meant was that while a variety of experiences came to those whom John baptized, in the case of Jesus of Nazareth, there occurred the event of the Christ descending into his three sheaths. I told you in the first of these lectures that this Christ is the same Being of Whom the Old Testament says:

And the Spirit of God moved (or brooded)
upon the face of the waters. [Gen. 1:2]

This same spirit—that is, the divine Spirit of our solar system—entered the threefold sheath of Jesus of Nazareth.

I shall now set forth what actually occurred at the Baptism by John; but inasmuch as this was the supreme event in *Earth* evolution, I must beg you to realize from the outset that it is necessarily difficult to comprehend. The minor events of *Earth* evolution are naturally easier to understand than the great ones. Who could doubt, therefore, that the mightiest one of all must present the greatest difficulties? I shall presently make various statements that may shock those who are insufficiently prepared; but even they should remind themselves that the purpose of the human soul's sojourn on earth is to keep constantly perfecting itself—in the matter of gaining insight as well as in others—and that what at first comes as a shock must in time appear wholly comprehensible. Were this not the case one would needs despair of the possibility for development in the human soul. As it is, however, we can remind ourselves daily that regardless of how much or how little we have learned, it is our task constantly to perfect our soul, that it may ever better comprehend this matter.

We have before us, then, a threefold human sheath, a physical, etheric, and astral body, and of these the Christ takes possession, so to say. That is indicated by the words resounding out of the universe:

This is my Son, imbued with my love, in Whom I manifest myself.

That is the right translation of this utterance. One can readily imagine that mighty changes must have taken place in the threefold sheath of Jesus of Nazareth when the God entered it; but you will understand, too, that in the old initiations great changes were involved, affecting the whole human being. You will recall that I described the last act of the old initiation for you. After the neophyte, initiated in the divine mysteries, had undergone long preparation by means of study and exercises, he was reduced to a deathlike state for three and a half days, during which his etheric body was separated from his physical body; and this enabled the fruits garnered by the astral body to express themselves in the etheric body. This means that the candidate rose from the rank of a "purified one," as the term is, to an "illuminated one" who perceives the spiritual world.

Even in those old times—or rather, especially then, when such initiations were still possible—one who had reached this stage had a certain power over his entire corporeality. When he returned again into his physical body he controlled it superbly in respect of certain finer elements. Here you might ask, in facing such an initiate, one who achieved so great a mastery over his various sheaths, even the physical body, could one notice this—did he show it?—

Well, it was observed by anyone who had acquired the faculty of that sort of vision. Others as a rule saw him as an ordinary, simple man and noticed nothing remarkable about him. Why? Simply because the physical body, as seen by physical eyes, is merely the outer expression of what underlies it, and the changes mentioned refer to the spiritual element that underlies the physical body.

Now, all the old initiates achieved a certain degree of mastery over their physical body as a result of the procedure to which they were subjected; but there was *one* capacity that no old initiation could ever bring under the dominion of the human spirit. Here we touch the fringe, as it were, of a profound secret, or mystery. In the structure of man there is one element to which the power of a pre-Christian initiation could not penetrate; the subtle physico-chemical processes in the skeleton. Strange as it may sound to you, that is the case. Previous to the Baptism of Christ Jesus there never had been a human individuality in earth evolution, either among initiates or elsewhere, with power over the chemico-physical processes in the skeleton. Through the entry of the Christ into the body of Jesus of Nazareth the Egohood of Christ acquired dominion even over the skeleton. And the result was that, as a unique event, there once lived upon earth a body capable of employing its forces in such a way as to incorporate the form of the skeleton—that is, its spiritual form—in *Earth* evolution. Nothing of all that man passes through in his earth development would endure were he not able to incorporate in *Earth* evolution, as a law, the noble form of his skeleton, were he unable gradually to master this law of the skeleton.

There is a connection here with an old popular superstition—indeed, old traditions are frequently associated with the occult. In certain circles it is customary to employ the skeleton as a symbol when death is to be represented. This

182

stands for the idea that at the beginning of *Earth* evolution all the laws governing the systems of the human organization other than the skeleton were so far advanced that at the end of the *Earth's* evolution they would be present again, though in a higher form; but that evolution would carry nothing into the future unless the form of the skeleton were taken over. The form of the skeleton conquers death in the physical sense, hence He Who was to vanquish death on the earth had to have mastery over the skeleton—in the same manner as I indicated this mastery over certain spiritual attributes in connection with lesser faculties. Man has control of his circulatory system only to a slight degree. In feeling shame, he drives his blood outward from within which means that the soul acts upon the circulatory system. In turning pale, when frightened, he drives his blood back inward into the center. In sorrow, tears come to his eyes. All these phenomena represent a certain dominion of the soul over what is corporeal; but far greater mastery over the bodily functions is enjoyed by one who has been initiated beyond a certain stage: among other powers, he has the ability to control voluntarily the movements of the various parts of his brain in a definite way.

The human entity, then, that was the sheath of Jesus of Nazareth came under the dominion of the Christ; and the will of the Christ, His sovereign will, had the power to penetrate the skeleton, so that it could be influenced, as it were, for the first time. The significance of this fact can be set forth as follows: Man acquired his present form, that he has by virtue of his skeleton, on the *Earth*—not during a previous embodiment of our planet; but he would lose it again had it not been for the coming of that spiritual power we call the Christ. He would carry over into the future nothing in the way of harvest and fruits of his sojourn on *Earth* had not Christ established His dominion over the skeleton. It was therefore a stupendous force that penetrated to the very marrow of the threefold sheath of Jesus of Nazareth at the moment of the Baptism by John. We must visualize this moment vividly, for it is one side of what took place.

In the case of an ordinary birth the attitudes deriving from a previous incarnation unite with what is given through heredity. The human individuality that had existed in former lives merges with what is provided for him as his corporeal-etheric sheath; in other words, something from the spiritual world unites with the principle that is physical, of the senses. Those of you who have frequently attended my lectures are aware that as regards outer appearances everything presents itself as in a mirror, reversed, as soon as we enter the spiritual world. So when a person is made clairvoyant by systematic methods, when his eyes have opened to the spiritual world, he must first gradually learn to find his way about, for everything appears reversed. When he sees a number, say 345, he must not read it as he would in the physical world, but backwards: 543. In like manner you must learn to observe, in a certain sense, everything else as well in reverse—not only numbers. Now, the event of the Christ uniting with the outer sheath of Jesus of Nazareth also appears to one whose spiritual eyes are open in reversed order. While in a physical incarnation something spiritual descends from higher worlds and unites with the physical, that which was sacrificed in order that the Christ Spirit might enter appeared above the head of Jesus of Nazareth in the form of a white dove. Something spiritual appears as it detaches itself from the physical. That is an actual clairvoyant observation and it would be far from right to consider it a mere allegory or symbol. It is a real, clairvoyant, spiritual fact, actually present on the astral plane to clairvoyant sight. Just as a physical birth implies the attraction of spirit, so this birth was a sacrifice, a renunciation; and thereby the opportunity was provided for the Spirit, Who at the beginning of our *Earth* evolution *moved upon the face of the waters*, to unite with the threefold sheath of Jesus of Nazareth and to strengthen and inspire it through and through, as described.

You will now understand that when this took place an area was involved far greater than the spot on which the Baptism occurred. It would be very shortsighted to imagine that an event associated with any being whatever is circumscribed by the boundaries visible to the eye. That is the powerful delusion to which men can succumb when they put their faith in the outer senses alone. Where is a man's boundary, as the outer senses see it? A superficial verdict would say, in his skin. That is where he stops in all directions. Someone might even add, If I were to cut off the nose that is part of you, you would no longer be a complete human being; which goes to show that everything of that kind is part of your being. But how short-sighted that is! When we limit ourselves to physical perception we do not look for any integral part of a man even ten to twelve inches or so outside his skin; but consider that with every breath you draw you inhale air from the general air of your environment. Well, if your nose is cut off, you are no longer a complete human being; but the same is true if your air is cut off. It is quite arbitrary to imagine that a man is bounded by his skin. Everything surrounding him is part of him as well, even in the physical sense; so that when something happens to a man at a given spot, it is not only the space occupied by his body that participates in the occurrence. If you were to try the experiment of poisoning the air within the radius of a mile surrounding the spot where a man stood, poisoning it virulently enough for the fumes to reach him, you would discover that the entire space within the mile radius takes part in his life processes.

The whole earth takes part in every life process. If this is

185

the case even in a physical life process, you will not find it incomprehensible that in an event such as the Baptism the whole spiritual world participated, and that much, very much, occurred in order that this might take place. If within the radius of a mile you poison the air surrounding a man to the extent of influencing his life processes, and if then another man approaches him, the latter will suffer an effect as well. This may differ, according to his proximity to the poisoned area. If he is at a greater distance, for example, the effect will be less; but some effect will nevertheless result. It will therefore no longer seem strange to you if today we raise the question concerning the possibility of there having been other influences resulting from the Baptism. And here we touch upon another profound mystery of which we are constrained to speak today with awe and reverence, for the preparation needed to understand such things will come to mankind only by slow degrees.

At the same moment when the Spirit of Christ descended into the body of Jesus of Nazareth and the transformation occurred as described, an influence was exerted upon the Mother of Jesus of Nazareth as well. It consisted in her regaining her virginity at this moment of the Baptism; that is, her inner organism reverted to the state existing before puberty. At the birth of the Christ, the Mother of Jesus of Nazareth became a virgin.*

Those are the two momentous facts, the great and mighty influences indicated, though cryptically, by the writer of the John Gospel. If we are able to read this Gospel aright, all this can be found stated there in one way or another; but in order to recognize its meaning we must link up with various

---

*This startling statement Dr. Steiner evidently did not wish to elaborate further here. He was to deal with it later in detail in the fifth lecture of the cycle given in Oslo in 1913 entitled *The Fifth Gospel*.

matters upon which we touched yesterday from other aspects.

We have said that in olden times people lived under the influence of endogamy. Marriage was entered into within the same tribe by blood relatives. Only as time passed did it become customary to marry outside the tribe into other blood. The farther back we go in time, the more we find people living under the influence of this blood relationship; and the flowing of the tribal blood through men's veins brought about the strong, magical forces of which we spoke. One who lived at that time and could look far back in his line of ancestry, finding there only tribally related blood, had magical force working in his own blood, making possible the influence of soul upon soul as described yesterday. And people knew that very well, even the simplest of them. But it would be utterly wrong to conclude from this that nowadays consanguineous marriages would produce similar conditions, that magical forces would come to light. You would be falling into the same error as would the lily of the valley if it were suddenly to announce: Henceforth I shall no longer bloom in May: I shall bloom in October! It cannot bloom in October because the necessary conditions are lacking. The same is true of the magical forces. They cannot develop in an era in which the requisite conditions no longer exist. In our time they must evolve in a different manner; what was described applies only to the older epochs.

The crude materialistic scientist can naturally not understand the idea that the laws governing evolution have changed; he believes that what he witnesses today in his physics laboratory must always have taken place in the same way. But that is nonsense, because laws do change. Those who have derived their faith from modern natural science would have marveled at the events in Palestine, narrated in the John Gospel, as something strange indeed. But those who lived at the time of Christ Jesus, when living traditions still remained

187

of an age in which such things were wholly within the range of possibility, were not particularly amazed at them. That is why I could say yesterday that no one was greatly astonished at what occurred at the Marriage of Cana in the nature of a sign.

And why should they have been astonished? Outwardly it was nothing but a repetition of something they knew to have been observed time and again. Turn to the Second Book of Kings, 4, 42–44:

> *And there came a man from Baalshalisha, and brought the man of God [Elisha] bread of the first-fruits, twenty loaves of barley, and full ears of corn in the husk thereof. And he said, Give unto the people, that they may eat. And his servitor said, Should I set this before an hundred men? He said again, Give the people, that may eat: for thus saith the Lord, They shall eat, and shall leave thereof. So he set it before them, and they did eat, and left thereof, according to the word of the Lord.*

There you have in the Old Testament the same situation we find in the feeding of the Five Thousand, narrated in a manner suited to that time. Why should such a sign excite wonder among people whose documents told them that it had happened before? It is essential that we understand this.

Now, what took place in a man who had been initiated in the old sense? He gained access to the spiritual world, his eyes were opened to the spiritually active forces—that is, he could see into the connection between the blood and the spiritually active forces. Others had a faint glimmering of this, but the initiate's vision reached back to the first ancestor from whom the blood had flowed down through the generations; and he could understand that an entire folk ego expressed itself in this blood, just as the individual ego is expressed in the individual's blood. That is the way an initiate saw back to the source of the blood stream that coursed through the generations, and he felt identified in his soul with the whole Folk Spirit whose physiognomy came to expression in the common blood of the people. Such a one was to a certain degree initiated, and up to a point he was master of definite magical powers in the old sense.

There is another thing we must keep in view. The male and female principles co-operate in the propagation of mankind in a manner that can be briefly characterized as follows. Were the female principle to dominate completely, man would develop in such a way as to keep constantly producing homogeneous characters: the child would always resemble his parents, grandparents, and so on. Forces that bring about resemblance are inherent in the female principle, while all that reduces it, that creates differences, lies with the male principle. When, within a folk community, you find a number of faces that resemble each other, you have what derives from the female element; but certain differences are to be seen in these faces enabling you to distinguish the separate individuals, and this results from the male influence. If the influence of the female element alone prevailed you would not be able to tell the individual persons apart; and if only the influence of the male element were in evidence you could never recognize a group of people as belonging to the same stock. So the manner in which the male and female principles co-operate can be stated as follows: the influence of the male principle individualizes, specializes, separates, while that of the female principle tends to generalize.

From this we can see that whatever pertains to a people as a whole derives from the female element; the force in woman carries over from generation to generation the factor which otherwise expresses itself in the continuous blood stream. A further characterization of the origin of the magical forces residing in the blood bonds could be given thus: they are linked with the female principle that courses through the entire people and lives in all its members.

Well, if a man had risen through initiation to the point of being able to wield the forces, so to speak, with which the common blood was inoculated through the female folk element, what was his essential characteristic? The old Persian initiation adopted certain names to distinguish the various degrees rising to spiritual heights, and one of these names must be of special interest to us. The first degree in the Persian initiation was termed the *Raven*; the second, the *Initiate*; the third, the *Warrior*; the fourth, the *Lion*; the fifth degree always bore the name of the people in question: a Persian, for example, who had risen to the fifth degree of initiation was termed a *Persian*.

First the initiate became a Raven, which meant that he could carry on a study of the outer world; and being a servant of those who dwell in the spiritual world he brought to that world tidings of the physical world. Hence the symbol of the Raven as emissary between the physical and the spiritual world—from the Ravens of Elijah to those of Barbarossa. One who reached the second degree already stood within the spiritual world; and one initiated in the third degree, having advanced past the second, is entrusted with the task of advocating the truths of occultism: he becomes a Warrior. An initiate of the second degree was not permitted to contend for the truths of the spiritual world. In the fourth degree the spiritual truths became established, to a certain extent, in the initiate. And the fifth degree is the one of which I said that here the initiate learned to control all that flowed in the blood through the generations, learned to deal with it by means of the forces descending with the blood through the female element of propagation. What name, then,

190

would be applied to a man who had experienced his initiation within the Israelite People? *Israelite*, just as in an analogous case in Persia he would have been called a Persian.

Now observe the following. Among the first to be brought to Christ Jesus, according to the Gospel of St. John, was Nathanael. The others, who were already followers of Christ Jesus, say to Nathanael:

> *We have found the Master, Him Who dwells in*
> *Jesus of Nazareth.* (John 1:45-50]

To which Nathanael replies:

> *Can there any good thing come out of Nazareth?*

But when Nathaniel is brought to Christ, Christ says to him:

> *Behold an Israelite indeed, in whom is no guile.*

An "Israelite" indeed, in whom truth dwells! Christ says this because He knows to what degree Nathanael is initiated. Whereupon Nathanael realizes that he is dealing with someone who knows quite as much as he does—in fact, with One Who towers above him, Who knows more than he does. And then, in order to stress the reference to initiation, Christ adds:

> *I saw thee before thou comest to me: before that*
> *Philip called thee, when thou wast under the fig*
> *tree, I saw thee.*

The term "fig tree" is here used in exactly the same sense as in connection with Buddha: the fig tree is the "Bodhi Tree." It is the symbol of initiation. What Christ says to him is, I recognize thee as one initiated in the fifth degree. The author of the John Gospel indicates that Christ ranked above an initiate of the fifth degree. Step by step this writer leads us on, in this case by showing us that in the body of Jesus of Nazareth there dwells one who stands above the fifth degree of initiation.

And more. We have just learned that a fifth-degree initiate commands the occult-magical forces residing in the blood flowing down through the generations. He has become one,

191

as it were, with the Folk Soul. Earlier we learned that this Folk Soul expresses itself in the forces inherent in woman. Therefore one who is initiated in the fifth degree will be dealing—in accord with the old conditions—with the female forces. This, of course, must all be pictured spiritually. But Christ's relation to these forces is an entirely new one. He is dealing with the woman who regains her virginity through the Baptism, who recaptures the new, sprouting forces of the virgin state. That was the wholly new factor which the writer of the John Gospel wanted to indicate by saying that a certain current flowed from the Son to the Mother. Everyone with occult knowledge at that time knew quite well that a son, provided he was initiated in the fifth grade, was able to employ magically the folk forces expressed in the folk element of his mother, but Christ demonstrated in a loftier spiritual manner the forces of the woman who had become virgin again.

Thus we see what led up to the Marriage in Cana. We see that what occurred there had to be brought about by an initiate ranking above an initiate of the fifth degree. We are also shown that this fact bore a connection with the folk forces inherent in the female personality. In a marvelous fashion the author of the John Gospel prepares us for what came to pass there. As has been said, we shall approach the miracle question itself later; but in the meantime you can readily imagine that freshly drawn water is different from water that has stood for a time, just as a flower freshly picked is different from one that has been wilting for three days. Differentiations of that sort naturally do not occur to materialistic observation. Water until recently united with the forces of the earth is very different from stale water. In conjunction with the forces residing in the freshly drawn water, one who is initiated as described can work through the forces which are linked with a spiritual relationship such as that between Christ and the Mother who has become virgin. Christ carries farther what the earth is capable of achieving. The earth can transform the water in the grapevine into wine. The Christ, Who has approached the earth and become the Spirit of the Earth, is the spiritual principle that is otherwise active in the entire earth body; so if He is the Christ He must be able to accomplish the same thing as the earth. And the earth, within the vine, transforms water into wine.

The first sign, therefore, performed by Christ Jesus as set forth in the John Gospel is one that links up, so to speak, with what could be accomplished in olden times by an initiate who controlled the forces extending through the blood ties of the generations, as we have just learned from the Books of Kings.

But now we find a continuing increase in the strength of those forces which Christ develops in the body of Jesus of Nazareth—not those that the Christ had within Himself. Therefore, do not ask, Can it be, then that the Christ has to develop? Certainly not. But what did have to be developed through the Christ was the body of Jesus of Nazareth, however purified and ennobled. It had to be guided upward step by step by the Christ; for into this body were to be poured the forces intended to manifest themselves shortly.

The next sign is the healing of the nobleman's son, and the following one, the healing of him who had lain sick for thirty-eight years by the Pool of Bethesda. What intensification have we here of the forces through which Christ worked on this earth? It consists in the fact that now Christ could influence not only those who surrounded Him, those actually present in the flesh. At the Marriage of Cana He caused the water to become wine as the people drank it. He worked upon the etheric bodies of those present; for by the infusion of His force into the etheric bodies of the people surrounding Him the water became wine in their mouths—that is, the water tasted like wine. Now, however, the effect was intended not alone for the body, but for the very depths of the soul; for only in that way could Christ influence the nobleman's son through the mediation of his father, and only thus could He penetrate the sinful soul of him who had lain sick for thirty-eight years. To send His forces into the etheric body alone would not have sufficed. The astral body had to be acted upon, for it is the astral body that sins. By exerting an influence upon the etheric body, water can be turned into wine; but in order to affect another personality it is necessary to penetrate to something deeper. And this demanded that Christ continue to work upon the threefold sheath of Jesus of Nazareth. Note well that Christ does not thereby change, thereby become another. He works upon the threefold sheath of Jesus of Nazareth; and this He does henceforth in such a way that the etheric body can become more independent of the physical body than it was previously.

So the time came when the etheric body in the threefold sheath of Jesus of Nazareth became freer, less closely bound to the physical body. This resulted in greater mastery over the latter: more powerful works could be accomplished, so to speak, in this physical body than hitherto—that is, powerful forces could be employed in it. The potentiality for this was given with the Baptism in the Jordan, and now it was to be further developed with special intensity. All this, however, was to proceed from the spiritual direction. The power of the astral body was to become so great in the threefold sheath of Jesus of Nazareth that the etheric body could acquire the control over the physical body that was indicated. Now, by what means can the astral body attain such power? By acquiring the right feelings, by devotion to the right feelings towards all that takes place around us; above all, by achieving the right attitude towards human egotism. Did Christ accomplish this with the body of Jesus of Nazareth?

194

Did His work result in the right attitude toward all the egotism He encountered, in exposing the fundamentally egotistical character of the souls present? Yes: the author of the John Gospel tells us how Christ appears as the purger of the Temple when he meets with those who do homage to egotism and defile the Temple by making it into a trading center. Thus He was able to say that His astral body had achieved sufficient strength to rebuild His physical body in three days, should it perish. This, too, is indicated by the writer of the John Gospel:

> *Jesus answered and said unto them, Destroy this*
> *temple, and in three days I will raise it up. Then*
> *said the Jews, Forty and six years was this temple*
> *in building, and wilt thou rear it up in three days?*
> *But he spake of the temple of his body.* [John 2: 19–21]

This indicates that the sheath which had been offered Him in sacrifice now has the power to control and master the physical body completely. Now this body, become independent, can move about at will, no longer subject to the laws of the physical world: regardless of the usual laws of the world of space, it can bring about and direct events in the spiritual world. Again we ask, does this occur? Yes: it is indicated in the chapter following the one in which the purging of the Temple is related.

> *There was a man of the Pharisees, named Nicode*
> *mus, a ruler of the Jews: The same came to Jesus*
> *by night, and said unto him . . .* [John 3:1–2]

Why does it say here, "by night?" The explanation that the Jew was simply afraid to go to Jesus by the light of day, so he crept through the window in the night, is as trivial as could be. Anybody can make up explanations of that sort. "By night" means nothing else than that this meeting between Jesus and Nicodemus occurred in the astral world: in the spiritual world, not in the world that surrounds us in our ordinary day consciousness. This means that Christ could now converse with Nicodemus outside the physical body—*by night*, when the physical body is not present, when the astral body is outside the physical and etheric bodies.

Thus the threefold sheath of Jesus of Nazareth was prepared by the Christ, Who dwelt in it, for the acts that were to follow, for what was to be infused into the souls of men. This implied a degree of sovereignty in the soul dwelling in Jesus of Nazareth that would enable it to act upon other bodies. But acting upon another soul is an entirely different matter from the type of influence we discussed yesterday. It comes to light in the next intensification, in the Feeding of the Five Thousand and in the Walking on the Water. To be seen in the flesh without being physically present called for something more; and so powerful had the force become, even at that stage, in the body of Jesus of Nazareth that the Christ was seen not only by His disciples but by others as well. Only, here again we must read the John Gospel carefully; for someone might take the standpoint of readily believing this sign in the case of the disciples, but not in the others.

> *The day following, when the people which stood on the other side of the sea saw that there was no other boat there, save that one whereinto his disciples were entered, and that Jesus went not with his disciples into the boat, but that his disciples were gone away alone;*
>
> *(Howbeit there came other boats from Tiberias nigh unto the place where they did eat the bread, after that the Lord had given thanks:)*
> *When the people therefore saw that Jesus was not there, neither his disciples, they also took shipping, and came to Capernaum, seeking for Jesus.* [John 6:22–25]

Let me emphasize that it says here, *the people who sought Jesus. The narrative continues:*

> *And when they had found him on the other side of the sea, they said unto him, Rabbi, when camest thou hither?*

That implies the same occurrence as in the case of the disciples. It does not say that every ordinary eye saw Him, but that He was seen by those who sought Him and who found Him, by virtue of an increase in their soul force. To say that someone saw another person does not imply that the person seen stood there in the flesh as a spatial figure visible to the physical eye. What in outer life is generally called "taking the Gospel literally" is really anything but that.

If you note that in all of this we have once more to do with what is essentially an intensification, you will understand that again something had to precede it, something to show that Christ had been working on the threefold sheath of Jesus of Nazareth in a manner to render its force ever mightier. His work was that of a healer: He was able to transmit His force to the other's soul. This He could only do by working henceforth in the manner He Himself describes in His conversation with the Samaritan woman by the well:

> *I am the living water.*

Earlier, at the Marriage in Cana He had revealed Himself as an initiate of the fifth grade, having dominion over the elements. Now, He makes it clear that He works in the elements and dwells in them. Later He manifests Himself as one with the forces active on the whole earth and throughout the world. This occurs in the chapter [5:21ff] dealing with Jesus, who has power over life and death by virtue of His power over the forces active in the physical body. That is why this chapter precedes the sign the performance of which called for a still greater force.

Then we see the force still increasing. Yesterday we pointed out that in the sign described as the healing of the man born blind Christ intervenes not only in matters pertaining to life between birth and death, but in that which passes from life to life as the individuality of the human soul. The man was born blind because the divine individuality in him manifested itself in its works; and his sight is to be restored by means of the force Christ infuses into him, a force that will wipe out that which happened—not through the man's personality between birth and death, nor as a result of heredity, but which was incurred by his individuality.

I have repeatedly explained that Goethe's beautiful aphorism, that the eye is formed by means of light, for light,* which proceeded from a deep understanding of the Rosicrucian initiation, has a profoundly occult basis. I pointed out that Schopenhauer was quite right in saying that there can be no light without the eye; but how does the eye originate? Goethe says truly that had it not been for light, no organ sensitive to light, no eye, would ever have come into existence. The eye was created by the light. A single illustration proves this: when animals equipped with eyes migrate into dark caverns they soon lose their sight through lack of light. Light is what formed the eye. If Christ is to imbue a human individuality with a force able to create in him the capacity for making the eye into an organ responsive to light, such as it had not been previously, there must reside in the Christ the spiritual force that lives in light. Let us see where this is indicated in the John Gospel. The healing of the blind man is preceded by the chapter in which we read:

Then spake Jesus unto them, saying,
I am the light of the world. [John 8:12]

The healing of the blind man is narrated only after having been anticipated by the revelation,

"I am the light of the world."

*In *Goethe's Natural Scientific Writings*, vol. 3, page 88 (3rd edition, Berne: 1947), edited by Rudolf Steiner.

Now turn to the last chapter before the Raising of Lazarus and try to visualize some of the disclosures made there. You need only consider the passage reading:

Therefore doth my Father love me, because I lay down my life, that I might take it again. No man taketh it from me, but I lay it down of myself. I have power to lay it down . . . If I do not the works of my Father, believe me not. [John 10:17–18; 37]

Everything said here about the "good shepherd" is intended to indicate Christ's feeling that He is one with the Father, that henceforth He will no longer think of Himself as "I" other than as He is imbued with the Father force. As earlier He said, "I am the light of the world," so now:

I renounce my ego force by receiving the Father in me, so that the Father may work in me, that the primordial principle may permeate me and then flow forth into another being. I lay down my life that I may take it again.

That is what precedes the Raising of Lazarus.

And now, keeping all these considerations in mind, try to grasp the John Gospel in respect to its composition. Notice that up to the Raising of Lazarus, not only is a marvellous intensification indicated in the development of the forces residing in the body of Jesus of Nazareth, but before each increase we are told exactly what it is that acts upon his body. Oh, you will find everything in the John Gospel so closely knit that, if only you understand it, you will realize that not a sentence could be omitted. And the reason that it was so marvellously composed is that it was written as we have said, by one who was initiated by Christ Jesus Himself.

Our point of departure today was the question, What occurred at the Baptism in the Jordan? and we found that the potential capacity for vanquishing death came into the world with the descent of the Christ into the threefold sheath of Jesus of Nazareth. We saw the change that came over the

199

Mother of Jesus of Nazareth with the coming of the Christ: through the influence exercised upon her at the Baptism she became virginal again. The assertion, then, that was to be vouchsafed mankind through the John Gospel is indeed true: When at the Baptism the Christ was born in the body of Jesus of Nazareth, the Mother of Jesus of Nazareth became a virgin.

That is the point of departure of the Gospel according to St. John; and if you grasp it in conjunction with the mighty cosmic influence exercised in the event that occurred on the bank of the Jordan, then you will also understand that an accurate description of such an event—the first description of it—could only have been achieved by one whom Christ Himself had initiated, by the risen Lazarus "whom the Lord loved," thenceforth always mentioned as the disciple whom the Lord loved. It was the risen Lazarus who bequeathed us the Gospel; and he alone was able so firmly to weld its every passage because he had received the mightiest impulse from the greatest initiator, from Christ. He alone could point to something that later Paul, through his initiation, comprehended in a certain sense: that at that moment the germ of victory over death had entered *Earth* evolution.

Hence the momentous words spoken of Him Who hung on the Cross:

Not a bone of him shall be broken. [John 19:36
quoting Psalms 34:20]

Why? Because the form over which Christ must retain His dominion was not to be desecrated. Had they broken His bones, a base human force would have interfered with the power Christ had to exercise even over the bones of Jesus of Nazareth. None must touch that form, for it was written that this should remain wholly subject to Christ's dominion.

This will serve as a starting point for a consideration of the death of Christ, which we will undertake tomorrow.

XI

The lectures thus far given in this cycle should have made it abundantly clear that spiritual-scientific research reveals the Christ event as the most significant one in the entire evolution of mankind, that we must recognize it as having introduced a wholly new impulse into the totality of *Earth* evolution. Something completely new entered this evolution of mankind through the Mystery of Golgotha, through the event of Palestine and everything connected with it before and after, and human evolution must needs have taken a totally different course had the Christ event not intervened. If we are to understand the Mystery of Golgotha we must further examine some of the intimate details of the gradual approach of the Christ Being itself. Naturally, even fourteen lectures do not suffice to tell all there is to be told about a subject embracing the whole world. The author of the John Gospel pointed this out when he said that there was much more to be told, but that the world could not contain the books needed to tell it [John 21:25]. So you will not expect fourteen lectures to mention everything connected with the Christ event and with its narration in the Gospel of St. John and in the other, related ones.

Yesterday and the day before we learned how the dwelling of the Christ Spirit, the Christ Individuality, in the threefold sheath of Jesus of Nazareth gradually made possible all that is described in the John Gospel up to and including the chapter on the Raising of Lazarus. Thus we saw that Christ's task was the gradual development of the threefold corporeality—the physical, the etheric, and the astral body—that had been offered up to Him by the lofty initiate Jesus of Nazareth. But in order to understand exactly what Christ wrought in this threefold sheath we must first get a clear picture of the interrelationship, in man, of the three principles of his being. Hitherto we have only indicated in rough outline that in the waking state the physical body, the etheric or life body, the astral body, and the ego are seen by clairvoyant consciousness as interpenetrating each other, forming an interpermeating whole, and that at night the physical and etheric bodies remain in bed, while the astral body and the ego are withdrawn. Today, in order to describe the Mystery of Golgotha more closely, we must enquire more fully into the exact nature of this interpermeation of the four principles of the human being during day consciousness. In just what manner do the ego and astral body enter the etheric and physical bodies upon awakening in the morning? I can best make this clear by means of a diagram.

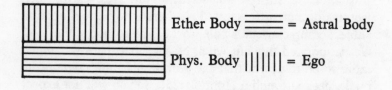

Suppose that in this drawing we had, down here, the physical body, and above it, the etheric body. In the morning, when the astral body and the ego re-enter the physical bodies from the spiritual world, this comes about in such a way that in the main (I beg you to take this qualification seriously) the astral body enters the etheric body, and the ego the physical body. In this drawing, then, the horizontal lines stand for the astral and etheric bodies, the vertical lines for the ego and the physical body.

I said "in the main" because naturally everything in the human being is interpenetrative: the ego, for example, is in the etheric body as well as elsewhere, and so on. But what is referred to here is the principal, the essential interpenetration, and the manner in which the latter prevails most completely can be represented by the diagram.

Next we must enquire, What, exactly, occurred at the Baptism? We have said that the ego of Jesus of Nazareth abandoned his physical, etheric, and astral bodies, leaving this threefold sheath for the Christ Being; so what remained of Jesus of Nazareth we can show in diagram as his physical, etheric, and astral bodies. The ego abandoned the physical body, and in place of the ego of Jesus of Nazareth there entered into this threefold sheath—occupying principally the physical body, though again not exclusively—the Christ Being.

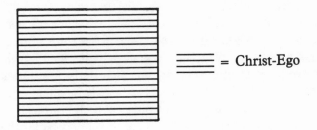 = Christ-Ego

Here we indeed touch the fringe of a deep mystery; for if we consider what really took place at this point we realize that it bears on all the immense complexities of mankind which we have indicated in the last lectures. I told you that everything people have in common, the generic factor, so to speak, in man within a certain group, is to be found in the female element of heredity. I said that the outer facial resemblance among members of the same people is carried down through the generations by woman. The male element, on the other hand, passes on the distinguishing features in man: it is the factor that makes him an individual entity here on earth, that places his ego upon a footing of its own. Great minds who are in touch with the spiritual world have always felt this in the right way, and we can really learn to know and appreciate the utterances of great men who were close to the spiritual world only by penetrating to these depths of cosmic facts.

Look once more at our first diagram and reflect as follows: We have an etheric body, and in it lives the astral body. The astral body is the vehicle of our conceptions, ideas, thoughts, sensations, feelings, and it dwells in the etheric body. But we have learned that it is specifically the task of the etheric body to work upon the physical body effectively, so to say, containing as it does the forces that form it. We must therefore conclude that this etheric body, permeated as it is by the astral body, contains all that makes man a man, all that imprints in him a definite form from within, as it were, proceeding from the spiritual elements. So that whatever produces resemblance among men derives from what works within, and is not merely external; in other words, not from anything bound to his physical body, but from elements associated with his etheric and astral bodies, for these are the inner principles.

For this reason, anyone who can see into such matters will sense that what permeates his etheric and astral bodies comes from the maternal element, whereas all that gives his physical body its peculiar form, imprinted by his ego—the ego dwelling in the physical body—is a paternal heritage.

"My father gave my build to me,
Toward life my sober bearing;

From mother comes my cheerful heart,
My joy in storytelling."*

These words spoken by Goethe are an interpretation of what I showed you in the diagram. "From my father I have my stature" refers to what develops from the ego; and the imagination, the gift of storytelling, inherited from the mother, has its being in the etheric and astral bodies. Verses by great poets are in no way adequately grasped by those who think they have understood them by means of trivial human concepts.

But now we must apply what we have illustrated to the Christ event. From this point of view we must ask, What would have happened to mankind if the Christ event had not taken place? If it had not occurred, the course of human development would have continued as we saw it commence with the post-Atlantean time. We learned that in very old times civilization rested upon a form of love closely linked with tribal relationship, with consanguinity. Those related by blood loved each other. And we saw how in the course of human evolution this bond was increasingly torn.

Now let us pass from the earliest days of human evolution to the time of Christ Jesus' appearance. While in most ancient epochs marriage was always consummated within one and the same tribe, you will find that during the Roman dominion—and that is the time of the Christ event—the custom of endogamy was increasingly ignored, that a great variety of peoples were thrown together as a result of the Roman expeditions, and that the "close marriage" had very largely to give way to exogamy, the "distant marriage." It was necessary for blood ties to lose their strength in the evo-

_____

*From "Zahme Xenien" VI, 32, in Poems, vol. 3, first section; published by H. Düntzer (Kurschner German National Literatur, Goethe's Works III, 1).

lution of mankind because men were destined to take their stand upon their own ego.

Assuming, now, that Christ had not come to provide new forces, to replace the old love engendered by blood ties with a new spiritual love, what would have happened? In that case love, the factor that brings men together, would gradually have vanished from the face of the earth. The love that unites men would have perished in man's nature. Without the Christ the human race would have lived to see the dying out of love of one person for another. Men would have been driven into their own segregated individualities. Looked at only from the point of view of external science, these things do not disclose the profound truths underlying them. If you were to examine—not chemically, but by the means at the disposal of spiritual research—the blood of present-day man and compare it with that of people who lived several thousand years before the appearance of Christ, you would find that it had changed, had taken on a character tending to make it less and less a vehicle capable of bearing love. Imagine, in ancient times, a man of insight who could see deep into the course of human development, who could foretell what would needs come to pass should only the one antiquated tendency persist without the intervention of the Christ event: how would the course of future evolution present itself to an initiate of that sort? What images would he have had to evoke in the human soul to indicate what would happen in the future if love in the soul, the Christ love, failed to replace the love arising from blood ties in the same measure as the latter disappeared? He had to say: If men become ever more isolated, more hardened in their own ego; if the lines separating souls become ever more marked so that souls understand each other less and less, then men of the outer world will fall increasingly into discord and contention, and the dissension of all against all will usurp the place of love on earth.

And this is indeed what would have ensued if evolution had proceeded on the basis of blood relationship *without* the intervention of Christ. All men would inevitably have been involved in the conflict of all against all which will come to pass in any case, but only for those who have not become imbued in the right way with the Christ principle. That is what a prophetic seer beheld as an end of the *Earth* evolution, and well could it fill his soul with terror: souls no longer understand each other, hence they must rage, soul against soul.

I have explained that only gradually can men become united through the Christ principle. In Tolstoi and Solovyev I gave you an example that showed how two noble spirits, each thinking to proclaim the real Christ, can hold such contradictory views that one of them considers the other the Antichrist—for that is what Solovyev believed Tolstoi to be. The conflict of beliefs at first present in the souls of men would gradually come to expression in the outer world, that is, men would rage against each other. That would be the inevitable consequence of the development of the blood principle. It would be pointless to object here that in spite of the Christ event we still see discord and contention on all sides, that we are still far from any realization of Christian love. I have told you that we are only at the beginning of Christian evolution. The great impulse has been given which will enable the Christ to inhabit ever more the souls of men in the further course of earth development, and to unite them in a spiritual way. What still exists today in the way of discord and contention, and will lead to even greater excesses, is a result of the fact that hitherto mankind has become permeated with the real Christ principle only to the most negligible extent. Conditions that have existed among men from time immemorial still hold sway and can be overcome only by degrees, inasmuch as the Christ impulse will flow into mankind but slowly and gradually.

That, then, is a picture of what would have been foreseen in pre-Christian times by one who had clairvoyantly penetrated the future course of human evolution. He could have put it this way: I have been vouchsafed a remnant of the old power of clairvoyance. In primeval times all men were able to see into the spiritual world by means of a dim, dull clairvoyance, which has gradually vanished. But the possibility still exists, like a heritage from those ancient times, to penetrate the spiritual world in an abnormal, dreamlike state. In this way there can be seen something of what lies beneath the outer surface of things.

All the old legends, fairy stories, and myths, which truly are fraught with a wisdom deeper than is to be found in modern science, tells us that in the olden times the capacity for entering exceptional states was very widespread. Call such states dreams, if you like; they nevertheless heralded events. But they did not provide sufficient wisdom to protect men from the conflict of all against all. The sage of old emphasized this in the strongest possible terms, saying, We are heir to a primeval wisdom which people of the Atlantean era were able to perceive in abnormal states. Even now there are isolated men who can discern it under the same conditions; and what is heralded there is the course the near future will take. But the revelations of those dreams inspired no confidence: they were deceptive and destined to become ever more so. This was how a teacher taught in pre-Christian times, and in that form did he proclaim it to the people.

That is why it is of significance that, appreciating the whole intensity and power of the Christ impulse one is led to the comprehension of a certain great truth. In a world lacking the Christ impulse, the isolation and segregation of men and their mutual antagonism would bring about something like a struggle for existence—similar to the materialistic-Darwinistic theory foisted upon us today—a struggle for existence such as reigns in the animal kingdom, but which should have no place in the world of men. Somewhat grotesquely we might say, when the earth has run its course it will present the picture of humanity painted by certain materialists in line with a Darwinistic theory borrowed from the animal world! Today however, when applied to mankind, this theory is wrong. It is correct for the animal kingdom because there no impulse governs which could transform discord into love. Through His deed, Christ, as a spiritual force in humanity, will refute all materialistic Darwinism.

But in order to grasp this, one must understand that in the outer sense world men can eliminate the antagonistic attitude arising from their differences of opinion, feelings, and actions only by combatting and adjusting within themselves all that would otherwise flow out into the external world. No one is going to quarrel with a different opinion in the soul of another if he first fights against all that must be combatted in himself, if he establishes harmony among the various principles of his being. He will confront the outer world as one who loves, not as one who quarrels. It is all a matter of diverting the conflict from the outer world to the inner man. The forces holding sway in human nature must battle each other within man.

Two conflicting opinions must be looked at as follows: This is one opinion, it is tenable. That is the other, it is also tenable. But if I recognize only the one and consider justifiable only what I want, resisting the other, then I shall be involved in a struggle on the physical plane. To affirm my own opinion alone is to be selfish; to consider my actions the only justifiable ones means being egotistical. If I consider the other man's opinion and endeavor to create harmony within myself, my attitude toward the other will then be a very different one. Only then will I begin to understand him. Diverting external strife into another channel—the harmonizing of inner human forces—that would be another way of expressing the idea of progress in the evolution of mankind. The possibility of inner concord, of finding the way to harmonize the resisting forces within, this had to be bestowed upon man by the Christ. Christ gives man the power first of all to eliminate discord within himself. Without Christ this could never be achieved. In respect of outer strife, the ancient, pre-Christian people rightly looked upon one special form of it as the ultimate horror: the child's strife against father and mother. Also, in the days when men knew what course evolution would take lacking the Christ-impulse, patricide was considered the most terrible and abhorrent of all crimes. That was made very clear by those wise men of old who foresaw the coming of Christ. But they also knew what the inevitable result would be in the outer world if the battle were not first waged in man's own soul.

Let us examine our own inner nature. We have learned that where the etheric and astral bodies interpenetrate, the mother holds sway, while the father comes to expression in the ego-permeated physical body. In other words, the mother, the female element, governs in all that pertains to the traits we share with others, to the generic, to all that constitutes our inner life in so far as it expresses itself in wisdom and in conceptions; whereas every quality arising from a union of the ego and the physical body, in the externally differentiated form—all that makes man an ego—derives from the father, the male element. What is it, then, above all things that the ancient sages, who thought along these lines, had to demand of men? They had to insist on a clear understanding of the relation of the physical body and the ego to the etheric and astral bodies: on a mental grasp of the maternal and paternal elements. By reason of having an etheric and an astral body man has the mother principle in him. In addition to his outer mother, the mother of the physical plane, he has, so to speak, the maternal element within him, the *Mother*. Besides his physical father, he has within him the paternal element, the *Father*. The proper adjustment of the relation between this inner father and inner mother is something that was held up to men as a lofty ideal to strive for. Failure to harmonize these two elements inevitably results in spreading discord from within out into the physical world with devastating consequences. Therefore, said the old sage: Man's task is to bring about harmony within himself between the paternal and the maternal elements. If he does not succeed, there will appear in the world what we must recognize as the ultimate horror.

What we have just expressed in anthroposophical phraseology, so to say, was proclaimed to mankind by the ancient sages somewhat as follows: In primeval times we inherited a primordial wisdom. Even today, men can participate in it when in an abnormal state. But the possibility of entering this state is becoming ever more remote, and even the old initiation cannot lead beyond a certain point in human evolution.

Let us once more consider this old initiation as we described it in the last lectures: what occurred there? Out of the complex composed of physical body, etheric body, astral body, and ego, the etheric and astral bodies were lifted out, but the ego remained behind. Hence there could be no question of self-consciousness during the three and a half days of initiation. It was extinguished and replaced by a form of consciousness from the higher spiritual world, instilled by the priest-initiator who guided the candidate throughout and placed his own ego at the latter's disposal. Now, what exactly was the result of this? Something occurred that was expressed in a formula that will strike you as strange; but when you have understood it, it will no longer seem so. It was expressed as follows: When a man was initiated in the old sense, the maternal element emerged and the paternal

211

element remained behind; that is, the candidate killed the paternal element within himself and united with the mother in him. In other words, he killed his father within him and wedded his mother. So when the old initiate had lain three and a half days in the lethargic state, he had united with his mother and had killed the father within himself. He had become fatherless and this had to be so, for he had to renounce his individuality and dwell in a higher spiritual world. He became one with his people. But what lived in his people was precisely expressed by the maternal element. He became one with the entire organism of his people; he became exactly what Nathanael was, what was always designated by the name of the people in question—in Jewry, an *"Israelite,"* among Persians a *"Persian."*

There can never be any wisdom in the world other than the wisdom proceeding from the Mysteries—no other is possible. Those who learn the corresponding wisdom in the Mysteries become messengers for the outer world and the latter learns from them what is beheld in the Mysteries. But it was acquired in line with the old wisdom which was attained by means of uniting with the inner mother and killing the father in oneself. But this hereditary wisdom cannot help man past a certain point in evolution. Something different, something wholly new, had to replace the old wisdom. Had mankind continued indefinitely to receive the old wisdom gained in this way, it would have been driven, as already stated, into the conflict of all against all. Opinion would be arrayed against opinion, feeling against feeling, will against will; and that terrifying, gruesome image of the future, where man would unite with his mother and kill his father, would come true. All this was portrayed in pregnant pictures, in great and mighty images, by the old initiates who, though initiated, looked for the coming of Christ; and the imprint of this wisdom of the pre-Christian sages has been preserved in the legends and myths.

We need only recall the name of Oedipus. Here, we can relate something in which the ancient sages expressed what they had to say on this subject. The old Greek legend, presented in so mighty and grandiose a way by the Greek tragedians, runs as follows: There was a king in Thebes, and his name was Laios. His spouse was Iokaste. For a long time they had no progeny. Then Laios enquired of the Oracle of Delphi whether he could not be vouchsafed a son and the oracle gave him the answer: If thou wilt have a son it will be one who shall kill thee. In a state of intoxication—that is, in a state of dimmed consciousness—Laios begot a son. Oedipus was born. Laios knew that this was the son who would kill him, he therefore resolved to abandon the child; and in order to insure his complete annihilation he caused his feet to be pierced. Then he was left to die. But a shepherd found the child and took pity on him. He brought him to Corinth, and there Oedipus was reared in the royal household. When he was grown he learned of the oracle's prophesy: that he would kill his father and wed his mother. There was no escaping it: on account of being taken for the king's son he had to leave the place where he was reared. On his way he met his real father and, without recognizing him, killed him. He came to Thebes; and because he was able to answer the Sphinx' questions and solve the riddle of the grisly monster that led so many to their death, the Sphinx had to kill itself. Thus, for the time being, Oedipus was his country's benefactor. He was made king and received the queen's hand in marriage—his mother's hand! Without knowing it, he had killed his father and united with his mother. He now ruled as king; but by reason of having acquired his rule in this way and of the horror that clung to him, he brought untold misery upon his country. In Sophocles' drama we finally encounter him as blinded, as one who has destroyed his own eyesight.

This is an image that originated in the old temples of wisdom; and what was meant to be expressed by it was that in a certain respect Oedipus could still make contact, in the old sense, with the spiritual world. How had he arrived at a relationship with the spiritual world? His father had consulted the oracle. Those oracles were the last heritage of the old clairvoyance, but they were powerless to establish peace in the outer world. They could not provide the harmony between the paternal and the maternal elements which man was to attain.

The circumstance that Oedipus solved the Sphinx' riddle indicates that he was intended to represent the sort of man who had acquired a certain old type of clairvoyance simply through heredity; that is, he knew the nature of man to the extent to which the last remnants of the old primordial wisdom could provide such cognition. But never could it suffice to stem the raging of man against man, as symbolized by the patricide and the union with the mother. Although in touch with primordial wisdom, Oedipus is unable, by its means, to see through the coherence of things. This old wisdom no longer induces seership—that is what the old sages wanted to proclaim. Had it bestowed vision in the sense of the old blood-ties, then the blood would have spoken when Oedipus contronted his father and his mother. But the blood no longer spoke! That is a graphic presentation of the disintegration of primordial wisdom.

What had to happen in order that once and for all the inner harmonious balance might be found between the maternal and paternal elements, between man's own ego possessing the father element, and the mother principle? The Christ impulse had to come.—And now we can peer from still another angle into certain depths of the Marriage in Cana of Galilee. We are told:

The mother of Jesus was there: And both Jesus was called, and his disciples, to the marriage.

214

Jesus—or better, Christ—was to be the great example for humanity of a being who had achieved the inner concord between himself—that is, his ego—and the mother principle. At the Marriage in Cana of Galilee He indicated:

Something passes from me to you. . .

This was a new form of passing from me to you. It was no longer in the old sense, but implied a renewal of the whole relationship. It meant the lofty and enduring ideal of inner balance achieved without first killing the father—without withdrawing from the physical body; it meant finding the balance with the maternal principle in the ego. Now the time had come when the human being learns to combat within himself the excessive power of egotism, of the ego principle; when he learns to correlate it with the maternal principle holding sway in the etheric and astral bodies.

So we find in the Marriage in Cana a beautiful image of the relation of the ego, the paternal principle, to the mother principle: it represents the inner harmony, the love, that exists in the outer world between Christ Jesus and His Mother. It was intended as an image of the harmonious inward balance between the ego and the maternal principle. This had not existed previously; it came about through the deed of Christ Jesus. But inasmuch as it came about through the deed of Christ, it brought with it the only possible refutation—that is, through the deed—of all that would inevitably have come to pass under the influence of the legacies of the ancient wisdom which would have led to the killing of the father and the uniting of the mother with her son.

Just what is it that the Christ principle combats? The old sage, contemplating the Christ and comparing the old way with the new, could put it this way: If the union with the mother is sought in the old way, no good can result for humanity. But if it is sought in the new way, as shown in the Marriage at Cana—if man unites with the astral and etheric

215

bodies dwelling within him in this way—then salvation and peace and fraternity will spread among men more and more as time passes and the old principle of killing the father and wedding the mother will be resisted. So the antagonistic element which the Christ had to eradicate was not the ancient wisdom, the latter did not need to be combatted. It lost its power on its own and gradually exhausted itself. We see how people like Oedipus fall victim to discord precisely by putting their faith in it. On the other hand, the evil would not cease of itself if the new wisdom were ignored; that is, if people clung rigidly to the old principle and remained insensible to the manner in which the Christ impulse acts. Not to cling to the obsolete principle, not to keep rigidly to the old lines, but to learn what had come into the world through Christ—that is what was felt to be the greatest step forward.

Do we find this, too, suggested anywhere? We do: legends and myths are indeed fraught with the deepest wisdom. There is a legend you will not find in the Gospels, but it is none the less a Christian legend as well as a Christian truth. It runs this way: Once upon a time there was a married couple, and for a long time this couple had no son. Then it was revealed to the mother in a dream—note this well—that she would have a son, but that this son would first kill his father and then unite with his mother, and that he would bring frightful disaster upon his whole tribe.

Again we have a dream, corresponding to the oracle in the case of Oedipus; that is, we are again dealing with what had come down from primeval clairvoyance. What was to happen was revealed to the mother in the old way. But did this revelation suffice to make her see clearly the conditions governing in the world? to avert the disaster? Let us ask the legend, which informs us further:

Under the influence of the wisdom gleaned in her dream, the mother took the child she had borne to the island of

216

Kariot and there abandoned him. But he was found by the queen of a neighboring realm, who being childless, reared him herself. Later the royal couple had a child of their own, and the foundling soon felt himself discriminated against; and being of a passionate temperament he slew the son of the royal pair. Now he could no longer remain; he had to flee, and he came to the court of Pilate, the Governor, where he was soon made overseer in the household. But one day he came to blows with his neighbor; and in the struggle he killed him, knowing not that it was his own father. Circumstances later led to his wedding his neighbor's wife, who, unbeknownst to him, was his mother.

This foundling was Judas Iscariot. When he became aware of his terrible position he fled again. And nowhere did he find compassion save in Him Who had mercy for all who approached Him, Who not only sat at the table with publicans and sinners but Who, though seeing all, took unto Himself even this great sinner; for it was His mission to work not only for the righteous, but for all men, and to lead them out of sin to salvation. In this way Judas Iscariot came into the environment of Christ Jesus. And he brought the calamity which had been foretold, and which was destined to be fulfilled,—as Schiller says: "An evil deed its own curse bears within: It multiplies, begetting evil brood."*—into the sphere of Christ Jesus.

Judas became the betrayer of Christ Jesus. True, everything that was destined to come about through him had already been fulfilled in the murder of his father and the marriage with his mother; but he survived, so to speak, as a tool, because he was to be the evil instrument for bringing about good, thereby performing one more act beyond the fulfillment of his destiny.

---

*From Friedrich Schiller's drama *The Piccolomini*; Act 5, Scene 1.

The individuality presented to us in the figure of Oedipus loses his sight, as a result of the evil he has wrought, the moment he realizes what he has done. But the other, whose identical destiny originated in his connection with the inherited primordial wisdom, does not become blind: he was chosen to fulfill destiny, to do the deed that would lead to the Mystery of Golgotha, that would bring about the physical death of Him Who is *"the Light of the World"* and Who enkindles the Light of the World in healing the man born blind. Oedipus had to lose his sight; to the blind man, Christ gave sight. Yet He died at the hands of one who, like Oedipus, was chosen to exemplify the gradual extinction of the ancient wisdom in mankind, to expose its insufficiency in the matter of bringing salvation and peace and love. For these to come, the Christ-impulse was indispensable, and the event of Golgotha had to take place. There had first to come about something whose outer reflection is shown us in the relation between the Jesus-Christ Ego and His Mother at the Marriage in Cana of Galilee.

And one thing more was needed as well. The writer of the John Gospel describes it as follows: There beneath the Cross stood the Mother, and there stood the disciple "whom the Lord loved," Lazarus-John, whom He Himself had initiated and through whom the wisdom of Christianity was to be handed down to posterity; he through whom man's astral body was to be so powerfully influenced as to render it capable of harboring the Christ principle. There in the human astral body the Christ principle was to live, and it was John's mission to pour the Christ principle into this astral body. But in order that this might come to pass, this Christ principle, raying down from the Cross, had still to unite with the etheric principle, with the Mother. That is why from the Cross Christ called down the words:

From this hour forth, this is thy
mother—and this is thy son. [John 19:26–27]

That means, He unites His wisdom with the maternal principle.

Thus we see the profundity, not only of the Gospels, but of all the interrelationships in the Mysteries. Truly, the old legends are related to the prophesies and Gospels of more recent times as is presage to fulfillment. In the legends of Oedipus and of Judas we are clearly shown that once upon a time there was a divine, primordial wisdom. But this wisdom vanished: a new wisdom has to come. And this new wisdom will carry men forward to a point that would never have been attainable through the old wisdom. The Oedipus legend tells us what would have had to occur without the intervention of the Christ impulse; and the nature of the opponents to the Christ, the rigid clinging to the ancient wisdom, is made clear in the Judas legend. But the principle which even the old legends and myths had declared inadequate is brought to us in a new light through the new revelation, through the Gospel. The Gospel gives us the answer to what the old legends expressed in images of the old wisdom. In legends we were told that nevermore can the old wisdom provide what humanity needs for the future; but the Gospel, the new wisdom, says: I bring tidings of what mankind needs, of what could never have come without the influence of the Christ principle, without the event of Golgotha.

XII

We have arrived at an important point in our studies—a sort of climax—hence we may expect to encounter various difficult passages in elucidating the Gospels. I may therefore be permitted at the beginning of these expositions, to preface the continuation of what was said yesterday with a short survey of the major features thus far treated.

We know that the nature of mankind's development was essentially different in remote times from what it is today, and we know that the human being shows an increasingly different form as our retrospect reaches farther and farther back to earlier conditions. It has already been mentioned that from our own time, which we may call the Central European cultural epoch, we can look back successively to the Greco-Latin time, to the Egypto-Chaldean period, and then to the era in which the ancient Persian people was led by Zarathustra. Beyond that we arrive at the remote Indian civilization, so very different from ours; and that brings us to a period of cultural evolution that followed immediately upon a great and mighty catastrophe. This cataclysm, running its course in tempestuous events in the air and in the water element, led to the disappearance of that continent which mankind had inhabited before the Indian civilization —ancient Atlantis, situated between Europe-Africa, and America—and to the migration of its people, westward to America and on the other side to the lands of Europe, Asia, and Africa, which had gradually taken on their present configuration. This Atlantean age, especially in the early part, produced human beings who were very differently constituted in respect of their soul from present-day mankind; and what interests us primarily in human evolution is precisely what pertains to the soul, for we know that everything corporeal is a result of psycho-spiritual development.

What was the nature of the soul life in this ancient Atlantean age? We know that at that time human consciousness was very different from what it became later, and that in a certain respect man had an ancient clairvoyance, but that he was not yet capable of any pronounced self-consciousness, of ego-consciousness. This is achieved only by learning to distinguish oneself from outer objects, and people of that time were not quite able to do this.

Let us imagine for a moment what would happen in our time if we were unable to distinguish ourselves from our surroundings—let us consider the matter in a concise way. Nowadays we ask, Where are the confines of my being? And with a certain justification we answer, from our present-day standpoint, The confines of my human entity are where my skin divides me off from my surroundings. People imagine that they consist only of what their skin encloses, and that everything else is made up of outer objects which they perceive and from which they distinguish themselves. They believe this because they know that if some part is removed from within their skin they are no longer a complete human being, nor can be. From a certain standpoint it is quite correct to say that if you cut off a piece of a man's flesh he is no longer a whole human being.

On the other hand, we also know that we inhale air with every breath. And to the question, where is this air, the answer is, all around us—everywhere where our environment makes contact with us: that is the air we will have within us in the next moment. Now it is outside us, now in us. Cut off this air, remove it, and you can no longer exist. You are less whole than you would be if the hand within your skin were cut off. So the truth of the matter is that we are not bounded by our skin. The surrounding air is part of us, it enters and leaves us, and we have no right arbitrarily to fix the skin as our boundary.

If people would come to understand this—it would have to be arrived at theoretically, as perception provides no means of observing it—it would lead them to ponder on matters not forced upon their attention by the outer world itself. If a man were at all times able to see the air current passing into him, spreading, being transformed, and passing out again, it would never occur to him to say, This hand is more a part of me than the air I inhale. He would count the air as part of himself, and would suspect hallucinations if he fancied himself an independent being capable of existing without his environment.

No such delusion could exist for the Atlantean, for his observation clearly showed him a different state of affairs. He saw the objects in his environment not in sharp outline, but surrounded by colored auras. He did not see a plant as we see it, but more as we see the street lamps on a foggy autumn evening: everything was surrounded by a great colored aura. That was because there is spirit—spiritual beings —in and among all things of the outer world, which the Atlantean could perceive with his dim clairvoyance of that time. As the fog fills the space between the lights, so there are spiritual beings everywhere in space. The Atlantean saw these spiritual beings just as you see the fog, hence they constituted for him a kind of vaporous aura investing all outer objects. These themselves were indistinct; but because he saw the spirit he also saw everything of a spiritual nature that streamed in and out of him. For the same reason he saw himself as a component of his whole environment. He saw currents flowing into his body from all sides, currents you cannot see today. Air is merely the densest substance that

222

enters us: there are far more tenuous ones. Man has lost the power of discerning spirit because he no longer has the ancient dim clairvoyance; but the man of Atlantis saw the spiritual currents streaming in and out, just as your finger, were it conscious, would see the blood coursing through it and would know that it must wither if it were torn off. Just as the finger would feel, if conscious, so the Atlantean felt himself to be a member of an organism. He felt the currents streaming in through his eyes and ears, and so forth; and he knew that if he were to force himself out of their reach he could not remain a human being. He felt as though poured out into the whole outer world.

The man of Atlantis saw the spiritual world, but he could not distinguish himself from it: he lacked anything like a strong ego sense—self-consciousness in its present sense. The opportunity to develop this was provided by the fading from his spiritual view of all that had emphasized his dependence upon his environment. The cessation of that awareness enabled him to develop his self-consciousness, his egoity, and to do this was the task of post-Atlantean man. After the great Atlantean catastrophe people were organized in such a way that the spiritual world receded from their consciousness, and that they gradually learned to see the outer physical world of the senses ever more clearly and distinctly. However, nothing that evolves in the world takes place all at once, but step by step; it proceeds slowly and gradually. And thus the old dim clairvoyance vanished slowly and by degrees. Even today, under given conditions, it is still found as an old heritage in certain people and in mediumistic natures. Something that had reached its climax in a certain era gradually becomes extinct. In the earliest period of post-Atlantean times, ordinary people still retained a great deal of the gift of clairvoyance; and what these people saw in the spiritual world was continually supplemented, expanded, and animated by the initiates who were guided to the spiritual world by the methods described in an earlier lecture, and who thus became the messengers of what in former times had been seen to a certain extent by all men.

Better than any external historical research, legends, and myths—especially those linked with the oracle sanctuaries—have preserved for us what is true of those old times. In the oracle temples specially selected people were directed into abnormal states—a dream state, or mediumistic state, as one might say—by reducing them to a state of consciousness duller and darker than the ordinary waking state. They were in a condition of diminished consciousness, where they were surrounded by outer objects which, however, they did not see. This was not like the ancient state of clairvoyance, but an intermediate state, half dreamlike, half in the nature of clairvoyance. Now, if information was sought concerning certain particular circumstances in the world, or the right mode of procedure in some special matter, the oracles were consulted; for in them was to be found the old dim clairvoyance as a heritage of the ancient faculty.

At the beginning of his evolution, then, man was endowed with wisdom. Wisdom streamed into him. But this wisdom gradually dwindled away. Even the initiates in their abnormal states—for they had to be led into the spiritual world by the withdrawal of their etheric body—could henceforth attain to only an unreliable observation of the spiritual world. As a result of these conditions, however, those who were not only initiated in the old sense, but who had advanced with the times and were prophets of the future, realized that a new impulse was indispensable for humanity. An ancient heritage of wisdom had been bestowed upon mankind when it descended from divine-spiritual heights, but it became ever more obscured. In the beginning all men possessed it, later only the few who were led into special states of consciousness in the oracles, finally only the initiates, and so forth.

The day must come—thus spoke the old initiates who knew the signs of the time—in which this ancient heritage will have dwindled to the point where it is no longer capable of leading and guiding humanity. This would mean that man would fall a prey to uncertainty in the world. It would express itself in his willing, his acting, and his feeling. And with the gradual dwindling of wisdom men would become their own unwise leaders. Their ego would wax increasingly strong, so that with the recession of wisdom every individual would seek truth in his own ego, would develop his own feelings and will—every man for himself—and men would become ever more isolated, more alienated from each other, and they would understand each other less and less. Since each man wants to do his own thinking—in thoughts that no longer flow out of a unified wisdom—none can understand the other's thoughts. Human feelings, no longer guided by universal wisdom, must eventually come into mutual conflict, as must also human actions. All men would act, think, and feel in opposition to each other, and ultimately mankind would be split up altogether into an aggregation of quarrelling and fighting individuals.

And what was the outer, physical sign that appeared as the expression of this development? It was the transformation mankind experienced in the blood. In very ancient times, as we know, endogamy was customary. People married only within the blood-related tribe. But this custom yielded increasingly to exogamy. The blood of mutually alien tribes became mixed; and that explains the decrease, the dwindling, of the heritage deriving from a remote past.

Let us once more recall Goethe's words which we quoted yesterday:

"My father gave my build to me,

225

Toward life my sober bearing.
From mother comes my cheerful heart,
My joy in storytelling."

We connected this assertion with the fact that what the etheric body comprises derives from the maternal element, as handed down from generation to generation, so that every man bears in his own etheric body the legacy of the maternal element, and in his physical body, that of the paternal element. Now, by reason of consanguinity, the inheritance, perpetuating itself from etheric body to etheric body, was very potent, and from it derived the old faculty of clairvoyance. The offspring of endogamy inherited with the related blood the old capacity for wisdom in the etheric body. But as blood became more and more mixed—as a result of increasing intermarriage among tribes—the possibility of handing down the ancient wisdom diminished; for as we said yesterday, human blood gradually altered, and the mixing of different bloods obscured the ancient wisdom more and more.

In other words, the blood—bearer of inherited maternal attributes—became ever less fitted to transmit the old faculty of clairvoyance. It simply developed in such a way that people became ever less able to see into the spiritual world. Physically considered, therefore, human blood altered in a manner to render it increasingly incapable of bearing the old wisdom that once had guided man so surely, falling instead more and more into the opposite extreme, becoming the bearer of egotism—that is, of a quality that leads men, as egos, to individual isolation and mutual antagonism. And for the same reason it gradually lost its power of uniting men in love.

We are, of course, still involved in this process of deterioration taking place in the human blood because, in as far as it has its origin in an ancient epoch, it will follow its lingering course to the end of *Earth* evolution. Therefore an impulse was needed in humanity capable of counteracting this condition. Through consanguinity men would be led into error and misery, as the old wise men tell us in legends and myths. Men could no longer rely on the legacies of an ancient wisdom: even the oracles, asked for information and advice, divulged only what led to savage conflicts and quarrels. The oracle had foretold, for example, that Laios and Jocasta would have a son who would kill his father and wed his mother. Nevertheless, in the face of this legacy of oracle wisdom, nothing could at that time prevent the blood from falling more and more a prey to error: Oedipus does kill his father and does wed his mother. He commits patricide and incest.

What the old sage meant was this: Once upon a time men possessed wisdom; but even had it been preserved, the development of the ego must inevitably have proceeded, and egotism would have grown so strong that blood would rage against blood. Blood is no longer fitted to lead men upwards when it is guided only by the ancient wisdom. And thus the clairvoyant initiate who gave us the original picture of the Oedipus legend wished to set up a warning for mankind, saying: That is what would happen to you if nothing came to supersede the old oracle wisdom. And in the Judas legend there is preserved even more clearly an indication of what the old oracle wisdom would have led to. Judas' mother, too, was prophetically told that her son would kill his father and wed his mother, thereby conjuring up untold misery. Yet it all came to pass in spite of the foreknowledge. This means that the primeval, inherited wisdom is not capable of saving man from the abyss into which he must fall unless a new impulse reaches mankind.

If we now look more closely into the causes of all this we must ask, Why was it inevitable that the ancient wisdom should become unfitted to dominate humanity? The answer to this question can be found by examining more carefully the origin of the old wisdom in its relation to mankind. I have already indicated that in the old Atlantean age a connection existed between the physical body and the etheric body of man that differed greatly from the later relationship. In regard to two of the principles of man's nature it can be said that the physical and etheric bodies are so related that they approximately coincide, especially in the region of the head; but this is only the case in our own time. Looking back to the Atlantean period we find the etheric head protruding far beyond its physical counterpart; the etheric body extended past the physical body, particularly in the head region. Now, in the Atlantean epoch human evolution proceeded in such a way that the outline of the physical and of the etheric body became more and more coincident, especially in the head: the etheric body kept withdrawing into the physical body, thereby naturally altering this member of the human being.

That, then, is the essential feature of this phase of human evolution: the etheric body of the human head withdraws more and more into the physical aspect of the head until the two come to coincide. Now, as long as the etheric body was outside the physical head it was subject to conditions quite different from the subsequent ones. It was in touch, on all sides, with currents, with other spiritual beings; and the substance of what thus streamed in and out provided the faculty of clairvoyance in Atlantean times. So the capacity for clairvoyance was due to the incomplete coincidence of the physical and etheric bodies in the head region, a condition admitting from all sides currents endowing the etheric head with clairvoyance. Then followed the time when the etheric body withdrew into the physical body. In a certain way—not completely—it tore itself away from these currents. It began to cut itself off from the currents which had provided the capacity for clairvoyantly penetrating the wisdom of the world. Conversely, when in the old initiations a man's etheric body was withdrawn, his etheric head became interpermeated once more with the surrounding currents, and he became clairvoyant.

Now, had this contact between the etheric body and the surrounding world been severed at one stroke, in the middle of the Atlantean age, the old clairvoyance would have vanished far more rapidly than was actually the case. No remnants of it would have remained for the post-Atlantean time, nor would mankind of a later age have retained any recollection of it. As it happened, however, man preserved a certain contact with the outer currents. Something else took place as well. This etheric body that had cut itself off from the currents of its environment retained, nevertheless, certain remnants of the former capacity for wisdom. Keep well in mind that at the end of the Atlantean epoch, after man had drawn his etheric body into himself, there remained in it a sort of fund, the residue of what had once come to it from without—a small saving, if I may use the term: as if a son had a father, the father is earning money, and the son draws upon him according to his needs. In the same way, man drew upon his environment for all the wisdom he needed, up to the time when his etheric body severed the connection. Keeping to our simile, let us now assume that the son loses his father, there remains for him but a certain portion of his father's money, and he earns nothing to add to it. In time he will come to the end of it and have nothing left. That is the position in which the human being found himself. He had torn himself loose from his father-wisdom, had added nothing to it through his own endeavor, and subsisted on it into the Christian era—indeed, even now he is still living on his inheritance, not on anything he has earned. He lives on his capital, so to speak. In the earliest part of post-Atlantean development a bit of the capital was still left, though without his having himself earned the wisdom; he lived on the interest, as it were, and occasionally requested an additional sum from the initiates. But ultimately the coin of ancient wisdom lost its currency; and when it was given to Oedipus it no longer had any value. This old wisdom did not save him from the most frightful transgression, nor did it save Judas.

That is what took place in the course of human evolution. How did it come about that man gradually exhausted his capital of wisdom? Because earlier he had already absorbed two kinds of spiritual beings into himself: the Luciferic beings, and later, as a consequence of these, the Ahrimanic or Mephistophelean beings. These prevented him from acquiring anything in addition to the store of old wisdom, for they acted upon his being as follows: the Luciferic beings tended to corrupt his passions and feelings, while the Ahrimanic, the Mephistophelean beings were more concerned with outwardly distorting his view of the world. Had the Luciferic beings not intervened in *Earth* evolution, man would not have acquired the interest in the physical world which draws him down beneath his true status. If, as a result of the Luciferic influence, the Mephistophelian, the Ahrimanic, the Satanic beings had not taken a hand, man would know, and would always have known, that underlying every object of the senses there is spirit. He would look through the surface of the sense world upon the spirit. But Ahriman infused into human observation something like a dark smoke cloud that prevents penetration to the spiritual. Through Ahriman's agency man is enmeshed in lies, in *maya*, in illusion. These are the two beings that prevent man from earning any increment to the store of ancient wisdom once bestowed upon humanity; and as a consequence, this heritage has dwindled away and gradually become wholly useless.

Nevertheless, in a certain other respect evolution held to its course. During the Atlantean time, the human etheric body merged with the physical body. It was man's misfortune, so to speak, to be forced to experience the influence of Lucifer and Ahriman in his physical body in this physical world just at a time when he was God-forsaken, as it were. It was his fate. The result was that the old heritage of wisdom became useless precisely by reason of the influence of the physical body, of living in the physical body. He gathered his wisdom from his father's treasury, so to speak—from the ancient fund of wisdom. His source of supplies was outside his physical body, because he himself was outside it in respect of his etheric body. This source had gradually dried up. In order to augment his fund of wisdom, man would have needed a treasury in his own body. But this he did not have. Consequently, in default of an inner source of wisdom, there remained less and less of it in his etheric body every time he abandoned his physical body at death. After every death, every reincarnation, the sum of wisdom in his etheric body was less; the etheric body became ever poorer in wisdom.

But evolution advances; and just as in the Atlantean age evolution was such that the etheric body withdrew into the physical body, so future development will proceed in such a way that man will gradually emerge again from his physical body. Whereas in a former age the etheric body kept drawing into the physical—ever deeper, up to the coming of Christ —the time then arrived in which the course of evolution changed. At the moment in which Christ appeared the etheric body began to retrace its course; and already in our present time it is no longer as closely bound to the physical body as it was when Christ was present on earth. As a result the physical body has become even denser than before. The human being, then, is moving toward a future in which his etheric body will increasingly protrude, and in time will extend as far as it did in the Atlantean epoch.

Here we can pursue our simile a bit further. If the son, who had formerly lived on his father's fund, spends it all and earns nothing additional, his prospects will become increasingly dismal. But if this man now has a son of his own —that would be the grandson—the latter will not be in the same position as his father. The father at least inherited something and could go on spending, but there remains nothing at all for the grandson, nor does he inherit anything: for the time being he is left with nothing whatever. In a certain way that describes the course of human evolution. When the etheric body entered the physical, bringing along a supply of divine wisdom from the treasury of the Godhead, it still provided wisdom for its physical body. But the Luciferic and Ahrimanic spirits prevented all augmentation of this wisdom in the physical body—contrived that none should be added. When now the etheric body begins to emerge again it takes nothing with it from the physical body. The consequence is that if nothing else had intervened man would be heading for a future in which his etheric body, though belonging to him, would contain no vestige of wisdom or knowledge. And with the complete desiccation of the physical body the etheric body would be destitute as well, for nothing could be drawn from the dried-up physical body. Therefore, if the physical body is not to desiccate in that future period, the etheric body must be provided with strength, with the strength of wisdom. Before emerging from the physical body the etheric body should have been endowed with the power of wisdom. Within the physical body it must have received something it can take out with it. Then, when it emerges—provided it has acquired this wisdom—it can react on the physical body, giving it life and preventing its desiccation.

The future evolution of humanity can take one of two courses, of which one is as follows: Man develops without Christ. In this case the etheric body could bring with it nothing from the physical body, because it had received nothing from it; it emerges empty. But conversely, the etheric body cannot animate the physical body, having nothing to give; it cannot prevent the attrition, the withering, of the physical body. Man would gradually forfeit all the fruits of his physical life: they could furnish nothing out of his physical body, which he would therefore have to abandon. But the very purpose for which man descended to earth was to acquire a physical body *in addition to* his other principles. The germ of the physical body originated in an earlier period, but without its actual formation man would never fulfill his mission on earth. Now the influences of Lucifer and Ahriman have entered the picture; and if man acquires nothing in his physical body, if his etheric body withdraws again with nothing to take with it—having even used up the old store of wisdom—then the earth's mission is doomed. The mission of the earth would be lost to the universe. Man would carry over nothing into the future but the empty etheric skull which had been abundantly filled when he originally brought it into earth evolution.

But now let us suppose something were to occur at the right moment which would enable man, as his etheric body emerges again, to provide something for it, to animate it, to penetrate it with wisdom as of old; the etheric body would continue to emerge just the same, but now, endowed with new life, new strength, it could employ these for vitalizing the physical body. It could send power and life back into it. But the etheric body itself must first possess these. It would first have to receive this strength and life; and if it succeeds in this the fruits of man's earth life are saved. The physical body will then not simply decay, but rather, this corruptible physical body will assume the configuration of the etheric body, the incorruptible; and man's resurrection, with the harvest reaped in his physical body, is assured.

An impulse had thus to come to the earth through which the exhausted treasure of ancient wisdom might be replenished, through which the etheric body might be endowed with new life, thus enabling the physical element—otherwise destined to corruption—to put on the incorruptible and to become permeated by an etheric body capable of rendering it immortal, of rescuing it from *Earth* evolution. And that is what Christ brought mankind—this pervasion of the etheric body with life. The transformation of the human physical body that would otherwise be doomed to death, its preservation from corruption, its ability to put on the incorruptible—all this is connected with the Christ. Life was infused into the human etheric body by the Christ impulse —new life, after the old had been spent. And looking into the future, man must tell himself: When my etheric body will ultimately have emerged from my physical body, I should have developed in such a way that it is wholly saturated by the Christ. The Christ must live in me. In the course of my earth development I must by degrees completely permeate my etheric body with the Christ.

What I have just described to you are the deeper processes that elude outer observation. They constitute the spiritual principle underlying the physical evolution of the world.

But what outer form did all this have to take? What was it that entered the physical body through the Luciferic and Ahrimanic beings? The tendency to decay, to dissolution— in short, the tendency to die. The germ of death had entered the physical body. Had no Christ come, this death germ would have developed its full power only at the end of *Earth* evolution, for then the etheric body would be for all time powerless to reanimate man; and at the completion of *Earth* evolution, that which had come into being as human physical body would fall into decay and the earth's mission itself would end in death. Whenever we encounter death today we can discern in it a symbol of the universal death that would occur at the end of *Earth* evolution. Mankind's ancient heritage dwindles but slowly and gradually, and the possibility of being born again and again, of passing from incarnation to incarnation, is due to the life fund that man was originally provided with. As regards his purely external life in the successive incarnations, the possibility for life to exist would not be fully exhausted before the end of *Earth* evolution; but as time goes on the gradual extinction of the race would manifest itself. This would occur piece by piece, and the physical body would continually wither. Had the Christ impulse not come, man would perish member by member as *Earth* evolution approached its termination. At present the Christ-impulse is but at the beginning of its development. Only by degrees will it make its way among men; and only future epochs will reveal—and continue to reveal to the very end of *Earth* evolution—the full significance of Christ for humanity.

But the various human activities and interests have not all been affected alike by the Christ impulse. There are today many such that have not been touched by it at all, that must await a future time. I will give you a striking example of one whole sphere of human activity which at present has not been influenced by the Christ impulse at all. Toward the end of the pre-Christian epoch—say, in the 6th or 7th Century before our era—the primeval wisdom and power were on the wane in so far as human knowledge was concerned. In connection with other phases of life that wisdom long retained a fresh, young forcefulness; but it declined most noticeably in the matter of knowledge. From the eighth, seventh, and sixth centuries B.C. there remained something that may be termed the remnant of a remnant. Were you to hark back even to the Egypto-Chaldean wisdom, not to say that of ancient Persia or India, you would find this wisdom everywhere permeated by true spiritual vision, by the fruits of primeval clairvoyance; and for those endowed to a lesser degree with this faculty the reports of the clairvoyants were available. Such a thing as science other than one based on clairvoyance never existed in the Indian and Persian epochs, nor in still later times; even during the early Greek period there was no science without a basis of clairvoyant research. But then the time approached when this fading clairvoyant research was lost to human science, and for the first time we witness the rise of a human science devoid of clairvoyance—or at least, a science from which clairvoyance was gradually cast out. Why does this clairvoyance disappear? Because even now, the etheric body begins to emerge once again on top. There, the first traces are making themselves felt.

Clairvoyance vanishes, as does faith in the revelations of clairvoyants; and during the 6th or 7th Century before the appearance of Christ we see established something we can call a human science, from which the fruits of spiritual research are increasingly eliminated. And this becomes ever more the case: in Parmenides and Heraclitus, in Plato and even in Aristotle—everywhere in the writings of the old naturalists and physicians—you can find ample confirmation that what is known as science was originally permeated by the results of spiritual research. But knowledge of the spirit steadily deteriorated and decreased. In connection with our psychic capacity, our feeling and willing, it still endures; but as regards our thinking it is vanishing.

Thus with respect to human thinking, to thinking in terms of science, the influence of the etheric on the physical body had already begun to wane when Christ appeared. Everything of that sort comes about gradually, step by step. Christ came and gave the impulse; but naturally not everyone accepted it at once, and particularly was it rejected in certain spheres of activity. In others it was received, but in the field of science it was positively spurned. Examine for yourselves the science that prevailed in the time of the Roman empire. Look it up in *Celsus*, where you can read all sorts of rubbish about Christ. This Celsus was a great scholar, but he understood nothing whatever about human thinking as affected by the Christ impulse. He reports:

"There is said to have lived at one time in Palestine a couple known as Joseph and Mary, with whom the sect of Christians originated. But what is told about them is all superstition. The truth is that the wife of this Joseph was once unfaithful to her husband with a Roman captain named Panthera; but Joseph did not know the identity of the child's father."

That was one of the most popular accounts of the time. If you follow our contemporary literature you will realize that certain people of the present have not advanced beyond the standard of Celsus. Certainly there are fields in which the Christ impulse can take root but slowly, but among those now under discussion it has to this day found no foothold at all. There is one part of man we see withering: it is in the human brain. But when it shall have been influenced by the Christ impulse it will revive science in a very different form. Strange as that may sound in this age of scientific fanaticism, it is nevertheless true. That part of the brain assigned to scientific thinking is doomed to a slow death. This illustrates the gradual disappearance of the ancient heritage from scientific thinking. Aristotle still possessed a relatively large store of it, but we see science gradually being drained of it; and science, by reason of the accumulation of external data, is becoming God-forsaken in respect of its thinking, having nothing left of the old fund. And we see further how it is possible that, no matter how powerfully we experience the Christ, we can no longer establish any contact between the Christ-impulse and what mankind has achieved in the way of science.

We have tangible evidence of this. Suppose that a man of the thirteenth century had been profoundly affected by the Christ impulse and had said: We have the Christ impulse; like a flood of mighty new revelations it streams to us from the Gospel, and we can permeate ourselves with it.—And suppose further that this man had made it his mission to create a connecting link between science and Christianity: even as early as the thirteenth century he would have found nothing in the current science that could have been used for the purpose. He would have had to hark back to Aristotle. Only by collaborating with Aristotle, not with thirteenth-century science, would he have been able to interpret Christianity. Science simply became increasingly incapable of making any contact with the Christ principle; hence the thirteenth-century scholars had to revert to Aristotle, who still possessed something of the old legacy of wisdom and could thus provide concepts capable of correlating science and Christianity.

But as science grew richer in data and observations it became ever poorer in ideas, until finally the time came when all concepts emanating from the old wisdom disappeared from it. Even the greatest men are, of course, children of their era as far as their scientific activity is concerned. Galileo, for example, could not base his thinking on absolute thought, he could only think as his age thought. His greatness consists precisely in his having established God-forsaken thinking as such, purely mechanistical thinking. An important revolution in thought sets in with Galileo. The most commonplace phenomena as explained by modern physics had quite a different explanation prior to Galileo's day than afterwards. Say, someone throws a stone. Today we are told that the stone retains its motion until the latter is counteracted by the influence of another force, the force of inertia. Before Galileo's time, a different opinion was held: people were convinced that if the stone was to keep moving it would have to be propelled—something active must be behind it. Galileo taught people to think in an entirely new way, but in a way implying that the world is a mechanism. Indeed, the ideal striven for today is a mechanical, mechanistic explanation of the world with the complete elimination of all spirit. And the reason for this is that those portions of the human brain, of the thought apparatus, which constitute the organ for scientific thinking, are already so shrivelled as to be no longer able to infuse new life into concepts, with the result that the latter become more and more poverty-stricken.

One could easily show that science, for all the isolated facts it keeps accumulating, has not enriched the life of mankind by a single concept. Note well that observations are not concepts! Do not imagine that such things as Darwinism and the like have provided humanity with concepts. That is something that others have done—not the scientists, but men who tapped quite different sources. Goethe was such a man: he enriched man's fund of ideas from altogether different sources. For this reason the scientists consider him a *dilettante*.

The fact is that science has not grown richer in concepts. Far more alive, loftier, grander are those of antiquity. The Darwinian concepts are like squeezed-out lemons. Darwinism merely collected the results of observation and then linked them with poverty-stricken concepts. This trend in science points clearly to the process of gradual death. In the human brain there is a part that is withering, and this is the part that in our time functions in scientific thinking. The reason for this is that the portion of the human etheric body which should animate this shrivelling brain has as yet not grasped the Christ impulse. No life will flow into science until the Christ impulse enters the portion of the human brain that is intended to serve science. That is a fact based on the great cosmic laws. If science continues in this way it will become poorer and poorer in concepts, and gradually these will vanish. And increasingly numerous will be the scientists who keep lining up their data, and who will be frightened out of their wits when someone begins to think. Nowadays it is a sore trial for a professor to discover a bit of thinking in a doctor's dissertation submitted to him by some candidate.

But we now have an anthroposophy, and this anthroposophy will increasingly make the Christ impulse comprehensible for mankind, thereby imbuing the etheric body with ever more life—with such a wealth of it, in fact, that the etheric body will cause the melting of that desiccated portion of the brain which is responsible for the present trend of scientific thinking. That is an illustration of the manner in which the Christ impulse, penetrating gradually into mankind, will reanimate the dying members of the body. The future of humanity would see the withering of more and more members. But the flowing in of the Christ-impulse will increase proportionately with the dwindling of each part; and by the end of the *Earth* evolution all the parts that would otherwise have perished will be revivified by the Christ impulse, which will have saturated the whole etheric body: the human etheric body will have become one with the Christ-impulse.

The first impetus for this gradual revitalization of mankind, for the resurrection of humanity, was given at a particular moment during a scene most beautifully described in the Gospel of St. John. Think of the Christ as coming into the world a wholly universal Being, and commencing His great work by means of an etheric body completely saturated with His spirit—for the transformation brought about in the etheric body of Jesus of Nazareth enabled it to animate even the physical body. At the moment in which the etheric body of Jesus of Nazareth, in Whom the Christ now dwelt, became completely a life giver for the physical body, the etheric body of Christ is seen transfigured. And the writer of the John Gospel describes this moment:

> *Father, glorify thy name. Then came there a voice*
> *from heaven, saying, I have both glorified it, and*
> *will glorify it again.*
> *The people, therefore, that stood by, and heard it,*
> *said that it thundered.* [John 12:28–31]

What is said is that those who stood by heard thunder; but nowhere does it say that anyone who had not been duly prepared had heard it.

> *Others said, An angel spake to him.*
> *Jesus answered and said, This voice came not*
> *because of me, but for your sakes.*

Why? That what had taken place might be understood by all who were near. And Christ clarifies the event:

> *Now is the judgment of this world: now shall the*
> *prince of this world be cast out.*

In that moment Lucifer-Ahriman was cast out of the physical body of Christ! There stands the great example which in the future must be realized by all mankind: through the Christ impulse the obstacles placed by Lucifer-Ahriman must be cast out of the physical body. Man's earth body must be so vitalized by the Christ-impulse that the fruits of the earth's mission may be carried over into the time that is to follow this Earth epoch.

XIII

Yesterday we contemplated the significance the Mystery of Golgotha has for human evolution on our earth. But as every event in the world is connected through literally endless interrelationships with the evolution of the whole cosmos, we will fully understand the essence of the Mystery of Golgotha only by throwing light on its cosmic significance as well.

We already know that the Being we designate the Christ Being descended to our earth from supra-terrestrial regions and that It was seen in Its descent, so to speak: in ancient Persia by means of the clairvoyant faculty of Zarathustra It was perceived in the sun, then by Moses in the burning bush and in the fire on Sinai, and finally by those who experienced the Christ event, in the presence of the Christ in the body of Jesus of Nazareth.

We know further that the events of this earth, and particularly the evolution of mankind, are related to our solar system; for we have shown that the development of humanity, in the form it has actually taken, could never have come about had not a cosmic body, in which our present sun and moon were still united with the earth, cast out first the sun and later the moon, thereby establishing for the earth a sort of position of equilibrium between sun and moon. Because man could not keep pace with the rapid development of the beings who sought the sun as their field of action, the earth had to be separated from the sun; and because a continued union of earth and moon would have entailed a rapid hardening, an ossification, for mankind, the moon, together with

242

its substances and beings, had to be cast out as well. This made it possible for humanity to develop in the right way. But we learned yesterday that a certain remnant of this tendency to rigidity has nevertheless remained; and it would have sufficed to lead mankind into a state of decay at the end of our *Earth* evolution had the Christ impulse not come. These considerations will give us an insight into our whole evolution.

At one time, then, sun, moon, and earth constituted *a single* cosmic body. Then came the time when the sun split off, leaving only earth and moon united. Finally our present moon withdrew, and the earth remained as the scene of human evolution. This occurred in the old Lemurian time, the period preceding the so-called Atlantean age which we have already discussed from various points of view. From that time forth, from the Atlantean into our own time, the earth has developed in such a way that the sun and the moon forces have acted from without. Let us now consider the further progress of earth development up to the time when the Christ impulse came, and let us concentrate on a quite definite moment of our earth development: the moment in which the Cross was raised on Golgotha and the blood flowed from the wounds of Christ Jesus. Let us focus our attention on this moment in the evolution of our earth.

Up to this point, all that mankind had experienced had been determined by the entry, into the inner being of man, of the combined powers of the Luciferic and Ahrimanic beings. We have seen that as a consequence of this intrusion man became amalgamated with the outer world in *maya*, or illusion: Ahriman prevented the outer world from manifesting itself in its true form, making it appear like a world consisting only of matter and solid substance—as though no spirit underlay all matter. For a long time, therefore—and this is still the case today regarding many aspects of earth development—the human being found himself in a state brought about by error, because he receives from his environment only the material sense impressions which he then elaborates in his conceptions. So by reason of this influence of Ahriman, or Mephistopheles, he has a false picture of the outer world and forms illusory and erroneous conceptions of the spiritual world.

But all spirit is bound up with physical effects, and we have seen what physical effects accompanied this distortion of outward perception. We have seen that, as a consequence of the Luciferic and Ahrimanic influences, human blood became ever less fitted to provide the faculty of seeing the outer world in its true light: a steady increase in illusion was bound up with the blood's deterioration, with the dissolution of blood as it had been in the age of consanguinity, with the blood's dispersion and destruction by miscegenation. No longer could man consult the old wisdom he had once possessed as a legacy, a wisdom that told him: It is an error to believe that the outer world is nothing but matter; for if you consult the remnants of the old wisdom you inherited, these will tell you that a spiritual world underlies the physical world.

But these remnants kept dwindling, with the result that man became ever more dependent upon the physical world in regard to his entire soul life and his knowledge. That is what transformed all of his physical impressions into delusions and deceptions. Had it not been for the intervention of the Christ influence, he would ultimately have lost his whole heritage of ancient wisdom by being gradually reduced to complete dependence upon the outer sense world and its impressions. He would have forgotten the existence of a spiritual world—that is what would inevitably have occurred. He would have become blind to the spiritual world.

It is now our duty to consider in all its gravity a truth

such as this: the danger of man falling into ever greater delusion and error concerning the outer world. It is not a simple matter to do this—to contemplate in all its implications and its seriousness such a fact as man's lapse into error regarding the outer impressions of the sense world. Try to understand what it means to recognize as *maya*, as delusion, all external impressions of the senses as they confront us in the physical sense world. We are asked to learn that phenomena and impressions, as they exist in the sense world and as they impress us, are false; and that we must learn to see their true form behind the external impressions they give.

There is one event to which it is especially difficult, as a rule, to apply the truth, to say to oneself: The form in which it confronts me in the outer world is untrue, is illusion—*maya*. Can you think what event I have in mind? It is death. As a result of the sort of impressions we have described, our comprehension has come to grasp only external physical events; and for this reason death, when faced in the physical world, bears certain attributes that render it impossible to contemplate other than from the standpoint of the outer physical world. Death is a phenomenon concerning which mankind has inevitably become entangled in particularly erroneous and harmful views. The inference we must draw from this is that the form in which death presents itself is but *maya*—a delusion.

Before our eyes in the outer physical world a great variety of phenomena present themselves. There are the stars that intersperse cosmic space, yonder, the mountains, the plants, the animals. Here is the whole world of our minerals; and here, too, we have man, together with all the facts we can gather by means of sense observation. And if we enquire into the origin of these phenomena, of this outer physical-sensible world which appears to us as a world of matter, we

245

must answer, Their origin is in spirit. Spirit underlies our physical-sensible world. Then, were we to seek the primordial form of spirit from which springs all that is physical and of the senses, we would have to call it the basis of all being. In Christian esotericism this is the aspect of divinity known as the Father principle. It underlies everything that is *creature*. So what exactly is it that was veiled from man when all things became obscured by *maya*, or illusion? It was the divine Father principle. Instead of the *mirage* of the senses, man should see everywhere and in all things the divine Father principle, of which all things and he himself are a part. The Father principle, then, to which belong all things as well as man, does not appear in its true form. Because of the decline in human faculties, of which we have spoken, we see the Father principle veiled by delusion, by *maya*.

What do we find woven into this great delusion? Among all the phenomena we perceive, one stands out as essentially fundamental: death. Therefore we should tell ourselves that the outer objects confronting our senses are in reality the Father principle, are expressions of the divine-spiritual Father element. And since death is interwoven in the totality of the sense world, it is something that pertains to the divine-spiritual Father principle. Owing to the nature of man's development, the divine Father principle has become obscured for him by many a veil, and ultimately by the veil of death. What must man seek behind death as in all sense phenomena? The Father, the cosmic Father! Just as he must learn to think of every object as being in truth the Father, so he must come to feel that death, too, is the Father. And why does a false picture of the Father appear to us in the physical sense world? Why is it distorted to the point of the grotesque image appearing to us so deceptively as death? Because the Lucifer-Ahriman principle has been infused into every phase of our life.

What was needed, therefore, to disabuse man of this false, deceptive view of death and to provide a true conception of it was enlightenment arrived at by means of the actual facts. Something had to occur whereby he could learn that what he had known about death, what he had felt about it—everything he had been impelled to do as a result of his conception of death—was untrue. An event had to take place which would show him the true aspect of death. Its false form had to be obliterated and its true one set forth. To substitute, through His deed, the true aspect of death for the false one, that was Christ's mission on earth.

Owing to the interference of Lucifer-Ahriman in human evolution, death became the distorted image of the Father. Death was the consequence, the effect, of the influence of Lucifer-Ahriman. So what had to be done by Him Who would rid the world of this false face of death? Never could human life have been released from this distorted form of death had not its source been removed—Lucifer-Ahriman. But that is something no earthly being could have accomplished. An earthly being can extinguish, within earth development, anything brought about by earthly beings themselves, but not the Luciferic-Ahrimanic influence. This could be driven out only by a being that had not been on the earth but out in cosmic space when Lucifer-Ahriman intervened, a being that came to earth at a time when Lucifer-Ahriman had already fully entered the human body.

Now, this Being did come to earth and removed Lucifer-Ahriman, as we have seen, at exactly the right moment—eliminated the cause of all that had brought death into the world. This deed called for a Being having nothing whatever to do with any causes of death among men. It had to be a Being in no way connected with any cause of human death—that is, with anything brought about by Lucifer and later by Ahriman, with any individual human deeds done under the

247

Lucifer-Ahriman influence—in short, with anything whereby men became guilty, fell a prey to evil. For the death of a being affected by any of these causes would have been justified. Only an undeserved death, undertaken by one without guilt —an utterly innocent death—could extinguish all guilty death.

An innocent Being, accordingly, had to suffer death, wed death, submit to death. By so doing He infused into human life those forces which will gradually create knowledge concerning the true aspect of death; that is, the realization that death as it appears in the sense world is not truth—that on the contrary, this death had to occur to provide for life in the spiritual world; that precisely this death forms, in fact, the basis of that life in the spirit.

Thus the innocent death on Golgotha furnished the proof, which will gradually be comprehended by humanity, that death is the ever-living Father. And once we have achieved the right view of death, once we have learned from the event of Golgotha that external dying is of no importance, that in the body of Jesus of Nazareth there dwelt the Christ with Whom we can unite; once we have realized what Christ achieved, even though we see the image of death hung on the Cross, in rendering death a mere external event, that His life in the etheric body was the same before death as it was after this death, and that therefore this death cannot touch life—once we have understood that here is a death incapable of extinguishing life but is, rather, itself life, then the Christ on the Cross becomes the eternal emblem of the truth that death is in reality the giver of life. The plant comes forth from the seed: death is not the destroyer of life, but its seed. It has been sown into our physical sense world in order that the latter may not fall away from life, but may be raised into life. The refutation of death had to be furnished on the Cross by a contradictory death, by a death that was innocent.

We must now enquire what, exactly, was brought about

by this event. From the previous lectures we know that as the fourth principle of his being man has an ego, and that as this develops, the blood is its outer physical instrument. Blood is the expression of the ego, hence with its steady deterioration the ego fell to an ever increasing extent into error, into *maya*, or illusion. Hence, also, man is indebted for the growing power of his ego to the circumstance that he is provided with blood. But this ego, in turn, he owes in its spiritual aspect to the fact of his having learned to distinguish himself from the spiritual world, of his having become an individuality. This capacity could not have been bestowed upon him otherwise than by temporarily cutting off his view of the spiritual world; and the agency that effected this was precisely death. Had man always known that death is the seed of life he would not have achieved independence for his ego, for he would have remained linked with the spiritual world. As it was, however, death appeared, gave him the illusion of being separated from the spiritual world, and so trained his ego to independence.

This ego principle, however, grew more and more independent: it exaggerated its independence, strained it past a certain point. And this condition could be counteracted only by the withdrawal of the force which had caused it. Hence the factor which would have induced exaggerated egotism, which would have fostered not merely the ego principle, egoism, but egotism—this factor had to be driven out. And this was accomplished in such a way that in the future it can be more and more eradicated from the individual egos as well; it was accomplished when death came on the Cross of Golgotha and the blood flowed from the wounds. In the blood flowing from Christ's wounds we have the factual symbol of the excessive egotism in the human ego. Just as blood is the expression of the ego, so the blood that flowed on Golgotha is the expression of excess in the human ego. Had not the blood flowed on Golgotha, man would have become spiritually hardened in his egotism and would have been doomed to the fate we described yesterday. But the blood that flowed on Golgotha gave an impetus for the gradual disappearance of the force that makes an egotist of the ego.

But every physical event has its spiritual counterpart, and as the blood flowed from the wounds on Golgotha there occurred a corresponding spiritual event. At this moment, it happened for the first time that rays streamed forth from the earth into cosmic space, where formerly there had been none. We must visualize, then, as created at this moment, rays streaming from the earth into cosmic space. Darker and darker had the earth become with the passing of time—up to the event on Golgotha. Now the blood flows on Golgotha—and the earth begins to radiate light.

If in pre-Christian time some clairvoyant being had been able to observe the earth from a distant cosmic body, it would have seen the earth's aura gradually fading out, and at its darkest immediately preceding the event on Golgotha. Then, however, it would have seen it shine forth in new colors. The deed on Golgotha suffused the earth with an astral light that will gradually become an etheric and then a physical light. Every being in the world continues to evolve. What is today the sun was first a planet. And just as the old *Saturn* became a *Sun*, so our earth, now a planet, will gradually develop into a sun. The first impetus in this direction was given when the blood flowed from the wounds of the Redeemer on Golgotha. The earth began to shine—for the time being astrally, visible only to the seer. But in the future, the astral light will become physical light and the earth will be a luminous body, a sun body.

I have explained repeatedly that no new cosmic body comes into being through the agglomeration of physical matter, but through the creation, by a spiritual being, of a new spiritual center, a new sphere of activity. The formation of a cosmic body begins in spirit. Every physical cosmic body was first spirit. What our earth will ultimately become consists at present of the astral aspect of its aura which began to ray forth from the earth at the time we are here considering: that is the first nucleus of the future sun-earth. But what a man of that time would have perceived with his misleading senses is a phantom: that has no truth, it dissolves, it ceases to be; and the farther the earth moves toward its sun state, the more will this *maya* be consumed and perish in the fire of the sun. But through having been suffused at that time with a new force, through the newly created possibility for the earth to become a sun, it became possible as well for this same force to permeate man. This was the first impulse toward what I described yesterday: the radiating of the Christ force into the etheric human body. And thanks to the streaming in of this astral force it could start absorbing new vitality such as it will need in the distant future.

So if you will visualize the period in which the event of Golgotha occurred and then compare it with a later period— that is, if you compare a future condition of humanity with that which prevailed at the time of the event of Golgotha— you will find that at the time the Christ impulse intervened, the earth of itself had nothing left to infuse into the etheric bodies of men. Some time later, however, the etheric bodies of those who had found a contact with the Christ impulse were irradiated: men who understood the Christ absorbed the radiant force that has been in the earth ever since—the earth's new radiance. They have taken the light of Christ into the etheric bodies of men.

What takes place, now that there is always something of the Christ light in human etheric bodies? What occurs in

251

that part of the etheric body in which the Christ light has been received? What happens to it after death? What is it, in fact, that gradually permeates the etheric body as a result of the Christ impulse? It is something that the Christ impulse has brought and implanted into the etheric body of man, and that did not exist there previously. Since that time, as an effect of the Christ light, the possibility exists in human etheric bodies for something new to appear, something that breathes life and is immortal, something that can never perish in death. While men on earth are still misled by the illusory image of death, this new factor will nevertheless be rescued from death, will have no part in it.

Ever since that time, then, something exists in the human etheric body that is not subject to death, to the death forces of the earth. And this something which does not participate in death and which men gradually attain through the influence of the Christ impulse, now streams back again—out into cosmic space; and in proportion to its intensity in man it generates a certain force that flows out into cosmic space. And this force will in turn create a sphere around our earth that is in the process of becoming a sun: a sort of spiritual sphere is forming around the earth, composed of the etheric bodies that have come alive. Just as the Christ light radiates from the earth, there is also a kind of reflection of it that encircles the earth. What is here reflected as the Christ light, appearing as a consequence of the Christ event, this is what Christ called the Holy Spirit. Just as the event of Golgotha provided the first impetus for the earth to become a sun, so it is true that, beginning with this event, the earth begins to be creative, surrounding itself with a spiritual ring which, in turn, will in the future develop into a sort of planet circling the earth.

Thus a momentous process that commenced with the event of Golgotha has since been unfolding in the cosmos. When

252

the Cross was raised on Golgotha and the blood flowed from the wounds of Christ Jesus, a new cosmic center was created. We were present when that occurred; we were present as human beings, whether in a physical body or outside this physical life between birth and death. That is the way new worlds come into being; and we must comprehend that while we behold the dying Christ, we stand in the presence of the genesis of a new sun.

Christ espouses death, which on earth had become the characteristic expression of the Father Spirit. Christ goes to the Father and unites with His manifestation, death—and the image of death now becomes false, for death becomes the seed of a new sun in the universe. If we feel this event, if we can feel this unmasking of death and feel that the death on the Cross becomes the seed from which a new sun will germinate, then we also experience powerfully how mankind on earth must have felt and sensed it as the supreme transition in human evolution.

There was once a time when men still possessed a vague, dim clairvoyance. They lived in a spiritual element; and as they looked back upon their lives—from their thirtieth to their twentieth year, from the twentieth to the tenth, and so on back to their birth—they knew that they had come to this birth from divine-spiritual heights. For them, birth was not a beginning: they viewed birth and death also as spiritual beings, and they knew that something of spirit dwelt within them which this death could not touch. Birth and death in their present meaning did not exist as yet. They only gradually acquired their untrue, deceptive form in the outer image of the Father. Death became the characteristic feature of this external aspect of the Father.

Then men, in contemplating death, saw it apparently destroying life. Death became more and more an image representing the opposite of life. While life brought a large measure of suffering, death was considered the greatest suffering of all. What view of death must have been held by one who saw earth events from without, saw how these earth events were reflected in humanity before the appearance of the Christ? If he had descended from divine-spiritual heights as a higher being with views differing from those of men, he would have been constrained, in contemplating mankind, to speak as *Buddha* spoke. This Buddha had come forth from his royal palace where he had been reared, and where he had seen only what promotes life. Now, however, as he came forth, he saw a suffering human being, then an aged man, and finally even a dead man. These experiences wrung from him the utterance: "Sickness is suffering, old age is suffering, death is suffering." That is indeed the way it was experienced by mankind; and in these words the common feeling burst forth from the great soul of Buddha.

Then Christ appeared. And by the time another six hundred years after Christ had passed—just as six hundred had passed between Buddha and Christ—there were people who understood, when envisioning the Cross and the dead Man upon it, that what hung upon the Cross was the symbol of that seed from which springs forth life in abundance. They had learned to sense the true nature of death. Christ has espoused death, entered this death that had become the characteristic expression of the Father, united with this death; and from the union of Christ Jesus and death springs the beginning of a new life-sun. It is a false picture that shows death as synonymous with suffering: it is *maya*, illusion. Death, if permitted to approach us as it did Christ, is in reality the germ of life; and in the course of future ages men will come to recognize this. What men will contribute to a new sun and a new planetary system will be proportionate to what they receive of the Christ impulse and then give

254

of themselves in sacrifice, thus steadily adding to the radiance of the sun of life.

Here the objection might be raised, So says spiritual science; but how can you reconcile a cosmology of that sort with the Gospel? Christ enlightened those who were His disciples. In order to prepare them for the most comprehensive revelations He employed the method that is indispensable if the loftiest truths are to be adequately understood: He spoke to His disciples in parables or, as it is worded in the German Bible, in "proverbs" (*Sprichwörter*)—that is, in metaphors and parables. Then came the time when the disciples, having steadily matured, believed themselves able to receive the truth without its being clothed in proverbs. The moment arrives when Christ Jesus is prepared to talk to His apostles without proverbs, without parables. The apostles want to hear the name, the significant name, for the sake of which He had come into the world.

> *Hitherto have ye asked nothing in my name: ask, and ye shall receive, that your joy may be full. These things have I spoken unto you in parables: but the time cometh, when I shall no more speak unto you in parables, but shall shew you plainly of the Father.*

Try to feel the moment approaching in which He would speak to His disciples of the Father.

> *At that day ye shall ask in my name: and I say not unto you, that I will pray to the Father for you: For the Father Himself loveth you, because ye have loved me, and have believed that I came forth from God. I came out from the Father . . .*

He had, of course, come forth from the Father's true form, not from the deceptive image.

255

> *I came out from the Father, and am come into the*
> *world: again, I leave the world, and go to the*
> *Father.*

Now it dawns upon the disciples, whose understanding has matured, that the world as it surrounds them is the expression of the Father, and that what is most significant precisely where the outer world is most densely shrouded in *maya*, in illusion, is equally the expression of the Father: that Death is the name for the Father. That is what the disciples realize. Only, the passage must be read aright.

> *His disciples said unto him, Lo, now speakest thou*
> *plainly, and speakest no parable.*
> *Now are we sure that thou knowest all things and*
> *needest not that any man should ask thee: by this*
> *we believe that thou camest from God.*
> *Jesus answered them, Now ye believe.* *
> *Behold, the hour cometh, yea, is now come, that ye*
> *shall be scattered, every man to his own, and shall*
> *leave me alone; and yet I am not alone, because*
> *the Father is with me.*
> *These things have I spoken unto you, that in me ye*
> *might have peace. In the world ye shall have trib-*
> *ulation: but be of good cheer; I have overcome the*
> *world.* [John 16:24–33]

Did the disciples know whither He was about to depart? Yes, from now on they knew that He would go to meet death, to wed death. Now read again what He said to them after they had learned the meaning of the words: "I came forth from death"—that is, from death in its true form, the life-

---

*TRANSLATOR'S NOTE:—This is Luther's translation and Dr. Steiner retained it verbatim in quoting. The King James version, as we know, reads: "Do ye now believe?" Either would be equally correct, according to the Greek, since as yet there were no interrogative marks in Greek.

Father—"and am come into the world: again, I leave the world, and go to the Father." And to this the disciples replied: "Now are we sure that thou knowest all things, and needest not that any man should ask thee: by this we believe that thou camest from God."

Now the disciples knew that the true form of death is founded in the divine Father Spirit; that death as it is seen and felt by men is a deceptive phenomenon, an error. Thus Christ reveals to His disciples the name of death behind which is hidden the fount of sovereign life. Never would the new life-sun have come into being had not death entered the world and let itself be overcome by Christ. Death, therefore, when contemplated in its true form, is the Father. Christ came into the world because a false reflection of this Father had arisen in death. Christ came to create the true form, a true after-image of the living Father-God. The Son is the after-image, the descendant of the Father, and His mission was to reveal the true form of the Father. Verily, the Father sent His Son into the world that the true nature of the Father be made manifest: life eternal, veiled behind temporal death.

All this is not only the cosmology of spiritual science. It is what is needed to extract the full, profound import from the Gospel of St. John. He who wrote that Gospel thereby established, so to speak, the loftiest truths of which he could say to himself that in these mankind would find sustenance for all future time. And in proportion as mankind learns to understand and practice these truths it will attain to a new wisdom and will grow into the spiritual world in a new way. But this will come about only by degrees. Therefore, it was necessary that in the meantime the guides of Christian development should provide for the creation of what may be called auxiliary books to function side by side with the Gospel of St. John, books not intended only for the most

257

receptive and understanding—such as is the John Gospel, meant as a legacy of Christ for all eternity—but suitable for the immediate present.*

Thus, there appeared to begin with a book from which people of the first Christian centuries could best learn, in the measure of their understanding, what they needed for comprehension of the Christ event. Even here, of course, there were but few in proportion to the whole of mankind who could glean from this auxiliary book the exact nature of what it contained for them. This first book of its kind, not intended for the innermost circle but still for the chosen ones, was the Gospel of St. Mark. This Gospel embodies precisely those features that held an intimate appeal, so to speak, for a certain type of understanding then prevalent (we shall come back to this). Then a time came when it gradually became less intelligible to men; human comprehension turned more in the direction of seeing most clearly the full force of Christ in its inner value for the soul and in a certain contempt for the outer physical world.

It was a period in which men were imbued with the feeling: Worthless are all temporal goods; true riches are found only in the properly developed inner self of man. This was the time when, for example, Johannes Tauler wrote his book, *Vom armen Leben Kristi* (Concerning the Piteous Life of Christ): the time in which the Gospel of St. Luke was the one best understood. Luke, a disciple of Paul, was one of those who gave Paul's own gospel a form adapted to the time, stressing the "piteous life" of Jesus of Nazareth, born in a stable among poor shepherds. We recognize the *arme*

---

*A few months later Dr. Steiner added significantly to what he said here on the subject of the four evangelists. See the lecture given at Berlin on November 1, 1909, the first of three appearing under the title *Deeper Secrets of Human History in the Light of the Gospel of St. Matthew*.

Leben Kristi mirrored in the Luke Gospel, as a second subsidiary book for the further development of humanity.

In our time there will be those who can best learn what they are able to understand, as it accords with our age, from the Gospel of St. Matthew. People of our period, though perhaps referring less frequently to the name "Matthew," will nevertheless select more and more what corresponds with the Matthew Gospel. The time will come when people will point out that it is impossible to understand the supersensible events that took place at the Baptism in the Jordan, as we have described them. That is an understanding which will come to many only in the future. We are approaching an epoch in which he who, in the thirtieth year of his life, received the Christ into himself, will be increasingly thought of as "the simple man of Nazareth"—even by theological research.

Those who feel this way about it, those to whom the simple man of Nazareth is of supreme importance and who attach less significance to the Christ than to the lofty initiate—those, in short, who want Jesus of Nazareth—will find the content and meaning of the Matthew Gospel especially significant. A materialistically thinking age can say: We open the Matthew Gospel and find a genealogic record, a table of heredity that shows us the ancestors of Jesus of Nazareth chronologically. It runs from Abraham down through three times fourteen generations to Joseph. Just as it says that Abraham begat Isaac, Isaac begat Jacob, and so forth, so it runs to Joseph and Jesus of Nazareth. The reason this is stated is to make quite clear the possibility of tracing back to Abraham the physical line of heredity of that body into which Jesus of Nazareth, as an individual, had been born. Leave out Joseph, and the whole table becomes meaningless. To speak of a supersensible birth in the face of this table robs the latter of every vestige of sense; for why should the

259

writer of the Matthew Gospel take the trouble to trace a line of ancestry through three times fourteen generations if he intended to follow this by saying that in respect of the physical flesh Jesus of Nazareth was not descended from Joseph? The only way in which the Gospel of St. Matthew can be understood is by stressing the fact that through Joseph the individuality of Jesus of Nazareth was born into a body which had actually descended from Abraham. The purpose of this table was to emphasize the impossibility of omitting Joseph, within the meaning of the Matthew Gospel. It follows that neither can Joseph be ignored by those who fail to understand the supersensible birth in the sense of the Baptism in the Jordan.

But the Matthew Gospel was originally written in a community which placed the greatest value not upon Christ, but upon the individuality that stood before men in the person of Jesus of Nazareth, the initiate. Underlying the Matthew Gospel was the initiate wisdom known to the Ebionite Gnostics, and this Gospel is based upon a document from that source as its model. Prime importance was placed on the initiate, Jesus of Nazareth; and all else connected with the matter becomes far clearer still by reason of its being embodied in the Ebionite gospel. But this is precisely what makes possible a certain approach to the Matthew Gospel— one which is not exactly demanded by it, for actually it is not implied, but which can be read into it: The Gospel of St. Matthew may be interpreted as implying that we are not dealing here with a supersensible birth. On the other hand, what is presented in the Matthew Gospel may be regarded as the symbol of a God—one who is simply called a God, one who, as a God, is really only a human being—even though this was not what Matthew meant. But those who nowadays base their standpoint upon Matthew—and they will do so more and more—will interpret the matter in that way.

In order that no man wishing to approach the Christ may be denied the opportunity of doing so, the Matthew Gospel provides for those who are unable to rise from Jesus to Christ: it is a rung in the ladder which they can ascend to Jesus of Nazareth. The mission of spiritual science, however, is to guide men upward to an understanding of the Gospel of Gospels, the Gospel of St. John. Every other Gospel should be regarded as complementary to it. In the John Gospel are to be found the reasons for the existence of the others, and we shall understand these aright only by studying them on the basis of the John Gospel.

A study of the Gospel of St. John will lead to a comprehensive understanding of what took place on Golgotha; to an understanding of the Mystery by means of which death, in the untrue form it had assumed in human evolution, was refuted. Men will further learn to grasp the fact that through the deed of Golgotha, not only was it revealed to human cognition that death is in reality the source of life, but man was provided with an attitude toward death which permitted him to infuse more and more life into his own being, until ultimately it will become wholly alive—that is, until he will be able to rise from all death, until he has overcome death. That is what was revealed to Paul when he saw the living Christ on the road to Damascus—when he knew: *Christ liveth*—as he gazed with his newly acquired clairvoyance into what constituted the environment of the earth. As an Old-Testament initiate he knew that until then the earth had lacked a certain light, but now he saw that light in it. Hence the Christ was present; hence also, He Who had hung on the Cross was the Christ in Jesus of Nazareth.

Thus there came to Paul, on the road to Damascus, the understanding of what had taken place on Golgotha.

XIV

Anyone not sufficiently prepared may well have found it very strange, in yesterday's lecture, to hear the name of the Father Spirit of the world linked with the name of death. You must not forget, however, what was said at the same time: that the form in which death appears to men in the physical world is not its true form, and that therefore the outer sense world, which appears to be inevitably subject to death, is for this very reason not the true expression of what really underlies it, of the divine-spiritual Being at its root. This is really equivalent to saying that man suffers from an illusion, a monstrous deception, a *maya*, concerning all that is spread out around him in space for his senses to perceive. Could he recognize the true form he would not perceive the sense image but would discern the spirit. Could he recognize death in its real aspect he would see in death the form this sense world would have to have in order to be the true expression of the divine Father Spirit.

In order that this earth-world of ours might come into being at all, an earlier, supra-terrestrial world had to condense into physical matter, into physical substance as we know it. In this way the outer world could become the expression of a divine spiritual world, a divine spiritual world which thus possesses what may be thought of as creations alongside and apart from itself. All previous manifestations of our cosmic existence were of a nature that was more or less a part of and within the divine Being. On the old *Saturn* there existed as yet nothing of our air, our water, our earth—that is, our solid bodies. *Saturn* was a body consisting exclu-

262

sively of warmth, a warmth-filled space. All the beings it harbored still dwelt in the bosom of the divine Father Spirit. And so it was too on the old *Sun*, although its condensation had advanced to the gaseous state. This air planet, the old *Sun*, contained all its creatures within itself, and that means, within the divine-spiritual Being. Even on the old *Moon* this condition prevailed.

It was only on the *Earth* that creation emerged for the first time from the womb of the divine-spiritual Nature and became something that existed alongside of it. But in this new element that arose and henceforth appeared side by side with the divine-spiritual Being—even constituting the garment, the sheath, the physical corporeality of man—all the retarded spirits who gradually ensconced themselves. This meant that it became a creation different from what it should have been as an image of the divine-spiritual Being. Having borne within itself all creatures—our present mineral, plant, animal, and human kingdoms—the divine spiritual Being sent them forth, as it were, spread them out like a tapestry, and this was now a reflection of the divine-spiritual Being. That is the way it should have remained. But into it moved the retarded element that had previously been expelled by the divine-spiritual Being, become interwoven with it. This in a way dulled the luster of creation: its worth was diminished from what it would otherwise have been.

This dimming commenced in the age in which the moon split off from the earth, the age of which we have said that if nothing else had occurred, and if the moon had not been cast out, the earth would have become waste even at that time. But man was to be fostered in such a way as to enable him to achieve his independence, and this called for embodiment in an earthly-physical substance. Beginning with the Lemurian age, then down through the Atlantean time, he had to be led to an ever-increasing ability to incarnate in some physical-sensible substance. But this substance now contained the retarded beings, so that man could not but incarnate in bodily sheaths inhabited by such beings.

In the Atlantean age, certain beings existed who were companions of the human beings. Man himself, as we know, was embodied at that time in a soft substance, and what today is his flesh was not at all as it is at present. The man of old Atlantis, where the air was wholly permeated by dense, heavy aqueous vapor, and where human beings were water beings, was constituted like certain present-day jellyfish of the sea, scarcely distinguishable from the surrounding water. Potentially all his organs were present, but they solidified only gradually. Only gradually did man acquire his bones, and so forth. The more tenuous material predisposition for the organs was there, but these hardened only in the course of time. In the early Atlantean period, then, there existed beings who in a sense were still men's companions, in so far as man was clairvoyant and could discern even those beings who had really established their habitation on the sun, but who streamed toward him in the sun's rays. For not only did physical sunlight come to man, but in this physical sunlight he saw beings approaching him; and when in a state comparable to sleep, he could say, Now I am outside my body in the sphere where sun beings dwell.

But then came the time, toward the middle and last third of the Atlantean age, in which the earth condensed more and more in regard to its physical substance, and man received the predisposition to develop his self-consciousness. Thenceforth, there were no longer any such beings for men to see, for these had to withdraw from the earth, to cease revealing themselves to men's earthly sight. More and more forcefully human beings were drawn down into dense matter by the Luciferic influence. In this way, it became possible for a being, whom we must term Lucifer, to take possession of the human astral body to such an extent that man inevitably descended ever deeper into a dense physical body. But at the same time, the beings who had formerly been his companions rose ever higher, refusing to have anything to do with the retarded beings; they broke away from them. While the Luciferic beings invaded the human astral body, the higher beings cast them down, saying, in effect, Ye shall not rise with us: get on below as best ye can!

One of these higher beings is represented in Michael, who cast the Luciferic beings into the abyss and assigned the earth to them as their sphere of action; and it was within the astral body of man that they sought to exercise their influence. "Heaven" was no longer the habitation of these beings. They had been cast down to earth by the beings whose scene of action was now found in heaven. All evil, however, all harm, has its good side and its place in cosmic wisdom. Thus it was inevitable that these beings had to remain behind in evolution in order to draw man down into physical matter, where alone he could learn to address himself as "I," to develop his self-consciousness. Without being enmeshed in *maya* he never could have learned this. But on the other hand, man would have perished in illusion if illusion and its powers—Lucifer-Ahriman—had succeeded in confining him permanently in illusion.

I must now express certain thoughts which I beg you to listen to with all possible circumspection; for only by further developing them and by taking them literally—though not in the literal sense of a materialistically minded person—can they be rightly understood.

What was the aim and intention of the Luciferic-Ahrimanic beings concerning the physical world? What did they want to bring about in all the beings now dwelling in the world, beings whom they were able to influence after they had united with human evolution in the Atlantean time?

265

These beings, Lucifer-Ahriman, intended nothing less than to keep all earth beings in the form of the dense, physical matter in which they are enmeshed. For example: when a plant grows forth from its root, sprouts leaf after leaf, and finally produces the blossom, it is Lucifer-Ahriman's purpose to foster this growth and expansion indefinitely; that is, to make this growing being resemble the physical form it inhabits, to preserve it as it is, thereby snatching it from the spiritual world. For were they to succeed in making this being of the spiritual world resemble the physical form, they would be wresting heaven from the earth, so to speak. In the animal kingdom as well the Luciferic-Ahrimanic beings have the tendency to make all animals resemble the body in which they live, and to cause them, within their material substance, to forget their divine-spiritual origin. It is the same in the case of the human being.

In order to prevent this, the divine-spiritual Father spoke: In their culmination, in man, the beings of earth have attained to external *knowledge* in their ego; but we cannot yet entrust them with *life*. For life would in that case take a course in which the beings would be torn from their divine-spiritual root in this life. The human being would become an integral part of the physical body and would for all time forget his divine-spiritual origin. Only by bestowing the boon of death upon all things attracted into matter could the divine Father Spirit rescue the memory of divine origin. Thus it became possible for the growing plant to shoot upward until the impulse of fructification entered, and then for its form to wither and a new one to spring from its seed. But in entering the seed state, the plant is for a moment in the divine-spiritual world, and the divine-spiritual world refreshes it. And all this applies pre-eminently to the human being. He would be banished and chained to the earth and would forget his divine-spiritual origin were not death spread over the earth—were he not provided with ever-fresh sources of strength between death and a new birth—in order that he may not forget his divine-spiritual origin.

Death? Yes, where indeed is death to be found on the earth? Let us enquire of some plant being that delights us. There we have a being that gladdens our eyes with its glorious blossoms—and within a few months it is no longer there. Death has claimed it. Or take an animal—perhaps one that has been faithful to us, or any other animal: in a short time it will be gone, taken by death. Consider the human being as he is placed in the physical world. After a certain span, death will come to him, he will no longer be; for if he continued to be here he would forget his divine-spiritual origin. Think of a mountain. The time will come when the volcanic action of our earth will have engulfed it; death passes over it. Seek as you will, nothing is to be found that is not interwoven with death. Everything on earth is steeped in death.

Thus death is the benefactor that snatches man out of a domain which would wholly estrange him from the divine-spiritual world. Yet it was necessary for man to come into this physical world of sense, for only there could he achieve his self-consciousness, his human egoity. Were he to keep passing through death without the capacity for taking something along from this realm of death, he would be able, to be sure, to return to the divine-spiritual world, but without consciousness, without egoity. He *must* enter the divine-spiritual world possessed of his egoity. That is why he must be able to fructify the earthly realm, the realm wholly permeated by death, in such a way that death becomes the seed of an ego principle in the eternal realm, the spiritual realm.

But this possibility of transforming death, which would otherwise mean annihilation, into the seed of eternal egoity was provided by the Christ impulse. On Golgotha, the true aspect of death was manifested to all mankind for the first time. As a result of Christ's having espoused death—Christ, image of the Father Spirit, Son of the Father Spirit—death becomes the well-spring of a new life—and, as we learned yesterday, of a new sun. And now that man has achieved an ego for all eternity, everything that formerly existed as his apprenticeship can henceforth vanish, and he can advance into the future with his rescued ego principle which will more and more be fashioned after the ego principle of Christ.

As an illustration of what has just been set forth, let us take a seven-armed candelabrum and light it step by step, and let us consider the first flame of its sevenfold unity a symbol of the first phase of human evolution, the *Saturn* phase. Every evolution proceeds in seven subdivisions, so in the first flame we see a symbol of the forces that flowed into man during the *Saturn* period. Passing to the second flame of this sevenfold candelabrum we have the symbol of the forces that came to man during the *Sun* phase. In like manner we can see in the third unit the forces from the *Moon*, and in the fourth, the symbol of everything that streamed into man from the *Earth* evolution. Now let us imagine the middle light as burning brightly, while the next three are but very dim. The middle light represents the time when Christ entered evolution. Never could the remaining candles be kindled, never could the next evolutionary epochs come about, had not the Christ impulse intervened in the evolution of mankind—indeed, they are still dark today.

If we were now to represent future evolution in the same symbolical way we should have to do it thus: as the light following the middle one kindles and increases in luster, the first one must be gradually extinguished. With the lighting of the next one, the second would die away, and so forth; for here is the beginning of a new *Sun* evolution. And when all the last lights are burning it is fitting that the first three be extinguished, because their fruits have flowed into the last

268

three, have passed over into the future. There you have a picture of past evolution which received its forces from the Father Spirit. Had the Father Spirit held to this course, all the lights would gradually have to fade out, by reason of the interference of Lucifer-Ahriman. But the coming of the Christ impulse kindled a new light—and a cosmic sun begins its course.

Yes, it was inevitable that death should form part of all natural existence, because this is interpenetrated by Lucifer-Ahriman. On the other hand, mankind would never have achieved its independence without Lucifer-Ahriman. Yet through Lucifer-Ahriman alone, this independence would have expanded to such an extent that in the end it would have led to the forgetting of our divine-spiritual origin. For this reason, death had to become an ingredient even of our physical body. We would never be able to carry even our ego principle over into eternity, if its outer expression, which is our blood, had not been permeated by death.

We have within us the blood of life—the red blood stream; and we have the blood of death—the blue blood. In order to provide life for our egoity, the life that flows in the red blood must at every moment be destroyed in the blue blood. Were it not so destroyed man would be so deeply submerged in life that he would forget his divine-spiritual origin. Western esotericism has a symbol for these two kinds of blood: two pillars, a red one and blue one. The one symbolizes a life flowing from the Father Spirit, but in a form where it would lose itself; the other represents the annihilation of the former. Death is the stronger, the more powerful of the two; it is the factor that brings about the destruction of that which otherwise would lose itself inwardly. But the destruction of what would otherwise lose itself means a call to resurrection.

Thus you see how an adequate interpretation of the John Gospel provides insight into the meaning of all life. What we have learned yesterday and today amounts simply to this: at that point of time which our Christian reckoning designates the new "Year 1," there occurred something of the most profound significance for the entire *Earth* evolution and, in as far as cosmic evolution is connected with the earth, for cosmic evolution as well. Indeed, with the event of Golgotha a new center was created. Ever since then, the Christ Spirit has been united with the earth. It had long been gradually approaching, but since that time it has been within the earth. Now, men's task is to learn to grasp this fact: that since the Golgotha event the Christ Spirit has been in the earth and in everything the earth brings forth. Human beings must learn that failure to recognize the Christ Spirit in all things means seeing them from the aspect of death, whereas finding the Christ in them means understanding them from the vantage point of life.

We are only at the beginning of the evolution that is specifically Christian. The future of this evolution consists in our seeing the whole earth as the body of Christ. For since that time, Christ has entered the earth and has therein created a new light center; He permeates the earth, shines forth into the world, and is for all time interwoven with the earth's aura. So, if today we see the earth devoid of its underlying Christ Spirit, we see what is decaying, rotting—its decomposing corpse. Split it up as we may into minute particles, unless we understand the Christ, we see but the disintegrating corpse. Wherever we see only matter, we see what is not true.

You do not find the truth by studying man as a being of this earth, for you will be studying only his disintegrating corpse. If you study this corpse you can be consistent in estimating the elements of the earth only by regarding the latter as composed of material atoms, regardless of whether these are spatially extended or whether they form force centers—that is not what matters. If we see atoms of which our earth is supposed to consist, we see the earth's corpse, we see that which is constantly disintegrating and which in time will no longer exist when the earth no longer exists— and the earth is in a process of dissolution. We shall see things in their true light only if we discern in every atom something of the Christ Spirit that has imbued it since the time we speak of. Of what does the earth consist since the Christ Spirit permeated it? Of life—right down to the atom. Every atom only has value, and can be understood, if you see in it a sheath encompassing spirit; and this spiritual element is a part of the Christ.

Now, consider anything whatever that pertains to the earth: when do you understand it aright? When you say, That is a part of the body of Christ. What was Christ able to say to those who would learn to understand Him? As He broke the bread made of the grain of the earth He could say,

This is my body.

And what could He say to them as he gave them the juice of the grape, which is derived from the juice of plants?

*This is my blood.**

Because He had become the soul of the earth, He could say of the solid substance, "This is my flesh," and of the plant's fluid, "This is my blood"—just as you say of your flesh, This is my flesh, and of your blood, This is my blood. And those who are able to grasp the true meaning of these words of Christ create for themselves thought images that attract the body and the blood of Christ in the bread and the wine, and they unite with the Christ Spirit.

In this way, the symbol of the Lord's Supper becomes a

---

*These words, and the communion ceremony, do not appear in the John Gospel, but in all the other three. However, John attributes similar words to Christ Jesus in His discourse on the Bread of Life. [John 6:48-5ͻ]

reality. Lacking in our hearts the thought that unites us with Christ we cannot engender the force of attraction that draws the Christ Spirit to us at Holy Communion; but by means of such a thought form the attraction is generated. For those, then, who need the outer symbol in order to perform the spiritual act—that is, to unite with the Christ—Communion will be the way until such time as their inner strength will have so grown, and they are so permeated by the Christ, that they can dispense with the outer physical agency. The Sacrament of Communion is the preparation for the mystical union with the Christ, the preparatory schooling. That is the light in which we must see these things. And just as everything evolves from matter upward toward spirit under the Christian influence, so those things which existed primarily as a bridge must then grow and develop under the influence of Christ. The Sacrament of Communion must rise from the physical to the spiritual plane if it is to lead to a true union with the Christ. One can do no more than hint at such matters, for only if they are received with a full sense of their sacred nature will they be rightly understood.

To recognize that through the event of Golgotha Christ entered the earth—this was a task set mankind. Men were to realize it more and more, and to become increasingly permeated by it. But this called for mediators; and one of the first great ones was he who had been Saul and became Paul. How far could Saul's knowledge extend, considering that he was a Jewish initiate? We can express it somewhat as follows: he could know what was contained in the Hebrew teachings. He knew that what Zarathustra had seen as Ahura Mazdao and what Moses had beheld as *Ehjeh asher ehjeh*—as Jahve or Jehova—in the burning bush and in the thunder and lightning on Sinai—he knew that this had come nearer the earth, had approached, and would one day occupy a human

272

body, and that in this human body it would effect a rejuvenation of the earth. On the other hand, he was influenced by the views of his time and by the Jewish law. He had witnessed the event of Golgotha but was unable to admit that He Who had died on the Cross was the bearer of the Christ. None of the events he had heard of or experienced could convince him that He Who was expected, according to the Jewish initiation, had been incarnated in Jesus of Nazareth.

Now, what would Saul have to experience to be convinced that the immortal Christ Spirit had really been present in the dying body of Jesus of Nazareth on Golgotha? From his Hebrew initiation he knew that after the Christ Spirit had dwelt in a human body and this human body had died, the Christ must be present in the earth's aura. Hence, it should be possible for the Christ to become visible to one able to see into the earth's aura with the eyes of the spirit. That he knew; but hitherto he had not achieved the capacity for seeing into the earth's aura. He was an initiate in wisdom, but not a clairvoyant. He did, however, possess the prerequisite for becoming clairvoyant in an abnormal manner, and he himself mentions this. He refers to it as "grace," bestowed upon him from above; he tells us that he was born prematurely —usually translated "out of due time." He was not carried the full time in the maternal womb, but descended from the spiritual to the physical world before being wholly immersed in all the elements of earthly existence; that is, he came into the world before the moment when ordinarily the unconscious ties which bind men to the spiritual powers are broken. The vision on the road to Damascus was made possible for one whose spiritual eyes had been opened through the agency of an untimely birth. His spiritual vision having been bestowed upon him as a consequence of his premature birth, he now gazed into the earth's aura and there beheld the Christ. Therefore the span of time during which this Christ had

273

walked the earth must have already lapsed. Here was proof that it was Christ Who had died on the Cross; for He Who, Paul knew, was to conquer death on the earth had appeared to him as a spiritual living being. Now he knew the significance of the event of Golgotha. He knew that Christ was risen; for He Whom Paul had beheld could never before have been seen in the earth's aura. Now he understood the words:

It is hard for thee to kick against the pricks. [Acts 9:5]
What are the "pricks?" Paul himself tells us:
O death, where is thy sting?* [I Cor. 15:55]
In vain would you kick against the pricks, for you would recognize only death. But henceforth you can no longer kick against death, for you have seen Him Who conquered death. In this way Paul became the apostle of Christianity who proclaimed most emphatically the living—the spiritually living —Christ.

What made it possible for the Christ to be seen in the earth's aura? The fact that in Christ Jesus—as in a primal impetus given earth evolution for the future—the etheric body was completely permeated by the Christ. The etheric body of Jesus of Nazareth could not be otherwise than wholly permeated by the Christ. Because this was so it exerted full mastery over the physical body, even to the extent of being able to restore the latter after its death; that is, it could appear in such a form as to contain again all that the physical body had embraced before death—but through the power of the etheric body. So when Christ was seen after His death, it was His etheric body that was seen. But for those who were able, as a result of the strength imparted to them through

---

*TRANSLATOR'S NOTE:—The German translations of the New Testament employ the same word for "pricks" and "sting" (*Stachel*). The Greek word kentron also means both.

274

the events in question, not only to recognize a physical-sensible body, but to see in an etheric body a real body with all the marks of a physical body—for such as these Christ was risen in reality. And in truth, He was.

We are further told in the Gospel that when a man has advanced to the stage in which his corruptible principle develops the incorruptible, he becomes endowed with higher vision. We are also told that those who had already achieved this higher vision as a result of self-development could see the Christ and know Him as such. That is told us clearly enough, but people lack the will really to read what it actually says in the Gospel. Take, for example, the first appearance of Christ after death. We read:

But Mary stood without at the sepulchre weeping: and as she wept, she stooped down, and looked into the sepulchre,
And seeth two angels in white sitting, the one at the head, and the other at the feet, where the body of Jesus had lain. And they say unto her, Woman, why weepest thou? She saith unto them, Because they have taken away my Lord, and I know not where they have laid him.
And when she had thus said, she turned herself back, and saw Jesus standing, and knew not that it was Jesus.
Jesus saith unto her, Woman, why weepest thou? Whom seekest thou? She, supposing him to be the gardener, saith unto him, Sir, if thou have borne him hence, tell me where thou hast laid him, and I will take him away. Jesus saith unto her, Mary. She turned herself, and saith unto him, Rabboni; which is to say, Master. [John 20:11-16]

Now, imagine you meet someone whom you had seen but a few days before: can you believe yourself incapable of

275

recognizing him? Can you imagine asking him whether he is the gardener, and where they had laid *him*—when he himself was the man you saw before you? But that is exactly what you have to impute to Mary—or to her who is here called Mary—were you to assume that every physical eye could have recognized Christ and seen Him as previously the physical eye had seen Him. Read the Gospels with their spirit in mind! No, the sacred power of words had first to penetrate the woman as a force: that was essential. Then the words echoed in her heart and rekindled all that she had witnessed. That was what gave her the spiritual vision to see Him Who was risen from the dead.

And does not Paul tell us the same thing? In the case of Paul it cannot be doubted that he saw Him with his spiritual vision when the Christ was once again on the spiritual plane, in the aura of the earth; and as proof that Christ lives he affirms that Christ has appeared. Then as appearances of equal importance, he mentions first:

> . . . that he was seen of Cephas, then of the twelve:
> After that, he was seen of above five hundred brethren
> at once; of whom the greater part remain unto this
> present, but some are fallen asleep.
> After that, he was seen of James; then of all the
> apostles. And last of all he was seen of me also, as
> of one born out of due time.
> For I am the least of the apostles, that I am not
> meet to be called an apostle. [1 Cor. 15:5-9]

Paul places the vision of the others entirely on a par with his own, which was made possible by his spiritual sight; hence he says literally:

> In like manner as I have seen the Christ, so has he
> been seen by the others also.

Their experiences, says Paul, engendered in them the power to see Christ as one arisen from the dead. Now we understand what Paul means. His viewpoint is at once recognizzable as the anthroposophic-spiritual viewpoint; for it tells us that there is a spiritual world, and if we contemplate it by means of the impulse given us through the power of Christ, we shall penetrate it in such a way as to find there the Christ Himself, Christ Who has passed through the event of Golgotha. That is the meaning of what Paul tells us. And it is possible for the human being—especially through what is known as Christian initiation—with patience and endurance gradually to become a successor to Paul, so to speak; to acquire for himself the faculties that will enable him to see into the spiritual world and spiritually to behold the Christ face to face.

In other lectures I have repeatedly set forth the first steps leading to a vision of the Christ Being Himself. The aspirant must live over again what is delineated for us in the Gospel of St. John. I will now merely indicate in briefest outline, in this connection, how man—if he resolves to pass through a certain gamut of feelings—can rise to the spiritual world in which, since the event of Golgotha, there shines the light of Christ.

We begin by saying to ourself, I observe the plant. It grows out of the mineral soil, grows and flowers. But if it could develop consciousness, as does man, it would have to bend down to the soil of the earth, the mineral kingdom from which it grows, and say, Among the present beings of nature thou stone art a lower being than I; but without thee, lower kingdom, I could not subsist. Similarly, were the animal able to sense the plant as the indispensable condition of its existence, it would have to confess, I, as an animal, am a higher being than thou, the plant; but without thee I should perish. Humbly it would have to bow down to the plant and say, To thee, a lower being, I owe my existence. And in the kingdom of man it should be thus: Everyone who has reached a given rung of the ladder should look upon those who in a spiritual sense stand beneath him, and say, True, ye belong to a lower world; but as the plant must bow before the mineral, and the animal before the plant, so should I who stand on a higher rung say: To thee, a humbler one, I owe my existence. Then, when for weeks and months —possibly years under the guidance of the right teacher—a man has completely immersed himself in such feelings of universal humility, he will know the meaning of the *Washing of the Feet*. He will have a direct spiritual vision of what Christ, as the higher Being, did in bending down to the Twelve and washing their feet. The whole significance of this event dawns on the disciple like a vision, and he knows that it took place. His enlightenment is such as to demand no further proof: he now gazes directly into the spiritual world and beholds Christ in the scene in question.

Then, stimulated by the teacher, this man can gain the strength to say, I shall courageously endure whatever sorrow and suffering this world may bring, and shall not complain. I shall steel myself to the point at which these no longer mean suffering and sorrow for me, because I shall know them for necessities in the world. And when he has become sufficiently staunch of soul, there springs from this contemplation the feeling of the *Scourging:* spiritually he feels it taking place in himself. And this opens his spiritual vision, enabling him to see for himself the Scourging as it is described in the Gospel of St. John.

Then the pupil is shown how to develop the strength for the next step, where he is able not only to bear the sorrow and suffering of all the world, but to say: I possess something so sacred that I stake my whole being on it. Should all the world overwhelm me with scorn and mockery, this remains holiest for me. No derision or disdain will keep me from cherishing it, though I stand alone. I profess it, and shall defend it. Then man experiences spiritually within him the *Crowning with Thorns*; and without the aid of any historical document his spiritual vision transmits to him this scene as described in the Gospel of St. John.

Then, when through proper guidance he has learned to regard his physical existence in quite a new light, to think of his own body as something external—when it has become a matter of course to feel and sense that he carries his physical body about with him as a material instrument—then he has reached the fourth stage of Christian initiation, the *Bearing of the Cross*. This has by no means made a frail ascetic of him: on the contrary, he learns to employ his physical instrument far more effectively than theretofore. When you have learned to regard your body as something you carry, you have arrived at the fourth stage of Christian initiation, the Bearing of the Cross. Therewith, you have attained to the enlightenment that enables you to see spiritually the scene in which Christ bears His Cross on His back, just as you have learned by the elevation of your soul to carry your body as you might a piece of wood.*

---

*It is worthwhile noting that only in the John Gospel is Christ described as bearing his own cross. The other three evangelists say that it was carried by Simon of Cyrene, Luke specifying (23:26) that Simon was just behind Christ in the procession to Golgotha. In his Hamburg cycle on the Gospel of St. John (Lecture 11) Steiner mentions also the appearance of the stigmata during the fourth stage of Christian initiation, and he gives the name of the Crucifixion to this stage.

One of the fullest and most precise pictures of this stage had been given by him earlier in Leipzig in 1906, this passage making clear that both the bearing of the cross and the crucifixion were involved. The passage reads as follows:

"It is very difficult to attain to the fourth level. The disciple must develop a feeling for the fact that his body has for him the same value as do all the objects surrounding him. He must learn to view it as something foreign; he must attain to the feeling: Not, I go somewhere, but I carry

Now something occurs which is to be regarded as the fifth stage of Christian initiation: it is called the "mystical death." Here, as a consequence of the inner maturity we have gained, everything that surrounds us—the whole physical world of the senses—appears to be extinguished. We are in darkness. And then comes a moment when this darkness is torn apart like a curtain, and we see behind this physical world into the spiritual world. At the same moment, however, something else occurs as well. We have learned to recognize sin and evil in their true forms; that is, in this stage we have learned the meaning of the *Descent into Hell*.

In the next stage we learn not only to regard our body as something alien, but also to feel everything else as being as much a part of us as our body, to look upon everything on earth as pertaining to us, as was a matter of course in ancient clairvoyance. Inasmuch as we all belong to one great organism, we further learn to regard the suffering of others as our own. Then, in proportion to our understanding of this, we are united with the earth, and we experience the act of being laid in the earth, the *Burial*. And by being united with the earth we have arisen out of it; for this experience has given us the first insight into the meaning of the words, *"The earth is in the process of becoming a new sun."*

The attainment of the fourth, fifth, and sixth stages of

---

my body there. Then, the disciple no longer lives in his body but he carries it, like the wooden cross. This exercise leads the disciple to seeing himself crucified on the cross. Outwardly, this level of initiation manifests itself in the appearance of the so-called stigmata. The disciple then receives real stigmata corresponding to the wounds of the crucifixion on those parts of his body, which actually become temporarily visible. These inner and outer experiences appear following the corresponding contemplation."

Notes from a lecture given July 10, 1906 from a series entitled *Populärer Okkultismus*.

Christian initiation enables us to see for ourselves the event of Golgotha, to merge with it. We no longer need documents: these served merely as rungs of the ladder.

Finally there is the seventh stage, known as the *Ascension* —in other words, the awakening in the spiritual world. It is rightly said of this stage that it cannot be expressed in any words of human language, that it can be imagined only by one who has learned to think without the instrumentality of the brain. The miracles of resurrection can be thought only when the physical brain is no longer needed as an instrument.

By reason of having had their spiritual eyes opened and of thus being able to see what took place, those who were present as believers when the event of Golgotha occurred could have seen the Christ in the way I have indicated—that is, if He had manifested Himself to their spiritual sight in the earth's aura. But even had Christ always retained, in a certain sense, the same form He had assumed at that time, the faithful would not have been able to see Him, had He— the Christ—not achieved something for Himself as well—by conquering death.

This brings us to a concept which is indeed difficult to grasp. The human being continues to learn incessantly as he develops his capacities, at whatever stage he finds himself. Not only man, however, but every being, from the humblest to the most exalted divine being, learns while developing farther and farther. What Christ did as a divine Being in the body of Jesus of Nazareth we have thus far described with reference to its fruits and its effect on mankind. But now we must ask, did Christ thereby also experience something within Himself that led Him to a higher stage? And the answer is, He did. Even divine-spiritual beings can experience what leads them to more advanced stages; and what He experienced —His ascent into a world still more exalted than the one in which He had previously had His being—this He revealed *in*

His Ascension to those who were His companions on the
earth. That is why the first six stages of Christian initiation
can be understood—though not perceived—by one who is
neither an initiate nor a clairvoyant, but who lives in dependence, for his thinking, on the physical brain; whereas the
seventh stage, the Ascension, can be comprehended only by
the clairvoyant who is no longer bound to the instrumentality of his physical brain, who has experienced for himself
what it means to think without the brain and to see without
the brain.

That is the way in which these matters are interrelated;
and such was the course of the world's development during
the period we have been privileged to discuss in these fourteen lectures.

We have already learned that Christ had indicated that
in the man who had been born blind and whose healing He
had brought about, there was to be revealed what had sinned
in him in an earlier life.* What Christ did, then, was to
teach the idea of reincarnation, in as far as people could
understand it. Karma, the extension of causes from one incarnation to another, that is what He taught. He taught as
one does with practical life in mind. What He meant was
this: There will be a future time in which all men will recognize karma. They will understand that when a man does evil
he need not be punished by an external, earthly power, for
the evil he did inevitably entails its compensation in this or
in some future incarnation. Then we shall only need to enter
this deed in the great cosmic book of laws, the *Akasha
Chronicle*, inscribe it in the spiritual world. Then we human
beings need not condemn him. We can entrust the judging

---

*This is a literal translation of what Dr. Steiner said. The word "what"
evidently refers to the individuality of the blind man in a former life.

of his deeds to the spiritual laws, to be inscribed in the spiritual world: we can leave him to karma.

> *Jesus went unto the mount of Olives.*
> *And early in the morning he came again into the temple, and all the people came unto him; and he sat down, and taught them.*
> *And the scribes and Pharisees brought unto him a woman taken in adultery; and when they had set her in the midst,*
> *They say unto him, Master, this woman was taken in adultery, in the very act.*
> *Now Moses in the law commanded us, that such should be stoned but what sayest thou?*
> *This they said, tempting him, that they might have to accuse him. But Jesus stooped down and with his finger wrote on the ground.* [John 8:1–6]

What was it He wrote? He inscribed the sin in the spiritual world, indicating that through the spiritual world the sin would find its compensation. The others, however, He reminded to ask themselves whether they were without sin; for only if they harbored nothing that called for compensation could they feel themselves to be in no way connected with the sin of this woman and therefore qualified to judge her. As it was, they had no way of knowing whether, in their previous life, they themselves might not have provided the cause of what had now come to this woman: they could not know whether in former lives they had induced what had now caused her to commit adultery; whether they themselves had committed this sin or laid its foundations in earlier incarnations. All is inscribed in karma. Jesus wrote on the ground which He had already permeated with His spiritual light; that is, He confided to the earth what should be the karma of the adulteress. What he meant was: Follow the path which I now mark out for you. Learn not to judge, but to leave what is in man to karmic adjustment. If we abide by this rule we will come to understand karma. Karma need not be taught as a dogma, for it is taught by facts. That was Christ's way of teaching.

Here we should pause to realize that such things could be written only by that one of Christ's pupils and disciples whom He himself had initiated: Lazarus-John. Hence it was this pupil alone who fully understood the power attained to by a Being Who, beginning with the Baptism, had gradually gained in His etheric body mastery over the physical body, to the extent of endowing the latter with ever new life. And for the same reason, this writer of the John Gospel knew that it was possible to transform what appeared to be water —through its being received into the human organs—into wine. He understood how the power of the etheric body could be effective in such a way that a few fishes and loaves sufficed to satisfy the hunger of many. That is what the author of the John Gospel told us, if only we take the Gospel seriously. Does he say anywhere that the few loaves and fishes were eaten in the ordinary physical way? No, you will not find that in the Gospel. He says clearly and distinctly, as you will see by taking every word literally, that Christ broke the bread; but also, that He offered up thanks to heaven:

> And Jesus took the loaves; and when he had given
> thanks, he distributed to the disciples, and the dis-
> ciples to them that were set down; and likewise of
> the fishes as much as they would. [John 6:11]

The meaning of these words as they appear in the original text, which is poorly reproduced in translation, is about as follows: The disciples passed on the loaves and the fishes, letting each do with them what he would. But none desired anything whatever save to feel, at this moment, what emanated as a force from the mighty etheric body of Christ Jesus. No one desired anything else.

284

And by what means was their hunger stilled? In the 23rd verse it says:

Howbeit there came other boats from Tiberias nigh
unto the place where they did eat bread, after that
the Lord had given thanks. [6:23]

It was though the agency of the prayer that the people had eaten the bread. They had eaten the bread without the physical act having taken place. Hence Christ Jesus could later throw light on what had occurred by saying,

I am the bread of life. [6:35]

What, then, had the people eaten? They had partaken of the power of Christ's body. And what could remain? Only the power of Christ's body; and the effect of this was so strong that afterwards one could gather something up.

According to occult teaching, every body consists of twelve members. The one uppermost is called the Ram; the adjacent one, the Bull; the one with the hands, the Twins; the chest is called the Crab; everything in the region of the heart is the Lion; below it—the trunk—is the Virgin; the hips, the Scales; below this, the Scorpion; and still farther down: the thigh, the Archer; the knee, the Goat; the lower leg, the Water-carrier; and the feet, the Fishes.

The human body, then, is divided into twelve members —and with good reason. Now, if the fragments were to be gathered up after the power of Christ's body had been used to satisfy hunger, they would have to be gathered in twelve measures.

Therefore they gathered them together, and filled
twelve baskets with the fragments of the five barley
loaves, which remained over and above unto them
that had eaten. [6:13]

They had not eaten the barley loaves. They had partaken of the power emanating from Christ. They had been satisfied by the power that radiated from Christ through His thanksgiving when He appealed to the spheres from which He had

285

descended. That is the sense in which we must understand the influence of the spiritual world on the physical world; and thus we can also understand the relation of the single incidents to the basic event, the evolution of our earth into a sun. They all take their place as mighty force-revealing events in the earth's process of becoming a sun. But it now becomes comprehensible that what communicated itself to the earth at that time as a mighty impulse can reach human beings only by slow degrees, that it can be infused into humanity but slowly and gradually.

As was indicated yesterday, the Gospel which in the beginning was best suited to convey the great truths to those able to receive them was St. Mark's Gospel. That was during the first centuries. It was men's task to reconquer through their own efforts the realms from which they had strayed. Let us try to understand how man himself descended from divine-spiritual heights to the lowest point, which occurred when the intervention of Golgotha provided an impetus to man's return to an upward striving. This acted like a mighty impulse, drawing man aloft again. He had descended from divine-spiritual heights and had sunk ever deeper; then, having saturated himself with the newly born spiritual light, he received from the Christ impulse the strength gradually to recover all that he had once possessed. And this he would have to accomplish in the following manner: In the time immediately following the Christ event he had to regain what he had lost during the last pre-Christian centuries, and this could be done with the help of the Mark Gospel.

What he had lost in a still earlier time had to be recaptured in the succeeding period by means of a Gospel directing his attention more to his inner life, and this was the Gospel of St. Luke. But we have also said that six hundred years before the appearance of Christ on earth, everything of a spiritual nature which had been vouchsafed mankind in

286

earlier centuries, and which had gradually been lost, was gathered together in the great being of Buddha. At that time, six centuries before Christ, the Buddha being lived, epitomizing everything that existed in the way of primeval wisdom—all that mankind had lost and that Buddha had come to proclaim. Hence it is narrated that when Buddha came into the world his birth had been foretold by his mother Maya. We are further told of one who had prophesied of the child that it would become a Buddha, the Redeemer, the Guide to immortality, freedom, and light. And there is many a Buddha legend reporting that as a twelve-year-old boy Buddha had strayed from home, and that he was found again under a tree surrounded by the poets and sages of Antiquity, whom he taught. In my book, *Christianity as Mystical Fact*, you will find set forth how in the Luke Gospel, six hundred years later, there crop up again the same legends that were told of Buddha; how his revelations reappear in a new form. That is why we encounter in the Luke Gospel what was already contained in the Buddha legends. So perfect is the agreement in such matters when seen in the light of spiritual science!

This should lead us to realize that a document such as the Gospel of St. John, and the others that complement it, are of an infinite profundity which we have studied in a series of lectures. If we could continue our lectures and make them twice as long, we could find ever new depths in the Gospels. Endless abundance would be disclosed could we extend the time indefinitely; and it would be borne in upon us that with the future development of mankind, still new and ever new depths in these documents will be fathomed. Truly, men will never exhaust their contents. There is nothing one has to read into them; we must merely prepare ourselves, by means of occult truths, to find out what they really contain. Then the whole universal complex of man-

287

kind, as well as the relation of this complex to the cosmos, will reveal itself to us; and we shall come to see ever deeper into the spiritual world.

But having heard a lecture cycle of such a nature, it is essential to realize that we have not just acquired a store of knowledge, a sum of isolated truths. Through indispensable, that would be the less important aspect: it is simply a matter of its being impossible to arrive at the deeper goal without it. No, the special fruit that should ripen for us as a result of these studies is that everything we have received through our mind, if we let it sink into our heart, should become a feeling for it all, should be transformed into feelings—even into impulses of the will. When all that we have understood and received through our mind becomes warmth of heart, it becomes a force within us, a healing force for spirit, soul, and body. And then we shall contemplate this past fortnight as follows: We have been immersed in the life of spirit and have acquired a great deal in many ways. Our gain, however, has not been a mere matter of empty concepts and ideas, but rather, of truths, concepts, and ideas capable of springing from our soul as living forces in our feelings and in our sensibilities. And these feelings and sensibilities will remain for us; we can never lose them, and we shall carry them with us in the world. We have not merely learned something; we have become more alive through what we have learned.

If, in taking leave of this cycle, we make such feelings our very own, spiritual science will fill our life. It will not withdraw us from our ordinary life, but will become for us something like an image of the loftiest concept presented in these lectures. What was set forth is this: Death in the world is inevitable, but the view we hold of death is erroneous. Christ taught us the true view of death, whereby death becomes the seed of a higher life.

Out yonder, beyond the sphere of these lectures, life

surges; everyday existence flows on and men live in it. Spiritual research detracts not from that life by an iota, robs it of nothing; but the view commonly held regarding this life before penetrating it with the eye of the spirit is erroneous, and this must appear to us as life's illusion. This illusion of life we must let perish in us; then the seed we have acquired by means of an illusion will blossom into a higher life. But only if we receive into ourselves the living, spiritual point of view can this come about. Far from making us ascetic in our lives, it is precisely thereby that we learn to know life in its true form, to master it in the right way, and to endow it with genuine fruitfulness. In proportion as we experience spiritual science itself in a Christian way we christianize life, and we experience a reflection of how death becomes a reflection of life. As we adopt spiritual science as our way of thinking, in the same measure will we—not become estranged from life, but rather, discover in what way our view of this life is faulty. Then, strengthened by a true conception of it, we shall enter it as active workers. There will be no withdrawing from life, for we shall have gained power and strength from studies that introduce us into the spiritual world.

If I have in some measure succeeded in so shaping these lectures that they may bear fruit in your lives, that they may contribute, even to a slight degree, to making you feel spiritual cognition as being an exaltation of life—living warmth in your feeling, thinking, and willing; in your working— then the light enkindled for us through our anthroposophical world view can glow as the fire of life's ardor, as the fire of life itself. And if this fire proves at all strong enough to endure and burn on through life, I shall have achieved my aim in undertaking this series of lectures.

May these feelings live on in your hearts as a subject of inner meditation!

Lecture Cycles on the Gospels Published in English

1908   The Gospel of St. John. Twelve lectures, Hamburg, May 18 to 31.

1909   The Gospel of St. John in Relation to the Other Gospels. Fourteen lectures, Kassel, June 24 to July 7.

1909   The Gospel of St. Luke. Ten lectures, Basel, September 15 to 26.

1909   Deeper Secrets of Human History in the Light of the Gospel of St. Matthew. Three lectures, Berlin, November 1 to 13.

1910   The Gospel of St. Matthew. Twelve lectures, Bern, September 1 to 12.

1910   Background to the Gospel of St. Mark. Thirteen lectures, Berlin and other cities, October 17, 1910 to March 13, 1911.

1911   The Spiritual Guidance of Man and Humanity. Three lectures, Copenhagen, June 6 to 8.

1911   From Jesus to Christ. Ten lectures, Karlsruhe, October 5 to 14.

1912   The Gospel of St. Mark. Ten lectures, Basel, September 15 to 24.

1913   The Fifth Gospel. Seven lectures, Christiania and Cologne, October 1 to 6, and December 17–18.

1914   Christ and the Human Soul. Four lectures, Norrköping, July 12 to 16.

The Five Basic Books

THEOSOPHY, AN INTRODUCTION TO THE SUPERSENSIBLE KNOWLEDGE OF THE WORLD AND THE DESTINATION OF MAN by Rudolf Steiner. The book begins with a beautiful description of the primordial trichotomy: body, soul, and spirit. A discussion of reincarnation and karma follows. The third and longest chapter of the work (74 pages) presents, in a vast panorama, the seven regions of the soul world, the seven regions of the land of spirits, and the soul's journey after death through these worlds. A brief discussion of the path to higher knowledge is found in the fifth chapter.

Paper, $6.95 #155; Cloth, $10.95 #154

KNOWLEDGE OF THE HIGHER WORLDS AND ITS ATTAINMENT by Rudolf Steiner. Rudolf Steiner's fundamental work on the path to higher knowledge explains in detail the exercises and disciplines a student must pursue in order to attain a wakeful experience of supersensible realities. The path described here is a safe one which will not interfere with the student's ability to lead a normal outer life.

Paper, $3.95 #80

CHRISTIANITY AND OCCULT MYSTERIES OF ANTIQUITY by Rudolf Steiner. An introduction to esoteric Christianity which explores the ancient mythological wisdom of Egypt and Greece. The work shows how this wisdom underwent a tremendous transformation into a historical event in the mystery of Golgotha.

Paper, $7.95 #33

PHILOSOPHY OF FREEDOM by Rudolf Steiner. Steiner's most important philosophical work deals both with epistemology, the study of how man knows himself and the world, and with the issue of human freedom. In the first half of the book Steiner focuses on the activity of thinking in order to demonstrate the true nature of knowledge. There he shows the fallacy of the contemporary idea of thinking, pointing out that the prevailing belief in the limits to knowledge is a self-imposed limit that contradicts its own claim to truth. The possibility for freedom is taken up in the second half of the book. The issue is not political freedom, but something more subtle; freedom of the will. There are those who maintain that man's thoughts and actions are just as determined as a chemical reaction or a honey bee's behavior. Steiner points again to the activity of thinking, from which arises the possibility of free human action.

Paper, $5.50 #116

OCCULT SCIENCE, AN OUTLINE by Rudolf Steiner. This work of nearly 400 pages begins with a thorough discussion and definition of the term "occult" science. A description of the supersensible nature of man follows, along with a discussion of dreams, sleep, death, life between death and rebirth, and reincarnation. In the fourth chapter evolution is described from the perspective of initiation science. The fifth chapter characterizes the training a student must undertake to become an initiate. The sixth and seventh chapters consider the future evolution of the world and more detailed observations regarding supersensible realities.

Paper, $6.95 #113; Cloth, $10.95 #112

Rudolf Steiner and Anthroposophy

MAN AND WORLD IN THE LIGHT OF ANTHROPOSOPHY by Stewart C. Easton. A new and revised edition of Dr. Easton's survey of Rudolf Steiner's Anthroposophy. This comprehensive volume of over 500 pages complete with index is an excellent guide to Steiner's thought and works. Chapter titles include: "History and the Evolution of Human Consciousness," "Individual Spiritual Development and Human Freedom" and "Man and His Life on Earth and in the Spiritual Worlds; Reincarnation and Karma."

Cloth, $21.00 #353

RUDOLF STEINER: HERALD OF A NEW EPOCH by Stewart C. Easton. Dr. Easton's interest in Rudolf Steiner dates from 1934, when he first came into contact with Steiner's work, and he has been involved in anthroposophical activities in one way or another ever since. A historian by profession, Dr. Easton brings together in this book innumerable facts and details of Steiner's life that have been previously unavailable to English readers. The result is an outstanding portrait of a unique personality that will satisfy a long-felt need.

Paper, $10.95 #427

Other Books on the Esoteric Path of Spiritual Development

RUDOLF STEINER AND INITIATION by Paul Eugen Schiller. The author is a research scientist and a lifelong student of Steiner's works. In this book, translated from the German by Henry Barnes, Schiller presents a systematic discussion of Steiner's writings and lectures on the path of knowledge. Among the topics discussed are: "Fundamental Moods," "Development of the Six Attributes," "Sense Free Thinking, Feeling, and Willing," "Meditation," "Body Free Life of the Soul," "The Rosicrucian Path of Initiation," and "The Level of Inspirational Cognition."

Paper, $5.95 #418

THE CALENDAR OF THE SOUL by Rudolf Steiner. This is Steiner's famous collection of 52 verses, one for each week of the year. By following the verses through the year the soul gains a deeper insight and penetration into nature and the course of the seasons. The translation was made by Ruth and Hans Pusch.

Cloth, $7.95 #28

THE STAGES OF HIGHER KNOWLEDGE by Rudolf Steiner. In these four essays Steiner describes the experience of the three higher stages of consciousness: imagination, inspiration, and intuition which are experienced by the student, as he progresses on the path to knowledge, and by the initiate. The six exercises for the heart center are characterized as a means of protecting oneself from the "danger of mischief from hurtful forces" which would arise if one practiced meditation without the exercises.

Paper, $4.50 #146

THE INNER DEVELOPMENT OF MAN by Rudolf Steiner. This is a one lecture introduction to the nature of esoteric training or path of knowledge.

Booklet, $.95 #72

PRACTICAL TRAINING IN THOUGHT by Rudolf Steiner (Karlsruhe, 1909). This most popular pamphlet has been translated into many languages and published in innumerable editions. It is known throughout the world for its clear and concise directions for improving memory, thinking habits and powers of concentration.

Booklet, $1.50 #120

293

Steiner Education

The WALDORF or STEINER SCHOOL movement is one of the largest private school systems in the world. There are numerous Steiner schools in the United States with programs from kindergarten through high school. The Anthroposophic Press offers the following titles on this important approach to education:

THE RECOVERY OF MAN IN CHILDHOOD by A.C. Harwood. Probably the best introduction to Waldorf Education available. The work shows how the Waldorf approach to education is harmonized with the developmental phases of the child. Chapter titles include: "Threefold Relation of Body and Mind," "The Map of Childhood," "The First Seven Years," "The Small Child at Home and at School," "The Temperaments," "Adolesence," and "The High School." The work is highly recommended to the parents of prospective students and anyone wishing a clear understanding of the Waldorf School Approach.

Paper, $7.95 #411

THE WALDORF SCHOOL APPROACH TO HISTORY by Werner Glas, Ph.D. This important work is addressed to parents, teachers, and the general reader interested in education. It is based on ideas which have been put to the test in the classrooms of the rapidly expanding Waldorf School movement. Chapter titles include: "The History of Civilization," "In the Quest of the Images From Plutarch to Bryant," and "Seventh Grade and the Calyx of Modern Consciousness."

". . . a careful account of one aspect of the teaching that goes on in these Rudolf Steiner schools . . ." (*Commonweal*)

Paper, $6.95 #482

EDUCATING AS AN ART edited by Ekkehard Piening and Nick Lyons. An important collection of essays on different aspects of Rudolf Steiner education written by prominent American Steiner School teachers. The essays cover such topics as the meaning of discipline, fairy tales in the first grade, the teaching of Norse Myths, an arithmetic play for second grade, the teaching of history, and the future of knowledge. Many fine photos.

Paper, $7.95 #275

Order Form

If you enjoyed this book and would like another copy or if you want to order one of the books described on the preceding pages, please fill out the form below and mail it to us: Anthroposophic Press, 258 Hungry Hollow Road, Spring Valley, N.Y. 10977

Name _____

Address _____

City _____

State _____ Zip _____

Book #	Title	Price	Qty.	Amt.

Postage and Handling $1.75

Total Enclosed